Xingyi - A Means To An End

By Mike Patterson

Copyright © 2012 by Mike Patterson, PHK Enterprises
All rights reserved.
ISBN-10: 0985855703
ISBN-13: 978-0-9858557-0-3

Disclaimer: Neither the author, nor any other people associated with this book, assume any liability for any reader attempting to perform any and all illustrated movements and/or illustrated drills, techniques or training methods of their own accord without qualified, proper instruction and supervision by a professional. Any reader should also be certified as physically fit by a physician before attempting any form of exercise.

Notice: Starting on page 156, this book also includes a trademarked program of training called R.S.P.C.T. (realistically structured progressive combat training). AKA - RSPCT

The choice to include the structure of RSPCT in no way constitutes a license for any reader to infringe upon my copyright of creation or the trademark that is R.S.P.C.T. You do NOT have my permission to teach nor include any portion of the R.S.P.C.T. program in your curriculum.

When faced with and pressured by a worthy adversary...
Rather than rise to your level of expectation,
You will instead sink to your level of true ability.

Mike Patterson

Dedication

This entire work is a dedication to my Shrfu, my mentor and my friend, Hsu Hong Chi. For without him, I would lack the tools, insights and knowledge from which to draw anything of substance. But while that is and will always be true, there are a few others to whom I would also like to dedicate this work.

First and foremost; To my lovely wife; without whose caring support, and occasional prodding, this book would have never been completed. She is, has been and always will be my proverbial rock in the sometimes stormy seas that are my life. Her insights have been invaluable in shaping my world view to what it has become.

Also; To all of my students... past, present and future. It is they who have been my continuous motivation to try and improve the way the arts have been communicated to me. As is it we, as teachers, that *serve them*.

A very special thanks to Alex Shpigel, and Brandon, who took time out of their busy schedules to assist in the photos for completion of this project.

A few notes on this text:

Since I come from an era that dates prior to the modern "PinYin" Romanization of the Chinese language, this book uses the old standard "Wade/Giles" Romanization instead. Hence you will see the art written as "Hsing I" as opposed to "Xingyi", "chi" instead of "qi", "chuan" instead of "quan", etc. Since I generally tend to explain the terms in equivalent English as I go along, this should not present much of an issue either way.

When references are made to the workings of the intercostal muscle structures of the ribcage, if I use the words "closing" or "opening" I am referring to the frontal rib cage only. It should be understood that the ribcage operates in a juxtaposed state, meaning that if the front *opens* the back will *close* and vice versa. This will not be stated each time as it is redundant for this work.

Specific terms:

Brace; to form a line of cohesive strength in the body allowing you to use the ground as ally.
Centerline; your central facing in relation to the opponent.
Costals; Abbreviated term referencing the intercostals muscle structures in the body.
Crane stance; a one legged stance typified by positioning one foot against the upper shin of the support leg.
Cross stance; a stance typified by having 70% of the weight on the front foot with that foot toed out to nearly 90 degrees, with the rear foot on the ball of the foot, heel raised and straight.
Double bamboo step; a footwork pattern where either the front foot moves first with the rear foot sliding up to the front foot's former location and the front foot then moving forward again. Or vice versa with the rear foot beginning such a movement to the rear.
Dragon stance; a stance typified by having 70% of the weight on the rear foot, front foot toed out, while rear foot is on the ball of the foot, heel raised and straight.
Full foot change; a footwork involving switching the positions of both feet simultaneously without leaping upward to accomplish the feat.
Frame (framing); the act of keeping your hands up, approximately aligned with your clavicles, elbows staying downward and close to the body.
Half foot change; a footwork involving switching the positions of both feet, dropping the lead foot back approximately 2/3 of the separated distance followed immediately by bringing the rear foot forward a full stride length.
Half fist; a hand position where the digits are folded in half creating an edge at the second joint.
Half step; a footwork involving shuffling of both feet one half pace, or just the rear foot as a follow step to a lead stride.
Intercostals; the fast twitch, short muscles that exist between the human ribs.
Iron Wall; A method where one leg is raised at an angle to redirect an incoming kick attack from the opponent.
Light foot; the act of suspending one foot, parallel to the ground, held in close proximity to the inner ankle of the supporting foot.
Load (loading); to establish kinetic potential of release of force.
Overhook; the act of draping one of your limbs over an opponent's limb or other body part.
Post(ing); the act of aligning your balance to one foot.
San ti shr; a stance configuration where 70% of the weight is on the rear leg with that foot toed out to 45 to 60 degrees with the front foot pointed straight forward and aligned with the body's centerline.
Shear; the act of taking force and momentum past you with a narrowly skewed vector.
Swing step; the act of stepping a foot in a circular arc to a toe in position while being posted on the other foot.
Thread (ing); moving one limb through a narrow opening, sometimes along the other limb.
Tiger foot; a stance with 90% of the weight on the rear leg and the front leg foot positioned on the ball of the foot approximately one and one half feet in front of you.
Twine (twining); the act of wrapping one of your limbs around an opponent's limb.

Statement of purpose.

I returned from Taiwan in the late 1970s and began teaching in the United States at the behest of my teacher. Throughout the next several years, as I continued to travel back and forth from the U.S. to Taiwan in continuation of my studies with Hsu Hong Chi, it never occurred to me to attempt accelerating my visits (I was already visiting every four months for one month at a time) for fear of losing my mentor in the Internal Martial Arts. It always seemed to me that there was no hurry. I had an excellent relationship and rapport with my teacher and I was still young, and he was but in his early 50's.

Once, during a conversation in early 1983, he remarked to me; "You never know what may happen. Maybe I die tomorrow." He must have seen the startled look that came across my face because he immediately patted my hand and said; "Don't worry. I probably outlive you."

When he suddenly passed away in late 1983, I was left literally dumb struck. An entire fleet of emotions swept over me in the following few years. These were the same gamut of emotions that all people experience when they lose someone very close to them. And as these feelings flowed forth and then began to ebb, another perspective began to emerge. This perspective was one of loss once again. This time it was not a feeling of loss for the man I loved, but rather a feeling of profound loss for the art that he carried inside him.

I slowly began to entertain the notion that I had also accumulated a great deal of information regarding the Internal Martial Arts. The growing perspective that all of us who diligently study the Internal Arts for long periods of time are but singular and fragile links in a chain which can be broken at any time by circumstance or fate was becoming pervasive in my mind. And as a result I began to consider that I should make every effort to record in whatever form possible the knowledge that had been transmitted to me.

This then is the purpose behind this book, the videos I have produced, the full contact teams I have trained, the WebSite I have authored and the school that I still run. This man called Hsu Hong Chi once was the vessel that housed profound knowledge. And once, while he was still alive, I made a solemn promise to him that I would attempt to propagate his Kung Fu family knowledge to the best of my ability. I am keeping that promise. And I hope that, wherever he may be, that this action somehow gives him some small pleasure.

With this book I wanted to achieve something practically useful. The problem I encountered in the writing was in terms of what content specifically to select and include. How to choose what granules were important enough to write down and what others should be given less weight. Time in practice tends to cause certain things to become auto generic to the point of "no mind" on the part of the practitioner. I want to say that I did not write this book with the intention of making "converts" to my perspectives. But rather simply to archive what I have learned and experienced in the forty plus years (at the time of writing) that I have walked this path called the Internal Arts.

My hope is that some may profit from the effort...

History

Hsing I Chuan is a very old "internal" art most often attributed to General Yueh Fuei, a famous Chinese military hero who died circa 1130 A.D. Although most scholars agree that General Yueh did not invent the art, he is often given credit as the founding father. It makes for a nice story and since scholars still cannot agree as to true origin, it is still a popular one.

The origins of this most ancient of Chinese systemized combative art forms are unknown. Yueh attributed a wandering Taoist as his teacher whom had no traceable name. And the history of evolution of the art is sketchy at best, although it seems certainly likely that it does pre-date Yueh's time frame. Some scholars believe the art should be dated at least as far back as the Liang Dynasty (550 A.D.) which is certainly possible. But verifiable records do not predate the 18th century. This does not, however, mean that original records may have not been destroyed or simply lost. Still, it seems most likely the myth of creation is attributed to Yueh because it makes for a colorful story. The art is so sophisticated and practical that it likely was several generations in evolution to its complete form.

What is known about Hsing I, is that it is one of the oldest and most famous systems of Kung Fu to ever come out of Chinese Culture. The skills of Hsing I masters are legendary, and their kung fu prowess is the subject of numerous tales and songs throughout Chinese History.

Suffice it to say that Hsing I is known as a most powerful form of Chinese Kung Fu and good teachers of this mighty art form are much sought after even today.

The Art of Hsing I is divided into three main schools of thought. They are the ShanXi School, the HeBei School, and the Honan School respectively. The ShanXi and HeBei methods are based upon the five forces of Taoist cosmology and the twelve animal styles, although the names of the animals sometimes vary a bit from family to family. And approaches to training also vary, sometimes significantly, from family to family even within the same lineage.

The ShanXi method is definitively more rare of the three main styles but is beginning to make its presence more known at the time of this writing. The Honan School is devoid of any actual physical representations of the Five Forces in form. They are conceptual ideas only, and the structure has only ten, more simplistic Animal movements contained.

For many years I had attempted to research the general history of the Internal Martial Arts in addition to researching my own family history. And after years of sifting through scant and questionable records I have ended up with more questions than hard answers. There are simply too many holes within sometimes vague and, at other times, personally motivated documents to be completely sure of too many things. Within my own research, I also discovered that there has been much "cross pollination" amongst the different families of Hsing I which further thwarts any effort to trace a specific lineage with complete accuracy. Many practitioners have had several teachers of prominence and not always within the same family line or style. At this point in time I do not personally believe that there is any such thing as a "pure" lineage of any one style or persuasion.

I once asked my teacher, Hsu Hong Chi, some questions about our family history. His reply was; "Where come from not important. Work, no work, is what important. That your concern." After 40 years (as of this writing) of practice, teaching, fighting and coaching, I have now come full circle and hold the same opinion as my mentor.

The research is nice on an intellectual level. But, what is truly important is practical skill. I have seen too many teachers and practitioners over the years that talk very well in terms of theory, principle and yes, history, *especially* history. Yet, they exhibit poor skill in terms of movement, technique and general internal ability. These days I spend my time practicing as opposed to researching the threads of history.

With all that said, the following family tree delineates the names of which I can be reasonably certain of given my research into the subject and all of the possible flaws notwithstanding. The names are listed in descending order of timeline starting with the eldest and working down to the latter generations, ending with myself.

Chi Lung Feng
Tsao Chi Wu
Tai Lung Pan
Li Lo Neng
Liu Chi Lan
Li Tsun I
Chang Chun Feng
Hung I Hsiang
Hsu Hong Chi
Mike Patterson

Li Tsun I

Chang Chun Feng

Over my years teaching to date, I have trained roughly four to five thousand individuals in our family disciplines. The list of individuals that have been certified as of the time of this writing is a short one indeed. Any person(s) who is claiming such license can be verified by contacting me directly through hsing-i.com. I always answer my email.

Hung I Hsiang

This will conclude this brief chapter on history. This is all that I am willing to say comfortably in relation to such things. The rest I will leave to those who fancy such pursuits.

For myself I am truly much more interested in effective practice at this stage of my life. "Where come from not important. Work, no work, is what important. That your concern."

Now, on with what works!

Hsu Hong Chi

Gan Hsin - Memories of Master Hsu

I am frequently asked by a variety of individuals to share tales and stories of my late teacher, Hsu Hong Chi, and my days with him on Taiwan.

The difficulty lies not in the telling of such tales, for there are so many accumulated over those fifteen years of knowing and learning from the man, but in which excerpts to pick. What snapshots to show someone in an attempt to illustrate such a multifaceted and, to me, larger than life human being. It seems so futile a method of communication, when attempting to describe such a beautiful spirit. Like showing someone a slide of the Grand Canyon. The picture cannot begin to compare to the experience of being there, involved with and awed by the moment(s) of direct interaction.

Master Hsu and Me in the mid 1970's

When I first met Master Hsu, he was standing outside of a movie theatre in *Shi Men Ting,* the shopping district of Downtown Taipei city. It just so happened that I had arrived on the same afternoon in which had been arranged a screening of his first Kung Fu movie entitled *"Major Brother."* It was a private screening, arranged solely for his students and close friends.

I remember thinking to myself, "This is a Kung Fu Master?" Where are the Dragon and Tiger brands on the forearms, the bald head, the bulging muscles? My Kung fu experience to date having been only with David Carradine's original series, I was expecting these things. I was disappointed to say the least. Seeing the movie, however, went along way toward restoring my dwindled faith in my future teacher. The movie was good. And he was great. My very young awareness had been vindicated temporarily. However, I was still skeptical. After all, had I not studied Karate, and Judo? I knew about the Martial Arts. (Or so I thought.)

The next day in the School, off of Chung Shan North Road in downtown Taipei not far from the famous Grand Hotel, I had my formal introduction to the Master. He knew about my limited experience in Martial Arts by way of my father. He walked directly up to me and said in his broken English, "So, you before study Karate, Judo, eh?" I nodded, and he continued. "So, you understanda power, eh?" This he said while executing a couple of Karate-like reverse punches,

Master Hsu, a senior classmate and Myself as a newly arrived pupil at a morning park meeting.

exaggerating the rotation of the hips and the extension of the rear leg for mechanical force. "Yes, yes!" I said excitedly. "That is what I learned before!" I experienced a warm feeling whereby the master had just acknowledged that what I had done prior was correct. That feeling lasted about five seconds. "This notta true power." he said, bursting by bubble of euphoria. "Come here. I show you true power."

He led me to the middle of the floor and turned me so that my back was oriented toward the far wall where there were rows of tatami (woven straw mats about two inches thick) mounted to the wall. I had silently wondered what purpose these pads on the wall would possibly have when I had seen them earlier that night. I was about to find out. The master told me to prepare myself so that I would not be harmed, by closing my teeth tightly and bracing my neck and spine muscularly. "Watch," he said. And I watched as he lightly placed both his hands on my chest. Then, it seemed to me that he sort of effortlessly flicked his wrists and I was suddenly airborne. I was literally hurled completely across the room and slammed into the tatami, their purpose now registering vaguely on my rattled awareness. I was unable to understand how a human being could generate so much power with so small a movement. It seemed to defy all logic and normal mechanics. It truly seemed like magic. And I resolved then and there that I had to stay with the man until I learned how he did that to me. Thus began a relationship that spanned nearly fifteen years.

It was not always easy in the beginning. The training consisted of Tien Kan (Heavenly Stem Linear Pa Kua) in sufficient repetition to drive the point home, 25 each side of each of the 24 exercises to warm up, interspersed with 200-300 pushups of various types, crane dips (a one-legged knee bend), and standing meditation. This was followed by tumbling and floor-work exercises, kicking drills, push hands, and some sparring. Very little technique was ever taught in the classes, which lasted from 8-10 p.m. nightly. If you wished to learn techniques, you had to be an inner door student.

My father, Master Hsu, Me at M.A.A.G. where I taught classes for him on Taiwan.

By the time I arrived on Taiwan, my father and Hsu Hong Chi had become very close, and my father was his top American Student at that time. Therefore, I was allowed in on his good graces. (Besides, he was my ride, I couldn't get home without him.) To say that I was extremely lucky, in this regard, would be a gross understatement. I have often counted my blessings.

If allowed, you stayed until sometimes as late as 2 a.m. in the morning and this is when Master Hsu taught other things, amazing things sometimes. He told many stories in the wee hours about a vast panorama of subject matter and he would punctuate his lessons with both physical and martial narrative and this is when the best techniques would come out.

Master Hsu could be a harsh man at times, in those days. When I first "pushed hands" with my teacher, I had little or no skill and as such suffered all of the problems that a new student faces in trying to perform the exercise properly. I was too stiff and I continuously floated my elbows too high. My teacher pointed this out right away, *"No lift elbow up, riba open, understan?"* He said. I did not understand until a few moments later when *WHAM!* Down came his right finger-tips across my left ribs. I felt like I had been whipped with four steel rods. *"I told you, no lift elbow, understan?"* Being thus stimulated, I thought I really had the idea now. But, *WHAM!* Again the steel rods came snaking down through my left ribs. And again the soft voice, *"Elbow must no up, understanduh?"* I never lifted my elbows again during push hands, *EVER.* "Pain good teacher." Master Hsu would always say. "You have pain, you learn to *MOVE,* quick!"

Another time, when I was a Green Belt, a student questioned Master Hsu about the power of Pi

Chuan (Splitting). It seemed that he could not derive any power from the movement so he felt it invalid. I must confess, I was having difficulty myself. But by this time I had acquired a healthy respect (and fear) for my teacher's hand. Hence, I did not ask too many questions that I felt might result in a direct demonstration. Preferring, rather to observe the effects of his power clinically.. from a distance.., on another pupil. I swear that sometimes my teacher was psychic. "Syau Mike! Lai, Lai!" (which means come here, but to me it meant *oh no*) I walked dutifully over to him. "Punch!" he commanded... I knew my teacher well enough by now to know that when given such an order, he meant it and he meant it in the most sincere way. So I launched a well rooted Peng Chuan (Crushing fist) at his heart.

In a surrealistic fashion I watched as my teachers hands descended in a blur toward my right arm. He lightly hooked only his pinkies on my arm, one at the inner wrist, and the other at the outer elbow, and with a loud *CRACK*, he promptly dislocated my shoulder. This happened with less than six inches of movement on his part. I immediately hit the floor. Both from the force of the blow and the pain it caused.

Without even a moment's hesitation, Master Hsu jumped down next to me, sat me up, and promptly realigned that same dislocated shoulder with another, less painful crack. Then, after seeing that I was fine, he turned to the other pupil who had asked the question in the first place, and asked, "Understand?" I learned both how to dislocate and relocate a shoulder on the same day.

Me receiving 1st place for my first Kuoshu win as my teacher, Hsu Hong Chi, looks from behind me.

What about the other pupil, you might ask? Well... he learned his own lessons. My teacher always taught on several levels at once. Everyone involved with the lesson learned something, each according to his/her own level. And he had this frightening (sometimes) ability to look into your innermost hidden thoughts and expose you to yourself, saying *Look! This is what you are!* I remember once at a seminar at my house in Lakeside, California, one of the then second generation pupils was asked a direct question to test his heart concerning how much money he had left in his wallet. The man began fanning the apparently pitiful amount of money he had in his wallet and attempting to count same. Suddenly, Master Hsu snatched the wallet out of his hand and started thumbing out a bunch of big bills from deeper in the wallet, opening secret panels in the wallet to reveal other big bills all the while saying "Oh. not too much money eh? Oh, Oh!" all the while laughing and giggling. Sometimes students would leave as a result of his penetrating insight. But if they listened to what he was trying to tell them, they would generally profit from his attempt to guide them.

Master Hsu had a tremendous dedication to his pupils. He sincerely believed in trying to teach something to everyone, no matter how minimal his interaction with them. I remember a time when, upon leaving a demonstration at a Chinese Military base, a belligerent M.P. questioned the validity of what we had demonstrated. He specifically taunted Master Hsu about the "Iron Body" demonstrations, saying that he did not believe that it was possible and casting aspersions or Chinese Kung Fu in general. Master Hsu dearly loved his Art and he could see the bully mentality in the M.P., so he casually invited the M.P. to strike the Black Belt of his choice as many times as he desired to quell his doubts. The M.P. chose Ah Huan, the smallest of us all (105 lbs.) My teacher, always the showman, did his best to egg the bully on, saying things like "Come on my grandma can hit harder than that." When the bully was sufficiently aroused and literally pounding on Ah Huan's body, Master Hsu gave Ah Huan the "High Sign" meaning to give the man "a lesson." On the next blow, the belligerent M.P. broke his wrist while punching Ah Huan in the stomach. As the M.P. knelt there on the road howling in despair, my teacher sidled up to him and said in a low, calm voice; "Now you believe, eh." Then he turned, as did we, and walked away.

I wish to emphasize at this point that my teacher was not as harsh as he was fair. It took awhile to see that. But the longer you were around the man, the more apparent this fact became. He just had a very strongly etched way of looking at things. He used to say that he hated deceit. He would say, *"I like everything cut and dried! I no like back door style!"*

Master Hsu, one of my students with 1st (Joe), Me, at an L.A. Kuoshu event in 1981.

I once saw a man crippled with a spinal problem. The man had been to all kinds of specialists according to his own words. But, alas, he had no results. A pupil brought the man to Master Hsu. He had only heard of my teacher (nicknamed *Magic Hands*) by his pupils and hoped that he might find help. He had very little money. My teacher asked him some cursory questions about his injury and then said, *"Okay. You give me two dollah, give Temple, I fix you. Hou bu Hou?"* (okay not okay) The man complied willingly. My teacher gently worked on this man's back. Ten minutes later he was pain free.

Another time, a man came to my teacher because of a chronic jaw dislocation. The man was very rich, liked everyone to know it, and had a $100.00 bill sticking out of his shirt pocket. My teacher asked him, "How much you pay?" The man said, "I have a $100.00." My teacher, knowing the man was trying to buy him and resenting the man's perspective, gave him a swift slap on the right side of his jaw and took the money from his pocket in one smooth movement saying "Okay, fix now." as he did it. The jaw was indeed fixed, and so had been the man.

I saw my teacher give of himself and his medicinal skills on countless occasions on Taiwan. I never saw him turn anyone away, nor did I ever see him fail to help someone. He used to say that to learn to fight, to hurt people was easy. Anyone could learn this in two to three years. But, to learn such skills is to become obligated to learn to help also. He used to say *"If know enough to take life, must know enough to save life. That is true mastery. Any less you only practice Kung Fu, no master yet."*

I was one of the few "round eyes" fortunate enough to learn Master Hsu's *Tui-Na* Bone Setting Skills. He used to teach by direct experience. A student would be injured and, barring any emergency, he would call me over. "Syau Mike, Lai." Then he would demonstrate what he wanted me to do on me, so that I could feel the technique. "Lai, Lai, okay now you fix." he would say...

Yeah, right I would think. "No worry." he would say. "You mistake, I fix." And he would wink. "Try, Try." He would urge. And so I would.

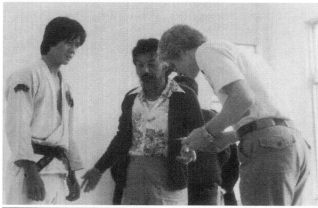

His fighting philosophy was direct, like the man. "Danger? Go!" he used to say while we were engaged in sparring practice. His great tactical knowledge was impressive to say the least. One time, a student was called up so that Shr Fu would be able to demonstrate the *pyan (changing angles)* attack of Pa Kua. The student described later how he was very excited at one point in the exchange because he thought he was actually going to be able to strike Shr Fu, and suddenly Master Hsu was behind him tapping him on the shoulder.

Master Hsu and Me as I am presented an award at Tan Chung University, 1982.

He was also very big on proper etiquette. My teacher's desk had a number of chairs around it arranged from nearer him to further away. I had many times as a young student in the school witnessed the game of musical chairs that the elder students played every time one of them walked in. You see, it was the tradition that the eldest present sit next to the Master. And then the next eldest, and so forth. Much like you see in traditional kung fu family photos, with the eldest next to the master, on the near right, and the next on the nearest left, and then alternate back and forth until all are seated, with the youngest students sitting the furthest away.

And so one day, Mr. Heh did not get up and move when Mr. Lai, his senior, came in to the room. This caused Mr. Lai (known for his Iron Palm) to anger and strike Mr. Heh most strongly. Mr. Heh went down gasping for air. This caused Master Hsu's son, Hong Yi, to run upstairs to get his father. Moments later, we heard Master Hsu's flip flops coming quickly down the stairs. He ran right over to Mr. Heh and began to resuscitate him. After the crisis was abated, and Mr. Heh was alright with his breathing normal, Master Hsu rebuked Mr. Lai lightly for losing his temper to such a degree. But then he really got angry at Mr. Heh for not paying proper respect to an elder brother under his tutelage. This was very important.

Master Hsu's perspective of the Student/Teacher relationship can best be summed up in his own words: *"You like study, I like teach. As long as you like study, I like teach. You no like study? Who lose? I lose? I no think so. I already know."* I firmly believe this is true. And I feel very fortunate to have had the opportunity and good fortune to have been able to study extensively with such an extraordinary man for nearly 15 years of my life. I will carry him with me for the rest of my days.

Building The Wall

 Many years ago my teacher, Master Hsu, said to me: "Kung Fu is like building a wall. Maybe you have a house, and you would like to build a wall all the way around. But, you cannot only build a wall. Because you must do your job, take care of your family, education... your life. So, some days you have no time, you cannot build even a single brick. Some days you have a little time, and you can build maybe one or two bricks. Some days, you have a lot of time, and can build many, many bricks. You should not worry, sooner or later, the wall will be built."

Let's face this fact. Studying Kung Fu is a long-term venture. Therefore the normal time/goal framework should not be applied to its study. The very act of doing so is most certainly self defeating. A pragmatic approach is the very essence of effective martial arts and therefore should be applied to *the study* of the martial arts as well.

First, you must recognize that you are dealing with *Self*. Self discipline, Self improvement, Self insight, Self achievement, Self enlightenment, etc. The only competition you are involved in, with regard to study, is against yourself. Once you have accepted this fact, the need to satisfy or compete with others is eliminated. This is not a race. No one is going to beat you to the finish line of your Self growth. True understanding cannot be rushed.

There are many factors which will affect the rate at which you progress. Your age, experience, athletic ability, practice habits, concentration while practicing, workload, family life, social life, academic life; the list is quite long. The main thing is just to continue to move forward. Every day, try to do something related to your practice. If you can accept this perspective, you will have minimal frustration along your path of learning.

Students often tell me that they would like to immerse themselves in study. Their thoughts are admirable but not very realistic. It is more prudent and appropriate to integrate your "studies" of the art within the rest of your life. Realize that there will inevitably be times when your "studies" will suffer. However, you should try and integrate your "practice" of the art into your daily routine. In this way you will continue to always move forward, and once you gather that momentum, you will not stop progressing.

My teacher used to say; "Good kung fu is found in the little things." And this is what he meant: Kung Fu is a complicated subject, and the thing to remember is to just keep at it... make it a part of your daily life. Practice your meditation a few brief minutes each night while lying in your bed before sleep. Practice your breathing while you are waiting for the bus or for your next appointment. Practice your balance while standing in line anywhere. Practice your horse stance while making a sandwich at home. Practice your hand speed just before, and again just after, turning off and on the light switch each time you enter or exit a room. Practice kicking control while slowly opening and closing doors at home with your foot. Practice your hand strength by carrying the grocery bags with one or two fingers each. Such possibilities are quite literally endless. I know, I know, it seems too simple, right? Well, let's take but one example:

how many times per day to you turn off or on a light switch? If every time you did one or the other you flicked your hand at top speed to within a fraction of an inch of the switch just once each time, how many times per year would you be practicing that strike? 3000? 4000? 5000? Master Hsu used to say "10,000 times practice and the technique is yours forever. 10,000 more and you have mastery of that technique." So, you do the math. That means maybe two to three years to mastery of any one type hand strike. How many more precious minutes wasted doing mundane tasks that could be made just as profitable?

We, in the martial arts, pride ourselves on the cultivation of awareness. What have you done to sharpen yours lately? I know, you must come to your institute to practice that, right? Wrong! Every day, all of us are in crowds of people everywhere we go. To practice visual awareness; try tilting your head slightly forward and use your peripheral vision to guide your steps and avoid jostling other people as you move through the crowd. At first, move very slowly and then later, more quickly. To train your audio awareness; try this exercise the next time you are at the movies. Try to zero in on a conversation near you. Isolate it from the other background noise and hear it clearly. Start at 10 feet distant, then gradually increase your range. Or, you can practice sensory awareness at home by putting on your clothes with your eyes shut. There are dozens of ways that your training can occupy the spare moments of your life. It only takes a little imagination.

Often students tell me that they have no time to do a "proper workout." What exactly is a "proper workout" anyway? The general consensus seems to be one that involves an hour or more of hard, sweat-breaking exercises combined with the practice of the every form and drill you know until your muscles ache and your body fatigues. No, that is an "aerobic" workout. A "proper workout" is anything in the realm of practicing a given skill to achieve greater ability within that particular area of study. For example: since the essence of form and fluidity within the form is simply synaptic conditioning of the nervous structures involved in carrying out a given motion, it follows that the more times you do the motion, the more smooth and refined it will become. So, you need not break a sweat at all to practice form, you need only go through the motions mindfully. This literally takes only minutes a day. Everyone has a few minutes to spare each day for practice in this manner. It can literally be done in the comfort of your office or living room. Now, of course, if you wish to develop speed and power in those same motions, then you must practice speedily and powerfully. This type of practice certainly will break a sweat. But, speed and power conditioning are dependent on familiarity, which brings us again back to just "going through the motions" mindfully. Realistically speaking, only about twenty five percent of your practice regimen need be devoted to the strenuous aspects of training. The bulk of skill is found in the easy familiarity of the movements. Overall, you should "train" in relation to what you wish to develop as skill sets. If you wish to fight competitively, then naturally you will need to up your conditioning and resistance aspects of training. If you wish to develop solid self defense skills, you will need to train said skills with a partner and with gradually less and less cooperation on his/her part.

Utilizing this type of approach to your training, even the busiest pupil can find a way to build his or her brick in the wall each and every day. And when in those are rarest of times you find yourself completely unencumbered with normal lifetime activity, well then you can really make some headway on that wall, huh?

Standing Meditation and "Energetics"
Foundation to Fruition

Standing practice is very important in our methodology. Again, no more, or less, important than anything else but we consider it a cornerstone of the overall matrix of training.

Meditation aspects aside, from standing practice we will initially learn to hold a position of "ease" in the body, meaning no antagonism and no tension. All muscle groups other than those needed to maintain the frame will be gradually shed away in terms of any tension. Appropriate "linkage" of the soft tissues and proper alignment of the skeletal system allow for cultivation of a relaxed, natural and fluid movement structure over time. This translates then to efficiency of motion via a corresponding "non antagonism" learned, which in turn can then translate to great speed of motion. Since acceleration is vital to kinetic potential, a properly relaxed and unified structure is capable of great force.

To us, the philosophy of "walking before running" can be applied to standing practice verses actual live movement. If you cannot relax during standing, you have little hope of truly relaxing during high speed dynamic movement, especially in the face of an adversary. Such was the opinion of the people who trained me and now my own as well.

In addition, standing practice when coupled with intention, has a way of activating the deeper connective tissues of the body in a unified and cohesive manner that is not easily achieved through other means. This then teaches the practitioner what a unified body should feel like and, when properly understood, will contribute to a solidity in motion that can truly become a force to be reckoned within any context of combat.

The energetic aspect of meditation is a subject of frequent discourse when one is a student of the internal disciplines. Each year I am deluged with a variety of different questions related to this central issue. I would like to lay out the general theme of this subject in this work for your digestion. But truly it is a subject worthy of a volume all its own and this is merely cursory.

There are three separate phases in the practice of "energetics" as they relate to the internal arts. These phases are much like the phases a plant undergoes as it grows through the seasonal changes of its life cycle and such things are closely tied to the theory of Chinese Medicine.

First, essence must be *"stored"* in the new plant so that it may gather enough strength to prepare itself for *"growth"*. And then, through modulated and balanced growth, a *"flourishing"* of the plant can be realized. Our energetic training follows a similar three stages in the developmental order. But, what practices are necessary for each given stage?

In the initial stage of *"storing"*, a student will practice the basic exercises and postures to open his/her body and begin to gather some additional energy into the system. It is important to pay strictest detail to body alignment while practicing for any positive gains to occur. This attention to detail is analogous to installing a plumbing system in that if you create a plumbing line that is unnaturally "crimped" or otherwise misaligned, one of two things will likely occur in that line. Either the area in question will develop a sediment deposit and clog, or, the escalating pressure will burst the pipe. This same thing can occur in the human body in the form of "stagnation" of circulation in the system. This is an altogether unfavorable condition, to be sure.

During this initial phase, it is necessary for the student only to practice the exercises with breath modulation and a relaxed, proper posture. It is not necessary to concentrate on any sort of a visualization. Just feel. Drop your mind into the practice and Relax. Sense everything. In time, you will begin to experience your own body and mind in a way that you had not known prior.

Once you have achieved a certain level of intuitive feeling for what you are doing, it will be time to move on to phase two. It is now time to begin working with your "I" or "Yi" (intention) to begin to motivate your being toward a positive integration of mind and structure. At this time, simple Chi Kung exercises can be most beneficial in gaining a better understanding of the harmony that exists within.

This is a necessary harmony of mind (the General), breath (the Tactics), body (the Terrain) and energy (the Soldiers). The better you understand clearly what you are doing, the better the result will be. The terrain (body) has already become known in phase one. And there will be a sense that the soldiers (energy) are there. But, the General (mind) must now be schooled in its own disciplines and tactics (breath) and the modified breathing methodology must be committed to autonomic memory so that concentration does not have to be diverted during the task at hand.

The seven energy centers are depicted above: Top front starting with Yin Tang or upper Dan Tien, then Middle Dan Tien and finally Lower Dan Tien. Then in the back; At bottom is Wei Lu (tail end), Ming Mien (gate of life), Yu Jen (jade pillow) and finally Pai Hui at the crown point.

Whereas before you were merely trying to feel the different energies in your body, now you will be attempting to enhance those feelings and gain more conscious control over them. This second stage is when initial visualizations are introduced and practiced. Though it is important to realize that without a sufficient length of time in level one practice, there will simply not be enough of a "charge" in the system to make any real progress in level two. So, whenever you feel that you are stagnating in your circulation trainings, consider that your "battery" may need some additional charging and go back to level one practice for awhile.

After a sufficient, concentrated time in level two, a serious student will finally gain the sensory awareness necessary for controlled access to his/her energy and will be able to circulate it freely throughout the meridian system at will.

It must be remembered that the proper method is to let the mind lead. And never to try to force the effort. The classics say; I (Yi), Li, Chi. The mind directs, the body obeys and the energy then follows. By analogy, think of a siphon action and you'll get the general idea.

Remember, it is important to remain focused during your meditations. You must let your awareness concentrate on your sensations of breath and then relax. You must *try without trying* and *do without doing* to be successful. Never strain your concentration. You must be casual, detached and open. Float with your sensations, but do not adhere to them. Your goal is to attain 10-15 minutes of no thought. Cultivate a detached emptiness. Be aware, but diffused.

It is time then to begin level three practice. This is where all the real benefits lie. Through advanced meditation techniques, the practitioner will gain greater control of the body's inner systems, helping to raise energy levels, increase immune systems to strengthen resistance, ease stress on the system as a whole, promote better digestion and assimilation for energy gains and benefit the psyche.

It is in this level that the entire discipline becomes a health regulating system, at once able to promote balance through harmony of the Yin and the Yang. Sensation and visualization are unified with form and motion yielding a powerful and unified mind/body workout.

This understanding and harmony will in turn promote more efficiency in the system which will then lead to greater strength, speed and focused control.

The subject of meditation is vast and very structured in the Taoist disciplines. It could easily be the subject of an entire work all on its own merit. The purpose of this brief chapter is only to introduce the idea of the importance of the tradition within the Hsing I discipline.

Once, when younger, I had deigned to ask my teacher some questions on the subject one particular rainy day in Taipei. In my mind, they were important questions. Even lofty to my limited perspective. He was looking up an herbal formula at the time, and after the third such question, he looked up from his desk squarely at me and said; *"You don't meditate much do you?"* I had to confess that, at the time, although I had tried many times I had been unable to maintain a focus for very long. And that had more often led to frustration and giving up than not on my part. He shook his head and said; *"If you no meditate, HALF you art, you miss! You like miss-ah half?!"* No, sir. I said. He then said; *"Then.. YOU MUST!"*

The rest of the conversation was pretty much filled with the advice I have rendered above. Do it for the sake of doing. Don't focus on goal or outcome. Just enjoy the journey.

Meditation may be the one short cut we have to greater proficiency in the arts. At the very least, the journey is interesting and rewarding.

Hsin, I, Li, Chi, Jin - The formula for success

Before we can get into discussing the theory and principles of practicing Hsing I, we must first by necessity, define exactly what we mean by "Hsing I" in the first place. Most people translate "Hsing" as form, but originally the character used was the character for "Hsin" or heart. It is not exactly known when the name was changed, but it is an important point to remember this original rendering, as it relates to the true nature of the boxing practice.

The character, "I" is usually translated as Mind or Will by most scholars. However, in our Western language this is far too vague. It should be distilled down ever further and rendered as "intention" to really begin to grasp the idea behind this method of Chinese Boxing.

This then, would give us a balance of "Hsin" Heart and "I" Intention within "Chuan" Boxing, yielding Heart Intention Boxing, as the original contextual rendering coined by the earliest of practitioners.

This also ties into a five word "formula" passed down in the songs of training regarding the formulation of unity, for expression of absolute unified power in the martial arts; Hsin, I, Li, Chi, Jin... Or... Heart, Mind, Body (physicality), Energy, Power.

A Chinese character can and does have many associative meanings. The problem we face in the West is that our language is linear. Chinese language is pictorial/symbolic. So when we see a translation of a character, we see whatever the translator "saw" in context of the translated material. But when a Chinese person sees that root character, he/she sees ALL the associative meanings at the same time.

Although "hsin" is usually rendered as heart and then tied to "desire," I am not positive that this is complete in terms of denoting the importance and/or the role that our seat of emotion plays in this equation. At least with regard to western practitioners. In the Western world, if you were to ask someone if they "desire" a million dollars, the answer would certainly come back as a yes. But ask that same person if they are actually doing anything about that desire and many would answer no they are not. Therefore, for us westerners, I think perhaps attaching the idea of a heart-felt "belief" may be closer to the mark.

When you combine your "belief" with an "intention" to do something, that will most certainly give rise to the "body" (physicality) of actually doing. This will then give rise to the kinetic, mental and spiritual "energy" necessary to accomplish the task at hand which will then give rise to the actual "power" of achievement.

This formula is not only applicable to the martial arts. It is also applicable to life in general and can be overlaid onto ANY undertaking. It is this author's opinion that the practice of such unity of emotion, idea and the physical act of doing can allow the accomplishment of any goal one may set themselves upon.

It is a learned, practiced and acquired skill set if one sets out with the notion to do exactly that.

The Importance of Ritual

A psychological anchor is formed in a very simple way, requiring only two components to be present in the process. The first is a powerful and profound state of mind, and the second is any repetitive act performed while in said mind state. In example, imagine that you are attending a funeral of a deceased loved one. Throughout the event, you are in a profound state of grief. Many people you know approach you and speak to you in a low tone of voice while touching you on the shoulder saying words to the effect of "it's alright, everything will be okay."

Years later, you are at a Christmas party and having the time of your life. A friend that you have not seen for many years walks up to you and touches you on the shoulder. In a low tone of voice the friend says; "How have you been? Are you doing okay?" Then suddenly you feel just as you did years before while at the funeral. What has just happened? The answer is that a psychological anchor has just been triggered. It was formed years before at the funeral. You were in a powerful profound state of grief (requirement No. 1 -- a powerful and profound state of mind). Many people who knew you and were concerned about you touched you on the shoulder and spoke consoling words to you in a low tone of voice (requirement No. 2 -- a repetitive act).

Martial arts abound with ritual practice methods designed to create and embed psychological anchors. We cultivate an exceptional focus of mind in performance of both Martial action and technique (component No. 1; a powerful and profound state of mind). And we hold this mind state while practicing over and over again our hsings (forms), katas, hyungs and ryus (component No. 2; a repetitive act performed while in said mind state).

| Relax, eyes stare forward. Calm the breath and feel. | Inhale and circle the hands up to join above the crown. | Exhale and lower the hands to Dan Tien, sink the body. | Inhale and uncoil the right hand upward and outward. | Step and half step into the left San Ti (three leg) Stance. |

In practice of the internal arts, this notion is exceptionally clear in its definition regarding the training. Hsin - I - Li - Chi - Jin (desire/belief - intention - movement - energy - power). This can be likened to an equation or formula for optimal performance. If all the parts are in place, in proper proportion and combination, that you will have something that is greater in the total than is in the individual parts alone. If not, you simply have individual parts.

This conceptual idea of training goes far beyond mere muscle memory. This type of practice creates, over time, a series of embedded psychological anchors. Because a psychological anchor requires only those two components present to effectively imprint on the psyche. In internal practice, "the profound state of mind" becomes a profoundly focused state of "no mind" such as is achieved through practice of meditation as opposed to an emotion such as grief or anger. The second component, which in a normal anchor could be something like clapping the hands in a certain way or being touched on the shoulder a certain way as in the above, instead becomes a specific sequence of complex motor mechanics such as is found in the internal martial arts training sequences. These things, practiced over time, create a forever kind of imprint to where ultimately, a person need literally only think the image and the technique flows out of them with all of its inherent properties of profoundly aligned and practiced body mechanics with both speed and accuracy.

This then, must be subsequently paired with live resistance drills of increasing reality to forever "marry" the imprinted skill set to the state of mind necessary in actual use in a real scenario. Too often in today's martial arts schools this last step is never done. Or, if it is touched upon it is not to the depth necessary to truly create a matrix of viable utility. This missing component of true skill training is causing a gradual denigration of the martial utility at large within traditional martial arts as a whole.

There exists a major disconnect in the way most people train their kungfu in America today. Meaning that they train form but not essence. And they do not train essence for fighting at all. At least most do not. The do the rituals/forms only.

It is insufficient to practice only "the ritual" and expect to gain martial ability. Although it is also true that "the ritual" aspect is an integral part of traditional training and for good reason as is outlined in the beginning of this chapter.

What makes these systems their own is the methods of power generation, tactical overlays, footwork, etc. as is true in any "system." It is the core components that tie all the parts together and make it work. But form is only the "textbook" from which to glean insight into such things. One must still train to "marry" the skills they gain through practice of their respective "art" to the actuality of the pressure of fighting. Things are different when another human being is of a mind determined to hurt you and you are well aware of that fact.

Beyond that, actual fighting is not film making and this is the second great misconception. You will rarely see the "picture perfect technique" in any actual fighting context. When you do, that is a true photo-op moment. In a competitive venue, for the first several years of any full contact competition, you see a developing use of principle in the evolving fighter. It is only after many years, when they become more calm in such a circumstance, that you may actually see more from them.

The street is another echelon entirely. Even a well seasoned full contact competitor MAY NOT be able to effectively respond in a street scenario. But they will be better prepared than most. To ensure that you will be able to respond in the street, such scenarios must also be present during your "marrying" process and they must come as close to actual as is allowable in training.

Pi Chuan

Splitting Fist

The Song Of Pi

From the mouth, come the two fists closely held.
Up to the eyebrow, drills the forefist.
Close behind the forefist, follows the hind fist.
Together with the crossing arms, the heart unites. Chi falls to Tan Tien as body moves,
hind foot forward as the arms separate.
In a hemisphere the Tiger's mouth opens while all fingers apart.
Forehand pushes to between eyebrow and heart.
Under the armpit, the hind hand stays.
Hand, nose, and foot form the three point set.
So as Pi Chuan tsuans upward, to the eyebrow, turned up the little finger.
Together sink the feet and hands, upthrust the tongue.
Advancing, changing styles, hind palm sinks downward.

In performance of Pi Chuan, the Splitting posture, there are several key elements that must be harmonized before the posture will feel balanced and powerful. Until these component parts are intuitively understood, the movements will feel only awkward at best. We will address the first two lines of the song first.

Initially, the fists must twist (tsuan) upward from their palms downward position at the waist, keeping near the torso so as to almost brush the skin, and then shoot outward from the level of the mouth. This will ensure a circular connected strength in the fist and the twisting will both augment power from central muscle groups and serve to coil the limb for power in the subsequent pulling action.

The third line reminds that the hind fist follows at the elbow of the striking fist to protect the ribs from attack and also to be closer to the opponent for secondary attack.

As this action is completed, and the thrusting from the rear foot dissipates, bring the rear foot up to light foot (foot level at medial ankle of support foot) position and feel the suspension from the Pai Hui (crown of head) point anchoring your center of balance.

"Together with crossing arms," begins the next line. And as the arms cross in preparation to perform the

palm separation, the mind stills and the intention takes shape. This is what is meant by "The Heart Unites". Be sure that the armpits remain open (about a golf ball's diameter) to keep the proper energetic/kinetic linkage.

The next section of the poem is very important in that it tries to impart to the reader the necessary harmony of mind and body as the intention is completed.

As you change styles into the Splitting palm, drop your mind to lower Tan Tien (a spot three fingers below your navel, residing inside the body cavity) and settle your frame as you perform the Tearing Silk action. In other words, it's all about core integration.

The next four lines of the song give details as to positioning of the posture. Tiger's mouth (the space between the thumb and index finger) must be open and stretched as is the whole hand. The attitude should be one of holding a six inch ball lightly. This shape is to aid the energetic aspects of the posture in practice. The forward hand should reside at a height that sits between the eyebrow and heart.

Regarding the line; "Under the armpit, the hind hand stays." This detail occurs immediately after the arms cross in transition into the Splitting Palm posture. The hind hand must circle through the armpit on its way down to the abdomen. This action creates a double interacting spiral, one vertical and one horizontal, in the torso and waist magnifying kinetic potential. At completion, the lead finger, nose and the lead toe should all be on a single plane, forming the

"three point set" of the San Ti (three leg) stance.

The final lines of the song relate to the first fisted posture of Pi Chuan and again reiterate that when you perform this part of the change to tsuan (twist) the striking hand so that the little finger is turned upward in relation to the fist. The tongue should always be pressed upward to the palate to insure the energetic connection of the Du and Ren pulses in practice. And the body and hind palm should sink downward in the "changing styles" of the Splitting palm to settle and ground the frame.

Pi Chuan is often called the soul of Hsing I practice. What you learn (or don't learn) in your Pi Chuan practice will transfer to every other part of your Hsing I Chuan.

The essence of Pi Chuan is Rising and Falling energy. When you advance to the light foot position, the whole body must be light and suspended while coiling every muscle fiber for the subsequent strike of the palm. Even the hand that is to become the striking palm is brought upward in a coiled position with the pinky turned upward.

When you advance forward, you must do so with solidity. Tan tien (core) motivates the strike and the whole body sinks/grounds at the spatial focal point. This is effortless power.

The Palm strike of Pi Chuan is mostly downward. The forward part of the stroke is largely a result of the corresponding foot movement. The strike must be performed like an axe stroke. The movement must be natural, allowing the force of gravity to act on the hand, and be coerced, guided and accelerated by the rest of the muscular/skeletal system.

Begin in San Ti Stance, Right Weight is 70% rearward	Coil the body downward suppressing the legs	Step the front foot forward, toe out, while bringing right fist up	Transition the rear leg to suspended position	Step and half step to change styles to left side San Ti

Coil the body downward suppressing the legs	Step the front foot forward, toe out, while bringing right fist up	Transition the rear leg to suspended position	Step and half step to change styles to right side San Ti

The state of mind must be pure and focused on only the movement currently being performed until completion. If you allow your mind to leap ahead to the next movement in an effort to gain more speed, you shall gain only disharmony and your movements shall lack power as a result of the absence of real intention. The conscious and subconscious mind must be linked together to manifest absolute power. There can be no disparity of command issued to the body.

The strength of Pi Chuan is imparted mainly through the waist and intercostal muscles. The half step of the rear foot does not allow for a "vector product" power in Pi Chuan as it does in some of the other elements. The kinetics are simply not there to apply this type of force. Rather the half stepping in Pi Chuan should be applied in synchronicity with the arrival of the body's center at it's pre-determined spatial point when the actual blow is delivered. Thereby maximizing the body's rooted connection to the ground. More solidity means less recoiled waste back into the body frame, yielding more potential power into the target.

Lastly, power originates in the waist, is rebounded through the legs, developed through the torso and manifest in the fingers. But Hsing I has been best likened to a whipping piece of rattan. It moves at once in a brisk wave, more like an impulse.

When practicing, remember to lead with the hands when performing Pi Chuan and connect them to Tan Tien so that the whole body moves as a unit. If you think of leading with the waist, you will move too sluggishly. The wave will be too big. It is simply not possible to think about the individual parts of the kinetic process and manifest it with any speed. The movement has to be like a pulse. The image of intent is formed and the body and energy obey that intention.

Remember quality over quantity in your practice. The internal arts are unique and they must be practiced in a unique and thoughtful way.

The important thing to remember in applying the splitting posture is to not be one dimensional in your thinking. Remember that each form of Hsing I can be applied from all five levels of application. Striking, throwing, chin na, striking the nerves, striking the points, all are viable.

The Splitting form is an archetype of that mechanic. And, yes, it can be applied from the form. But it can also be overlaid with the "Three Basin" theory giving you three different mediums to work from influencing angle and position of attack. It can also be explored from the "Seven Stars" theory, yielding a multitude of additional expressions of "Splitting" in the form of the Head, Shoulder, Elbow, Hip, Knee, Foot and Hand. *Try using Pi by employing just a half step out of guard to close and come over the top of the opponent's guard.*

My teacher used to say "You know one, you know ten." He was fond of expounding the fact that a change of hand position, angle, or footwork was necessary to adjust the technique to an ever changing situation of fighting. "As long as principle is correct, it's ok." he used to say. I believe very strongly in this. This is what makes Hsing I such a completely fascinating system.

Note: *Movement can never be accurately portrayed in still form. For more information on both the movement structures and possible applications of Pi Chuan (splitting fist), please refer to our instructional DVD products "Hsing I Five Force Elements" and "Hsing I Five Force Combinations." These can be found at hsing-i.com*

Tsuan Chuan

Drilling Fist

The Song Of Tsuan

Fore Hand "Yin Palm" presses down.
Hind Hand "Yang Fist" upward tsuans.
Up to the eyebrows the fists tsuan, elbows embrace heart while hind foot moves.
Stare at fore fist, four limbs stop.
Tsuan Chuan moves and styles changed.
Fore foot steps first, hind foot next, hind hand "Yin Palm" down the elbows kept.
Step by step the three points set.
Fore Hand "Yang Fist" hit the nose.
Little finger upward turned, heart by elbows protected.
Tsuan Chuan punches nose when advancing.
Fore Palm downward pressed with wrist, then upward turned as steps forward.

Tsuan Chuan is perhaps one of the most frequently over simplified forms of the five fists/ forces, as most students interpret this as an extended boxing style upper cut. This is in error as a comparison for several important reasons.

Let's discuss the poem line by line as the song of Tsuan is quite revealing of Hsing I subtlety.

The first three lines of the poem jump right into the primary idea of the "Water" Fist which is to "Tsuan" (drill). The first two lines remark of the "yin palm" (palm down) pressing while the "yang fist" (palm up) strikes upward while twisting "Tsuan." This is to be done on a narrow central axis (elbows embrace heart) while advancing on the opponent.

The fourth line then talks about two key elements of Hsing I practice "Stare at fore fist" alludes to the focused intention of mind at the moment of strike. It is vital that the mind is 100% committed to the strike. There can be no disparity of focus when the energy is discharged. The whole body power and mental intention must unite as one.

The second part of line four, "four limbs stop", remarks on the "body stop on four sides" principle from the 'Eight Fundamentals classic', in relation to back-lashing kinetic energy as a

result of issuing/Jing. Physics teaches us that for every action there is an equal an opposite reaction. The body, being as elastic as it is, will experience a "backlash" effect from the tremendous amount of energy being extended at the point of issuing. Therefore it is necessary to train the body to solidify its mass upon issuing force. With practice, this will allow the maximum amount of force to be transmitted from a solid base, having minimal backlash. I sometimes use an analogy for my students of slinging wet mud from a shovel. You learn quickly to get the shovel moving and then suddenly stopping its forward momentum to allow the wet mud to slide off the shovel. In analogy, your body is the "shovel" and your hands are the mud that issues from it. You must move the body then suddenly and completely stop!

Lines five and six then reinforce the idea of movement while striking. This is again a major point of Hsing I boxing. Not only does the momentum gained through movement give the potential for more power but it is entirely practical as well. Since it is a given that if one must fight, the desire is to end the encounter as soon as possible. It only makes sense to move into the opponent immediately when possible to make a pre-emptive strike.

Line seven remarks once again on the "three point set" as found in other poems. And this is something that cannot be told enough. Alignment on a single plane of the lead forefinger or knuckle, the lead toe or bubbling well (kidney #1), and the nose must always be observed. This keeps your potential kinetic energy centered and balanced for optimum efficiency. Plus, you protect your center at the same time which is where your enemy will be coming and where you get hit! I don't know about you but those are good enough reasons for me.

Now, line eight is where the reader has to be really paying attention because line eight tied to line three gives you an often overlooked key to the Water Fist.

"Up to the eyebrows the fists tsuan" plus "Fore Hand Yang Fist hit the nose" = ?....... (any ideas?) Obviously since the drilling action must first rise to the height of the eyebrows before ending up hitting the nose there is a slight arcing curve at work here that is usually overlooked because the novice interprets the striking fist action of Tsuan as an uppercut.

Line nine is then talking about the first action of Tsuan which is the open handed thrust of this Hsing-I style. The stipulation here is that the little finger is upturned during this action so that a coiled compression is formed in the muscles of the forearm in readiness for a strong hooking pull preceding the actual fisted attack.

Line ten reiterates two previously discussed points for blatant emphasis, namely hit the nose with whole body power while advancing forward.

Line eleven finishes by alluding to the focused intention of the down hand being through the wrist and not through the palm. And then finally line fourteen one last time tells you that the essence is a drilling 180 degree twist as the attack is made.

Remember that the strength of Tsuan Chuan is imparted equally from the legs, waist and costal spaces. The movement is extremely powerful as the kinetic energy can be applied with a vector product from the rear leg and combined with a forward momentum not unlike the crashing of a wave on the surf.

| Begin from San Ti Shr (three leg stance) | Step the front foot forward, toe out, while piercing forward | Step and half step to change styles to right Tsuan fist | Step the front foot forward, toe out, while piercing forward | Step and half step to change styles to left Tsuan fist |

In application, do not be one dimensional in your thinking. Remember, each form of Hsing I can be applied from all five levels of application. Tsuan can again be overlaid with the "Three Basin" theory, or the "Seven Stars" theory, yielding a multitude of additional expressions of "Drilling" in the form of the Head, Shoulder, Elbow, Hip, Knee, Foot and Hand. *Try using Tsuan to attack the ribs under the guard and then immediately firing the other drilling hand over the opponent's guard as he drops his elbow to stop the first attack.*

Again; "You know one, you know ten." A small change of hand position, angle of insertion, or footwork may be necessary to adjust the technique to an ever changing situation of fighting. As long as principle is correct and the proper force from the body is being employed, it's still the art of Hsing I. This understanding is what makes Hsing I so adaptable.

Note: *Movement can never be accurately portrayed in still form. For more information on both the movement structures and possible applications of Tsuan Chuan (drilling fist), please refer to our instructional DVD products "Hsing I Five Force Elements" and "Hsing I Five Force Combinations." These can be found at hsing-i.com*

Peng Chuan

Crushing/Penetrating Fist

The Song Of Peng

Peng Chuan starts with three points set.
"Hu Yen" upward high as heart.
Hind Hand "Yang Fist" under armpit stays, fore foot forward, hind foot next.
Shape like "T", the two feet are firm, body turns while looking straight.
Upstraight standing when foot lift, lifted foot with toes pointing side wise.
Hands and feet come down swiftly at same pace,
fore foot crossed then hind one follows naturally.
Peng Chuan still have tongue at palate.
Fore Arms elbow curved to upthrust.
Punch to the armpits when advancing.
Be quick and firm, the hind foot follows.

The song of Peng opens by reminding the reader about the three points set with the line "Peng Chuan starts with three points set". This, of course has been mentioned in other songs prior, so you might be wondering why it is being brought up yet another time?

Indeed, to have a good Peng form, the student must epitomize the concept of the three points and complete solidification of center. Without this, the blow will be weak and ineffectual.

The principles of the "Three Stops" from the "Eight Fundamentals" must be fully understood to be successful with Peng Chuan.

Specifically, the principle of "Body Stop On Four Sides" which means that at the moment the energy of the punch is issued the body must solidify in order to project the shock wave outward while allowing no recoiling effect back into the body mass causing a loss of potential energy.

Again, an analogy of this principle that I often use is one of slinging wet dirt or snow from a shovel. If you have ever had the "pleasure" of doing this, you'll remember that you could not simply toss the substance up and over

your shoulder like you do with dry dirt or powdery snow. If you tried, what happened was the mud/snow clung to the shovel blade all the way until it was right over your shoulder. And then you spun completely around from both the momentum and the weight of the filled shovel, or, the substance then fell off and right on to you.

Instead, you had to develop a special technique of starting the shovel forward and then suddenly stopping it so that the wet substance slid off the end of the shovel and on to the ground.

In this analogy, you must visualize your body as being the shovel and the hand that is striking is the mud/snow. Move the body forward and throw the fist out from the body. Then stop the body, so that the fist keeps moving forward with momentum and none of its energy comes recoiling (falling) back onto you.

Of course, be sure to obey the other postural fundamentals also, or you may injure yourself. There is a tremendous amount of potential energy in properly trained relaxation. Be sure to keep the shoulders relaxed, the elbows down and the spinal locks in place so that the recoil does not reflect onto you. This is a large part of the "Body Stop On Four Sides" principle.

The second line; "Hu Yen upward high as heart," reveals a "keyed" remark in reference to the ascendance of the fist to heart level within the matrix of the arc formed just before the downward/forward strike. This allows the adept to create tremendous downward compression from the drop of body weight and the closing of the intercostal muscles upon strike.

The third line, "Hind Hand Yang Fist under armpit stays, fore foot forward, hind foot next,"

reveals that the withdrawing hand is not passive but pulled back actively to reside under the armpit, creating tremendous torque from the body as it turns sideways simultaneously, while the fist extends and the feet come together in the half step.

Lines four and five; "Shape like 'T', the two feet are firm, body turns while looking straight" and "Upstraight standing when foot lift, lifted foot with toes pointing side wise" refer to the open posture of Peng and enforces the ideas of turning the body fully, forming the san ti stance position and staying firm or grounded in execution.

The sixth line of the poem reflects on the essential synchronization of timing the step with the punch: "Hands and feet come down swiftly at same pace, fore foot crossed then hind one follows naturally." And the second part of this line admonishes the reader to remember to move "naturally." Forced muscular power is not true power.

Line seven reminds that proper breathing and posture are always important considerations in combat, by prompting you that "Peng Chuan still have tongue at palate." This is not only an allusion to the Taoist practice of the "central circuit" for health. But also the simple practicality in breathing is to keep the mouth closed, teeth together and "tongue curled" so that you don't get a broken jaw upon entry to engagement for your trouble.

Line eight; "Fore Arms elbow curved to upthrust." is a good comment to the beginner who tends to over-straighten his/her arm in the Peng Chuan form. The text clearly states that the elbow is "curved to upthrust" meaning the point of the elbow is down.

The final lines, "Punch to the armpits when advancing" and "Be quick and firm, the hind foot follows" remind you of the attempt to master the downward/forward compression of the blow and that the practice should be vigorous, or quick and firm.

The power of Peng proceeds largely from the rotation of the waist. It is possible to apply a vector product force from the rear heel as the half step occurs, therefore the legs play a major role as well. The intercostals play a lesser role. But by no means should the available

compression power be overlooked or ignored as this is where the "down" or crushing aspects come from.

Remember that Hsing I cultivates "whole body power" in all of its actions and forms. Every piece should be in place. Nothing should be excluded from the practice, or your shapes will not be complete. Everything is about translating momentum from the thrust of the legs, through the core and into the projecting limb.

Peng Chuan is an excellent counter blow. *Try using the movement as an interceptive or "stop" hit against the opponent's advances.* Peng also lends itself well to combinations, with both itself, using angular closing, and/or other fists in high/low sequences.

Remember, "you know one, you know ten."

Begin from San Ti Shr (three leg stance)	Step forward, close stance while punching right	Step and half step while punching left	Step forward, close stance while punching right	Step and half step while punching left

Note: *Movement can never be accurately portrayed in still form. For more information on both the movement structures and possible applications of Peng Chuan (crushing/penetrating fist), please see our instructional DVD products "Hsing I Five Force Elements" and "Hsing I Five Force Combinations." These can be found at hsing-i.com*

Pao Chuan

Pounding Fist

The Song Of Pao

Elbows tightly embracing the body as foot lifted.
Fists in Yang fist must be tight.
Forehand be cross hind hand.
Form the "T" shape.
Fists first stay beside the navel. "Chi falls to Tan Tien as style changes, keep the three point set in place."
Fist outward, high as heart, fore fist "Hu Yen" upward while hind fist tsuans up to eyebrows with "Hu Yen" downwards and elbows too.
Pao Chuan must have foot lifted up.
Fore fist tsuans up as foot drops.
"Crossing steps" as fist and foot sink together.
Thus follows the hind foot on.

Pao Chuan is one of the easier motions in Hsing I to explain and to practice. It is also one of the more useful self defense motions, as it is a refined modification of a base instinct to shield the face when being attacked.

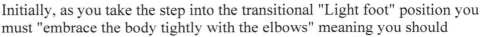

Initially, as you take the step into the transitional "Light foot" position you must "embrace the body tightly with the elbows" meaning you should anchor your fists at your Spleen and Liver gates and form a rounded outward position with the arms so that the elbows form a protective shield of the body against outside kicking techniques as expressed in the second line, "Fists in Yang fist must be tight."

At the same time you should be "condensing" your body to prepare a position of stored force in readiness to strike with the pounding position.

The third line; "Forehand be cross hind hand" refers to the crossing arms motion made in the transitional phase of Hsing I's Pao Chuan in this style.

The fourth line, "Form the 'T' shape," references the shape relationship of the parrying arm and striking fist. However, it should be noted that in this method the parry is actually a "warding off" redirecting movement of the arm, first inserted against and then positioned at a forty five degree angle to deflect effectively.

A 90 degree angle leaves the arm kinetically weakened in relation to downward force, so the idea of a "T" is more of a starting point for reference only.

The fifth line attempts to describe the necessary components of the strike itself. As the strike is made, you must sink your concentration so that Dan Tien motivates the strike and your strength is centered and balanced within the "Three Point Set." You must solidify the three locks of the spinal column and lock the hips forward so that the power emanates from the center, as if your Dan Tien were connected by an imaginary pole to your target, rather than striking from the arm alone. This ensures a whole body effort in the stroke.

As you perform the action, the striking fist should shoot to Heart height with the "Hu Yen" (tiger's Eye) up (vertical fist) while remaining curved at the elbow, relaxed at the shoulder, and secure and natural in the rotation of the shoulders. At the very end of the strike, the pinky should be brought up sharply to facilitate upward Jing/release of force.

The parrying fist should Tsuan (drill) forward to the eyebrows and then rotate outward for deflection while keeping the "Tiger's Eye" and the elbow downward. This construct, when properly applied, allows one to catch the incoming force and dissipate it upward and outward , often turning the opponent partially away and exposing the flank.

In transition, as stated in line seven, the foot is up to facilitate a quick change of direction. If the foot were placed on the ground it would tend to promote a stop in the flow of kinetic energy and decrease potential power. This "light foot" position also allows for low line kick on entry.

The practitioner is reminded in line eight that the drilling of the blocking fist should commence at the time that the front foot steps so that leverage is at its strongest during the movement. Then, as the "Crossing Steps" (angling half step) occurs, the weight must sink and so must the bottom of the striking fist (palm/wrist area) to facilitate a well rooted strike and to sharply bring the pinky up, promoting upward Jing. This point is very important to the kinetics of Pao.

The final line is almost written like an epitaph for the opponent, "Thus follows the hind foot on," which is again referencing the infamous Hsing I half step. And it is stated rather "matter of fact" at that.

Remember, as in all the fists, the state of mind must be pure and focused on only the movement being performed until completion. If you allow your mind to leap ahead to the next movement in an effort to gain more speed, you shall gain only disharmony and your movements shall lack power as a result of the absence of intention. The conscious and subconscious mind must be linked together to manifest absolute power. There can be no disparity of command issued to the body. I advise practicing at different speeds to accomplish this. Try holding each transition posture briefly to experience the feeling of coiled solidity, especially take note of how the "kua" (inguinal muscles) feel, before exploding with the strike.

The strength of Pao Chuan is imparted in equal parts from the legs, the waist and the torso. The posture allows a wide angle vector product to be applied from the leg to the striking fist at the moment the half step hits the ground. There should exist an applied synchronicity between the vectoring of leg force, the waist rotation and the expansion of the costal spaces to propel the fist in a kinetic wave.

Remember as you move, stay rooted, but be light. Try to explode in a controlled fashion. It is not good to strive for power without control. You want to be solidly connected, but still able to change in a heartbeat. Static strength is easily defeated. The Hsing I adept cultivates fluid strength. Tangible and intangible must become one in the same. The element of fire is in constant flux, flaring up here and there, burning brightly and then gone. Attaching to and licking up the opponents limb to gain entry. Only the lingering smoke reveals its path.

Again, because it cannot be said enough.. Do not be one dimensional in your thinking when you consider possible applications. Each form of can be applied from perspectives of striking, throwing, chin na, striking the nerves, striking the points, and this can be overlaid with the "Three Basin" theory giving you three different mediums to work from influencing angle and position of attack. It can also be explored from the "Seven Stars," theory, yielding a multitude of additional expressions of "Pounding" in the form of the Head, Shoulder, Elbow, Hip, Knee, Foot and Hand. The technical expression must not be limited to the "form." The form is merely the means of cultivation that particular mechanic and kinetic potential within that stroke.

You might try following Pao with Pi immediately upon entering the inside of an opponent's guard at closing. This is a quite natural two step combination upon reception.

The instinct of protecting the head is strong in all people. This method of Pao can be trained easily and adapted from that natural instinct with little effort. But you may spend a considerable time developing the mass involved power potential in Pao. Work it meticulously and it will reward your effort with a viable technique useful for simultaneous defense and counter.

| Step 45 degrees and draw hands to ribs | Thread left to centerline, still light foot | Step and half step 45 degrees, parry left, strike right | Step 45 degrees and draw hands to ribs | Thread right to centerline, still light foot | Step and half step 45 degrees, parry right, strike left |

Note: *Movement can never be accurately portrayed in still form. For more information on both the movement structures and possible applications of Pao Chuan (pounding fist), please refer to our instructional DVD products "Hsing I Five Force Elements" and "Hsing I Five Force Combinations." These can be found at hsing-i.com*

Heng Chuan

Crossing Fist

The Song of Heng

Forehand "Yang Fist", hind fist "Yin", hind hand just below the elbow keeps.
Foot lifts up as fists move, body be firm and "Chi" is settled.
Tongue curls up and air exhales, feet close as scissors when style changes.
Half turn the body while feet/hands move, hind hand twists up and thrusts out.
Steps down, fists "Yang" and three points set, nose and feet are specially linked.
Heng Chuan always keep hind fist "Yin".
Forehand "Yang Fist", elbows protect heart.
Left and right arms thrust out as bows. Feet/Hand sink together with tongue curled.

The "Crossing Fist" is by far the most difficult of the fists to learn to perform properly, let alone powerfully. But once perfected, it is one of the most useful of techniques in the system.

To understand Heng Chuan, you must consider three things. First, the element association, Earth. This will tell you something about its base nature as opposed to the other elements. When you think of Earth (and I mean the stuff we walk, play and live on), what qualities come to mind? Words like solid, firm, consistent... This gives you a clue as to performance of the movement. Heng Chuan should be solid and consistent in its power from start to finish. There should be no sudden acceleration contained in the action, unlike some of the other elemental movements. The crossing fist should be just as powerful at the beginning as it is at the end of the action. This is what gives it such remarkable versatility as a technique.

Second, consider its weapon association, the bullet. Kinetically, an old style bullet spirals into an outward projectile force with a graduated acceleration from the source. In this case, your core.

This is what is alluded to in line four of the poem, "Half turn the body while feet/hands move, Forehand twists up and thrusts out." This describes a large moving spiral. Not unlike the planetary motion of the Earth itself. And notice that the poem says "thrust" as this is often not fully understood. People want to "wipe" their fist across instead and this is not correct.

Third, consider the name of the movement itself, the "Crossing Fist." This gives you a clue about the application of the motion. Crossing your center, your opponent's center, your limbs, his limbs, both of your limbs, etc.

Now, going through the remaining lines of the poem in order:

Line two "Foot lifts up as fists move," which again means to keep the "light foot" in transition to ensure swift changes from side to side and to again allow for low line kick on entry, just as you find in Pao. And the second half of line two "Body be firm and Chi is settled" which alludes to the "I" (intention) of complete solidity in execution.

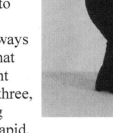

Line three; "Tongue curls up and air exhales" is again a reminder to keep the "fuse" in contact to permit free circulation of the Taoist "central circuit." But also once again, the simple practicality of always keeping the mouth closed, teeth together and "tongue curled" so that you don't receive a broken jaw or severed tongue upon engagement with the opponent by not doing such. And the second part of line three, "Feet close as scissors when style changes" refers to the squeezing inward of the two "kua" (frontal hips/inguinal area) to insure the rapid, accelerated projection of kinetic energy from the Dan Tien area and core stabilization.

Then in line five, "Steps down, fists 'Yang' and three points set, nose and feet are specially linked." This is to, as always, make the practitioner aware of the importance of maintaining your central alignment in Hsing I Chuan, what we call the "wedging" theory. The second half of the line, however, gives a small glimpse into the "secret" relationship of the "I" (intention) and the "whole body power" that Hsing I is famous for in application. The nose (and eyes) should follow the direction of the stepping and orientation of the body center.

And in line six, "Heng Chuan always keep hind fist Yin," we have a reminder of the necessary anchoring of Heng chuan's spiral power which I had mentioned earlier. The hind fist must push down sharply to help anchor the body because of the outward spiral of the attack. If this is not done, the body will tend to "float" and lose balance.

Line seven, "Forehand Yang Fist, elbows protect heart" is a reminder to keep the shoulders and elbows down to enable easy projection of your power/jing and to protect your heart cavities from attack. If the shoulders float upward, you will deliver force primarily from the arm and torso only. The shoulders should stay in their natural seat on execution.

The final line; "Left and right arms thrust out as bows" means to maintain the golf ball size space in the armpits to insure good energy circulation, and a coiled readiness in the frame for issuing kinetic energy. And the second half of the final line; "Feet/Hands sink together with tongue curled" reminds you that true root is achieved through a relaxed dropping of body and mind. But also again, a practicality in breathing is to keep the mouth closed "tongue curled" so that you don't get a broken jaw upon entry for your trouble.

The kinetic power of Heng Chuan is imparted primarily from the waist and costal spaces. Direct compound vectoring, such as in a vector product of force, is not possible in a spiral. So the role of the legs in this form is to both add thrust potential and then to assure solidity of the root at the moment of impact. More solidity means more potential power. You must be well anchored to ensure that none of the projected energy of the movement rebounds back into you, thus weakening the technique.

For application of Heng Chuan, try to again remember to be broad minded in your quest for viable techniques. Do not be one dimensional. And instead think from all five levels of application; to strike, to throw, to lock, to hit the nerve,

and/or specific points. Again, this perspective can then also be overlaid with the "Seven Stars" theory, thus yielding a multitude of additional expressions of the "Crossing" fist in the form of the Head, Shoulder, Elbow, Hip, Knee, Foot and Hand strokes.

Since Heng Chuan is equally powerful through the whole movement, it can be applied as a hammer fist to the inside, or a strike with the eye of the fist to the outside, or a throw to the outside, or a forearm strike to the inside, or a forearm strike to the outside, or an oblique fisted strike to either the outside or inside of the opponents body/guard, or, well you get the picture.

Heng Chuan is exceedingly useful in separating the opponent's guard to create opportunity. Or try slipping in underneath the opponent's guard obliquely at the exact right time. The skewed angle of attack is often not seen as a result of visual interference by the opponent's own guard.

| *Step 45 degrees, move left arm across center* | *Step and half step while crossing right hand strike* | *Step 45 degrees, move right arm across center* | *Step and half step while crossing left hand strike* | *Step 45 degrees, move left arm across center* |

Note: *Movement can never be accurately portrayed in still form. For more information on both the movement structures and possible applications of Heng Chuan (crossing fist), please refer to our instructional DVD products "Hsing I Five Force Elements" and "Hsing I Five Force Combinations." These can be found at hsing-i.com*

Ma Hsing

Horse Form

The Theory and Principle of the Ma (Horse) Hsing (Form)

The purpose of the following series of twelve chapters is to delve into the methodology behind the proper practice of the Hsing I twelve animals hsings. I will be discussing the prescribed method as taught to me through the late Master Hsu Hong Chi, and delving into the individual animals from the perspectives of kinetics and applied force, as well as potential strategy of combative application.

When a practitioner is working with one of the animal hsings (forms), the attempt must be made to capture the essence of the heart (emotion), and the essence of the intention (idea), of each respective animal associated to the form. In other words, it is not enough to simply perform the gestures without the intensity of the animal behind them. Without this essential essence, they are just empty movements. It could be said if practiced without these qualities that what you are practicing is external boxing within a Hsing I frame.

So then, what is the heart (emotion) of a Horse? And what is its Intention (idea)? Well, let us look at what the masters who went before us said.

The classic writings of Hsing I define the Ma (horse) Hsing as the following: *"The horse is a domestic animal. It can transport heavy loads, and is the fastest and surest way for men to travel on land. The hsing is related to the Mind. Practiced properly, it will bring good morale to the mind, dissipating anger/temper. Otherwise, it will produce diverse effects. Some people favor Ma Hsing because it can match all kinds of Kung Fus while the opponent is unable to win."*

Obviously, the first reference should give us a clue as to both the strength and the solidity of the technique once it is fully developed, *"It can transport heavy loads, and is the fastest and surest way for men to travel on land."* The reference here indicates that there are three predominant qualities contained in the form. Those of strength (power), speed (explosive movement) and sure footedness (root).

The second reference is to the health giving benefits and states in a rather matter of fact fashion, *"The hsing is related to the Mind. Practiced properly, it will bring good morale to the mind, dissipating anger/temper."* Then admonishes that improper practice may result in negative effects; *"Otherwise, it will produce diverse effects."* I think it is difficult for the average Westerner to understand that proper practice or improper practice of a concordant motion and breathing pattern could possibly affect the mind in either a positive way, or a negative way. But it is my experience that it can, and does. Let's face it, we have learned much about the mechanics of anatomical function, but we are still in the dark ages when it comes to understanding how the mind works by itself alone or in interaction with the body. Strides are being made, but we still have much to learn in this area. And the Chinese have long believed in such a connection. This belief pervades traditional Chinese medicine.

The final reference in the classics pertains to a minor lesson in combative strategy; *"Some people favor Ma Hsing because it can match all kinds of Kung Fus while the opponent is unable to win."* This indicates two things, one is that the horse movement can "match" other movements or styles. And the second is that the opponent will be "unable to win." The untold meaning here is found in the range of the horse movement structure which is designed for medium to long range tactical attack or counter application. If the distance is understood, the long reach of the horse technique makes it difficult to get around and/or close.

The horse hsing is the first animal learned in the Hsing I system taught through my family. It contains a unique "double pumping" action of the legs one after another which simulates the galloping action a horse uses to gather momentum and speed. Developing this type of leg work is considered essential in our family method in relation to other animals taught later on in the system with regard to total development of the practitioner.

By way of anecdote, permit me to share one story here: Years ago when I was first studying with my teacher, I had occasion one day to be practicing (or at least attempting to practice) the Fhu (tiger) Hsing when Master Hsu entered the room. Seizing the opportunity, I asked my teacher why I had been having such a difficult time gaining any perceivable power in the form. Without asking any one thing about my Tiger form at all, Master Hsu commanded me, "Let me see your Ma, (horse) form." I blushed immediately since that was the form I practiced the least.. besides I had learned that movement long ago in one of the fundamental forms "Ba Shou," or so I thought. But, I showed it to him just the same, as I could not have refused. After I completed the form, he looked at me and said, "You no good practice this form." I grinned sheepishly, since  he of course was right. He followed that statement with, "I know, because you before already learn this one, eh? Ba Shou number three have this one." Hmmm, I thought. He continued, "I before have same same make this mistake." He shook his head, "You cannot same same make my mistake." Whereupon he began to illustrate the differences to me of the foot work, concept, strategy, etc. of the two types of motion. Similar to my beginner's mind, but distinctly different. Chief among the difference is the afore mentioned "galloping" action of the legs.

My teacher used to strap two chest protectors on a student and then, extending his arm straight and rigid, he would use only the leg pumping action of horse and launch a blow into a student sending him flying with the impact generated by the leg action alone. I can now duplicate the same feat, but not without very long practice and attention to detail through my Ma Hsing work. And you know what? My Tiger isn't too shabby either.. he was right again.

| Condense downward and then shift mass forward | Raise fists, transition to light foot | Step and half step while exploding the strike forward | Condense downward and then shift mass forward | Raise fists, transition to light foot | Step and half step while exploding the strike forward |

When practicing the Ma (horse) form, one must be cognizant of four main phases of motion and the transitions between the four. In our method, in phase one, the practitioner condenses the body downward, compressing the intercostal muscles, loading the rear leg, and descending both hands downward. The forehand will be at the level of the Heart, and the hind hand shall stay at the level of the solar plexus region no more than six inches behind the forehand. In phase two, the body shifts from rear to front leg, while expanding the intercostals and expressing both hands along with the body motion forward and slightly upward. In phase three, then, the rear leg comes up next to the hind leg and resides in the light foot position (horizontal and level with the medial malleolus of the inner ankle), and the arms are brought to the fisted "insertion" position, while the intercostals contract yet again. In final phase four the body explodes outward, picking up additional drive from the secondary leg, expanding the intercostals and then rapidly contracting them at the end of the movement while simultaneously solidifying the half step at the precise moment of impact on the imaginary or real target.

Practiced correctly, the Ma Hsing yields power that is exemplary of all of Hsing I's concepts as a very powerful boxing art. Both legs are using their maximum thrust to develop momentum in the action. The intercostal muscles are being used in two and a half full compressions with following expansions. The waist is being held in reserve until the final phase of the movement series, when it is being snapped forward for sudden acceleration of the actual blow itself. All of the key motion components are utilized in just the right sequence for maximal kinetic potential. Simply beautiful.

Tactically, Ma Hsing is equally well suited for attack or counter offense. As an attack slipping Pi Chuan fist (the first action of our method's splitting technique) over the opponents guard and then, as he uses rising energy to fend off continuing into Ma underneath his lead hand, can be a very powerful and difficult to defend attack.

And equally true, using Ma to explode into a counter offensive "stop hit" against an opponent who is strongly attacking the high lines can be a most effective dissuading technique.

It is indeed true, what our Hsing I ancestors said, *"Some people favor Ma Hsing because it can match all kinds of Kung Fus while the opponent is unable to win."*

Note: *Movement can never be accurately portrayed in still form. For more information on both the movement structures and possible applications of the Ma Hsing (horse form), please refer to our instructional DVD product "Hsing I Twelve Animals Vol. 1." This video can be found at hsing-i.com*

Yao Hsing

SparrowHawk Form

The theory and principle of the Yao (SparrowHawk) Hsing (Form).

The classic writings of Hsing I define the SparrowHawk in the following manner: "*A kind of Eagle with a smaller trunk. Flies over the forest and dives in to the ground with great speed to prey on birds, snakes, monkeys, and even small deer. It has a fierce and savage nature. If the Hsing is practiced properly, breathing will be filled in the Hypogastrium for good use. If not, the Hsing will appear awkward.*"

The first reference is a physical description of the actual motions contained within the form. The sparrowhawk form embodies a side to side, almost diving, motion which necessitates the body to first be opened and then rapidly closed as the body turns and positions itself for attack. The utility of the motion lies in the oblique nature of the attack itself. The rising up action both opens the body of the practitioner from a mechanical perspective and also has the appearance of opening the body to attack from the opponent's perspective. This ploy is a deliberate illusion which will entice the opponent to attempt to attack the center line. This will then create the circumstance which will allow the practitioner to utilize the second motion which is a rapid change of the body position "diving" in under the arm to attack the throat. If you have ever witnessed the graceful actions of a hawk circling and then rapidly diving on its prey then you can easily appreciate the reference given. There is great speed present in the condition of this body change manifesting in a truly "fierce and savage nature."

The second part of the writing gives direct reference to the method of the employed Taoist breathing technique to mobilize energy. If the breath is utilized properly, the Dan Tien (core) will become energized and ready to release upon the change from passive to active within the context of the form. The inhalation should be concordant with the opening of the body while the exhalation should be concordant with the rapid closing (diving) of the body as it begins the attack phase of the motion. This will allow motivation of both mind and kinetic energy to be concordant with natural mobilization of the body energy as it occurs on exhalation. As the classics admonish, if this is not done "the Hsing will appear awkward" as a result of a scattered breathing pattern and a resultant scattered mind.

The sparrowhawk Hsing is the second animal learned in the Hsing I system taught through my family. It exemplifies the earth (heng) crossing energy within the context of the diving and attacking action. The unique downward lateral compression of the first phase links to a continuous spiraling expansion of the second phase yielding tremendous oblique power.

When practicing the Yao (sparrowhawk) form, one must be cognizant of the three primary phases of motion contained within the form. In phase one, the practitioner expands the intercostal muscles in preparation for the second phase of condensing and wrapping the lead hand inward. As phase two begins, the lead foot will toe out to 60 degrees allowing the body to both compress and turn laterally while both hands move with the waist in the same direction. At the very end of phase two, the rear heel will leave the ground in transition for preparation of phase three. In phase three, the waist will accelerate the lateral rotation and continue the spiraling of the hands outward while the rear foot steps through lightly at 30 degrees off center to form the attack frame. The end frame should cause the lead hand to reside at the throat level while the rear hand resides Palm down at mid chest.

| Beginning from left stance, San Ti Shr | Overhook the left hand and toe out, closing the costals | Cross-step through at 30 degrees while striking right | Overhook the right hand and toe out, closing the costals | Cross-step through at 30 degrees while striking left |

Practiced correctly, the Yao Hsing yields a power that is primarily waist and intercostal driven. The Dan Tien acts as the focal center point for the rotation of the body core while the closing phase links to the opening phase in one continuous action. Since Yao Hsing is primarily based on earth energy the expression of power should be smooth and continuous.

Tactically speaking, Yao Hsing is counter offensive. It can be utilized in the vein of slipping an

incoming linear attack while simultaneously attacking the opponent's throat, or to neutralize an attempted grab by attacking the elbow directly to apply a lock submission. There are numerous other tactical expressions as a result of the oblique movement structure contained within the Yao Hsing form.

As the classics say, "It has a fierce and savage nature."

Note: *Movement can never be accurately portrayed in still form. For more information on both the movement structures and possible applications of the Yao Hsing (sparrowhawk form), please refer to our instructional DVD product "Hsing I Twelve Animals Vol. 1." This video can be found at hsing-i.com*

Ing Shyung Hsing

Eagle Bear Form

The Theory and Principle of the Ing Shyung (Eagle/Bear) Hsing (Form)

The classic writings of Hsing I define the Ing Shyung (Eagle/ Bear) form as the following: *"Sluggish and dumb in appearance, but very powerful with thick and shaggy fur. Therefore, it is negative outside and positive inside. The Hsing properly practiced will bring circulation of breathing, the positive breathing up and the negative breathing down."*

It should be duly noted that the shape of the form is truly "Bear." The aspect within the form attributed to the "Eagle" has only to do with the specific hand shape utilized in practice and certain applications. This hand shape emphasizes seizing and grasping capabilities by using the palmer strength of grip. The fingers are kept together and used opposite the thumb to maximize the engagement of the strong muscles and ligaments of the forearm and palm/hand.

Now, with regards to the song; what the first line of the quote is referring to should be obvious to anyone who has seen the form of Eagle/Bear. The appearance of the form tends to look somewhat cumbersome at first glance. But if you look a bit deeper, the immense power contained within the movement becomes clear.

The second line of the quote refers to the energetic aspects of the motion. The Eagle/Bear is receptive in the first frame of motion to allow adherence to the opponent's incoming limb. Once the attachment is made, the limb can be easily grasped in the strong grip inherent in the Eagle aspect of the form and the opponent's balance can be controlled to create the opportunity to deliver the powerful stroke of the Bear. Therefore, this is a direct reference to a Yin exterior and a Yang interior.

The third line references the central circulation, meaning the Chi rising up the Du pulse and then descending the through the Ren pulse as per traditional Taoist teaching. The breath should be concordant with the two phases of motion, the inhalation timed with the receptive phase and the exhalation time with the active phase.

The Eagle/Bear Hsing is the third animal form learned in the Hsing I system taught through my family. It contains an aspect of issuing energy downward which is quite difficult to perfect. But once perfected is extremely powerful because the body mechanic also employs the force of gravity, with concordance of descending the body mass, as the stroke is delivered.

When practicing the Eagle/Bear form, the following five phases must be observed. In phase one, the lead hand fans backward, driven from the front leg, as the center shifts to the rear and the waist rotates toward that side. Then in phase two, there is a half step taken with the front foot while the hand continues to circle around and ascend through the middle to softly intercept. In phase three, the rear hand sweeps up while the rear foot moves to the front and waits in a Tiger foot position. These first three phases have encompassed first an opening, then a closing, and then opening once again of the intercostal muscles. Now, in the fourth phase, the lead foot steps outward at a 45 degree angle while the lead hand overturns and makes a grabbing action. Once the foot is placed the body rotates, bringing the striking hand with its rotation while still elevated, until residing directly over the strike zone. Throughout this fourth movement, the intercostals have remained open in preparation for the impending strike. Phase five will now encompass a rapid closing of the intercostals and a sinking of the body to deliver power to the striking hand. The strike should be delivered in a loose, whipping fashion. First brace the legs; then rotate the waist; then close the costals; then descend shoulder; then the elbow; and finally the hand in one coordinated downward whip. The end frame should cause the body to reside in a front bow position with the lead foot slightly toe in and the striking hand residing just inside and level with the knee. Meanwhile the rear hand has overturned, pulling downward and resides palm up and fisted at the waist.

Beginning from left stance, San Ti Shr	*Step at 45 degrees, pierce left hand forward from centerline*	*Bring rear foot to light foot, sweep the right hand upward*	*Step at 45 degrees, grab, pull overturn and strike downward*	*Small lead step, pierce right hand forward from centerline*
Bring rear foot to light foot, sweep the right hand upward	*Step at 45 degrees, grab, pull overturn and strike downward*	*Small lead step, pierce left hand forward from centerline*	*Bring rear foot to light foot, sweep the right hand upward*	*Step at 45 degrees, grab, pull overturn and strike downward*

Practiced correctly, the Ing Shyung Hsing yields a power that is predominantly driven from the waist and intercostals with the legs playing the role of transport and stability. The movement of the form is essentially a longer and broader "Pi" (Splitting) based energy and as such should be practiced accordingly.

Tactically speaking, Ing Shyung Hsing can be utilized both offensively and counter offensively. In the former, the lead hand can be used to bridge the opponent's guard creating a space for the striking hand to penetrate the center line yielding a very powerful downward palm strike to the face, head, clavicle or back. In the latter, the lead hand can be used to intercept the opponent's first strike, binding and controlling the hand, while the rear hand can be either instantly attached to the opponent's elbow or shoulder for a hyper extensive lock. Or in the alternative, the rear hand can wait, enticing the opponent to kick what appears to be the exposed center line. And as the kick comes, the rear hand can sweep up underneath, wrapping the opponent's kicking leg and creating the opportunity to throw. There are numerous other tactical variations on the same two themes yielding different strike configurations and additional throwing configurations.

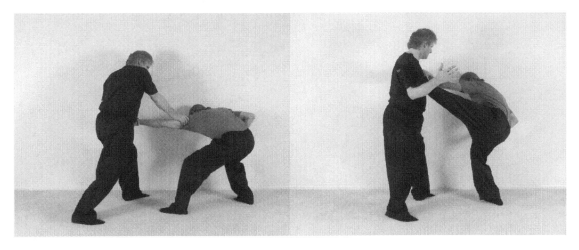

As the classics say, "it is very powerful."

Note: *Movement can never be accurately portrayed in still form. For more information on both the movement structures and possible applications of the Ing Shyung Hsing (eagle/bear form), please refer to our instructional DVD product "Hsing I Twelve Animals Vol. 4." This video can be found at hsing-i.com*

Dou Gi Hsing

Cockerel Form

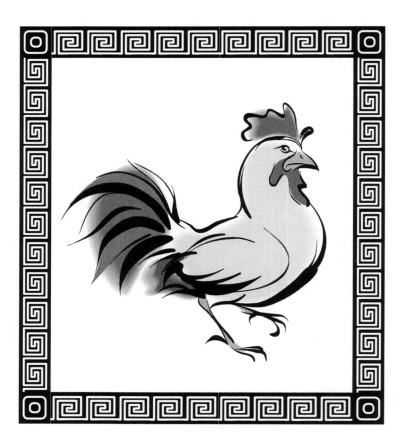

The theory and principles of the Dou Gi (Cockerel) Hsing (Form).

The classics of Hsing I define the Cockerel form in the following manner: *"Domestic fowl very useful to humans. Most Cocks possess physical power and courage. Some fight to the death. The Cock standing on one leg is used in most branches/schools. Proper practice helps the spleen and stomach. Incorrect practice will cause weakness in the earth element."*

In the first few parts of the reference, the typical straight insights into the form and method are revealed in the writing. The first line itself directly references the overall utility of the form. The Cockerel form employs a hand change that is greatly analogous to a boxer cover up, thus becoming extremely useful in a variety of circumstances when the opponent is pressing you.

The mainframe of the form employs three very useful movements. In sequence, these are a Tsuan Chuan drilling punch (somewhat like a boxing upper cut but not exactly), followed by both hands raising and covering the face and head in a narrow frame. And then, as the foot change completes, turning into a very powerful double Palm strike to the center line. In addition to this, the references of "physical power and courage" and "fight to the death" relate to the very *in your face* foot changing found within Cockerel which allows for a simultaneous evasion and counter attack against low line maneuvers from the opponent. Essentially, this footwork allows you to come and go simultaneously. And because of the dynamics of the foot change, the "coming" aspect is propelled with tremendous and sudden momentum.

The final part of the writing gives the correlation to the spleen and stomach Meridians (earth element) relating that proper practice will help these corresponding structures, and that also conversely, improper practice "will cause weakness." This relationship is direct in that the motion structure itself, done properly, initiates a motion based stimulation of the body's energy through the corresponding structures.

The Cockerel Hsing is the fourth animal learned in the Hsing I system taught through my family. Its movement structure dwells on close quarters foot changing to evade and counter the opponent's actions while simultaneously remaining in position to deliver telling blows. Although the mechanics of the foot change are not easy to master it is perhaps one of the most useful tactical movements against low line attacks and well worth time spent in practice.

When practicing the Dou Gi (Cockerel) form, one must be cognizant of the three primary phases contained in the main change. In phase one, the intercostals expand as the energy is driven from the rear heal. The Tsuan Chuan (drilling fist) is delivered to the mid-line and the weight shifts forward. Then, during the second phase, as the wrists are brought upward, the body must stay relaxed as the intercostals both close and then open again to motivate the action. It is during the second phase that the foot change occurs. The foot change itself must be motivated not only through the legs but by a rapid contraction of the abdominal muscles as well, sharply bringing the knee upward. The receding foot should be dropped back two-thirds of the stride length as the changing leg is brought rapidly upward. The overall effect of phase two should be that of a well timed cover up of the bodies vital areas. The intention should remain forward as should the weight. This then sets the stage for phase three which should proceed with a full step plus half step while the intercostals both close then open slightly to create an accelerated upward "pop" of the palm heels into the target zones.

| Beginning from left stance, San Ti Shr | Shift the weight forward and strike with the rear hand | Half foot change, raise knee and hands together | Step and half step while both palms strike forward and up | Shift the weight forward and strike with the rear hand |

| Half foot change, raise knee and hands together | Step and half step while both palms strike forward and up | Shift the weight forward, rear hammerfist while twisting body | Shift, pivot 180 degrees, rear hammerfist while twisting body |

| Raise front arm while rear foot cross kicks forward | Step to cross stance, strike right elbow downward | Full foot change, right arm strike forward, left arm shears rearward | Half foot change into San Ti Shr as ending frame, repeat |

The turn of the Dou Gi form has its own unique properties. The first hammer fist should both cross inward and project forward, creating a shearing effect. Then, while performing the second hammer fist, a 180 degree pivot of the body is required. One should take care that the right foot is positioned straightforward in relation to the new direction upon completion of the pivot to protect the foot and knee during the next change. While performing the cross kicking technique, be sure to keep the frame small to avoid the opponent being able to penetrate the guard. Then, as the downward elbow shape is being formed, be sure to rotate the palm toward the body thus ensuring that proper position is achieved for the stroke. Also, be conscious of closing the front while the back expands in preparation for the final movement of the turn. In regards to the final movement, be sure that the body expands equilaterally in the feet, springing up in a flat ascension as opposed to leaping up and then settling down. Be mindful that the last movement of the turn is composed of both forward and lateral energy.

Practiced correctly, the Dou Gi Hsing will yield an agility in the practiced foot change that will be extremely useful in close quarters combat both as an evasive maneuver and a means of magnifying sudden, momentum based force. Dou Gi Hsing is based largely in both drilling and splitting energies with an influence of pounding and so should be practiced accordingly.

Tactically speaking, the Cockerel form provides an excellent means of simultaneously evading and countering the opponent's close quarters low line attacks or bridging low line attacks. For example, the foot change can be used to both slip a low line round kick and provide the instant impetus for a punishing high line counter strike. The mainframe of the form itself provides some straightforward and practical

combat strategies found within the direct trap and attack to the high line. In addition there is the "cover up" strategy to shield rapidly incoming strikes to the high line with the added bonus of a hooked wrist and hand for quick, redirection and control strategies. As the classics say "very useful to humans."

Note: *Movement can never be accurately portrayed in still form. For more information on both the movement structures and possible applications of the DouGi Hsing (cockerel form), please refer to our instructional DVD product "Hsing I Twelve Animals Vol. 2." This video can be found at hsing-i.com*

Sir Hsing

Snake Form

The theory and principle of the Sir (Snake) Hsing (Form).

The classic writings of Hsing I define snake as the following: *"It can move very quickly on grass or rolling areas. It can bend and wind its body as it likes. It is long in shape, so can attack with either head or tail. (Ancient Chinese battle formation). The Hsing properly practiced can make good use of waist strength. It will do people good when the body produces a kind of breathing resulting from rubbing of the positive and negative Chi."*

The first reference gives an indication of the potential speed contained within the snake form. This much is self explanatory and needs no elaboration.

The second and third lines reference the implied flexibility of the Sir Hsing and potential ability to evade with one part of the body while attacking with another. (There is even a reference given to an ancient Military formation which indeed utilized the same concept in warfare).

The fourth line references what proper practice of the form will bring to the practitioner in terms of waist strength. Because of the rapid, diagonal and twisting motions combined with the opening and closing forces found in the Sir Hsing, the practitioner will eventually develop great flexibility and strength in the waist. This, of course, will be applicable to a wide range of skills in the future. Throwing skills would be a good example of applied waist strength gained.

The final part of the writing once again references the attached health benefits to the practice of the animal Hsings. In this reference, the correlation is made to the "rubbing of the positive and negative Chi." This again correlates to the Du pulse (positive) and Ren pulse (negative) respectively. The inhalation cycle would be correlated with the ascension of the breath along the Du pulse followed by the descent of the breath along the Ren pulse on exhalation.

The Snake Hsing is the fifth animal learned in the Hsing I system taught through my family. As stated above, "the Hsing properly practiced can make good use of waist strength." The Snake form embodies three of the five key words of classical Hsing I training; Yao (to shake), Guo (to wrap or bind) and T'suo (to cut).

When practicing the Sir (Snake) form, the practitioner must be cognizant of four main phases of motion. The first phase embodies the principle of "Yao" (to shake). The lead hand should first move inward and across the center line as the weight shifts slightly to the rear. This movement should be accompanied by a closing of the intercostals to properly prepare the body for what

Beginning from left stance, San Ti Shr	Step forward 45 degrees, sweep left hand up and across	Grab, pull down and cut while closing the stance	Step forward 45 degrees, push rear hand forward and brace	Half step rear foot, strike groin, shear forehand back

Step 45 degrees, sweep right hand up and across	Grab, pull down and cut while closing the stance	Step forward 45 degrees, push rear hand forward and brace	Half step rear foot, strike groin, shear forehand back

comes next. The lead foot should then toe out slightly in preparation for the weight shifting to the forward leg. The Dan Tien should then fire (twist rapidly), motivating the rotation of the core and the subsequent expansion of the intercostals as the weight shifts into the front leg. Done properly, all of this in concordance will create a kind of movement which when utilized against an opponent's attempted grab of the limb or high line attack will literally "shake" the opponent's center, exposing the flank.

The second phase of motion embodies both wrapping/binding and cutting principles. For the purposes of discussion, it is convenient to break this movement in into two respective parts. In the first part of the movement, the lead hand wraps around the opponent's limb to first seize and then twist to create the beginning of a bind. While the rear hand attaches to the opponent's elbow in a crescent configuration to control and hyper extend the opponent's limb, completing the bind. Then, the second part of the movement comes into play. The lead hand pulls the opponent's limb to the waist while the rear hand gives substantial downward pressure on the opponent's elbow. Simultaneously, the Dan Tien (core) motivates the waist into rapid rotation toward the lead hand side while the intercostals compress and the mass of the body is dropped rapidly toward the ground. At the final stage, just as the hyper extensive lock is completed, the control hand residing on the opponent's elbow is rotated 90 degrees to cause the palm to face away from your body's center, thus rending and separating the joint.

The third phase of motion exemplifies the "bracing" concept taught in my family. As you move out into the forward frame, you should brace the body into the rear leg by forming a straight line from the back of the head, down through the spinal column, along the back of the rear leg to the heel of the rear foot. This will allow a potential to strike simultaneously with the lead shoulder, the rear hand, or the head, either individually or in combination. To insure that the structure is strong, it is of paramount importance that the hips are tucked forward and the lower spine is straight (lower lock) solidifying the link to the ground.

The fourth and final phase of motion results in a primary attack to the low line of the opponent. As the half (trailing) step is brought up and the body solidifies to the ground, the lead hand shears down and back across the rear thigh while the rear hand is brought rapidly forward and upward to the groin level. The core of the body will rapidly rotate with the movement of both hands. Assuming a right side change, the left intercostals will close while the right open slightly (Yin and Yang).

Practiced correctly, the Sir Hsing will strengthen the power of the waist substantially. The Dan Tien (core) will motivate each of the four phases in combination with opening and closing power of the right and left intercostals in alternation. This form is primarily influenced by the elements of Crossing, Splitting and Pounding.

Tactically speaking, Sir Hsing is useful for short to medium range binding and controlling methods (much like the concept of a Snake constricting its prey). Because of the combination of rapid up to down, side to side and opening and closing actions it can also be extremely useful for medium range trapping. The Snake form's individual pieces make for various stand-alone techniques yielding numerous other tactical considerations. As the classics say "It can bend and wind its body as it likes."

Note: *Movement can never be accurately portrayed in still form. For more information on both the movement structures and possible applications of the Sir Hsing (snake form), please refer to our instructional DVD product "Hsing I Twelve Animals Vol. 3." This video can be found at hsing-i.com*

Tow Hsing

Tortise/Alligator Form

The theory and principle of the Tow (Tortoise/Alligator) Hsing (Form).

The classic writings define Tortoise/Alligator as the following: *"One of the most lively animals, especially in water. They can swim at great speed. This Hsing relates to the kidneys within the body. When the Hsing is practiced properly, it can strengthen bones and ligaments. If not, the actions of the body seem awkward."*

The first two lines of the reference relate the physical characteristics of the creature called Tow. The writing gives two key phrases of "one of the most lively" and "great speed." The side to side spiraling action found in both the advancing and retreating steps within the Tow Hsing can indeed harbor great strength and speed. This 45 degree twisting step has numerous low line tactical expressions and does appear lively, light and quick when seen in performance.

The third line of the reference gives the relationship of Tow Hsing to the water element, naming the kidney (which is the Yin organ) as per Chinese five element medical theory.

The final two lines of the reference relate the benefits to the body in terms of the "bones and ligaments." Besides the bones being a further five elemental relation to water (Kidney/Urinary bladder), the movements of Tow Hsing also serve to strengthen the same two structures in the body as a result of the twisting stepping pattern and rapid rotation of the frame terminating in the light foot position of Hsing I ending each change. This is no easy feat and proper practice requires tremendous linkage/strength to the grounded foot. The method of practice will tax those body structures in performance. Hence, the yield of bone and ligament strength.

The Tow Hsing is the sixth animal learned in the Hsing I system taught through my family. It is primarily of the Water element but also contains a strong Earth influence. Both qualities are performed in harmony with each change of the form. Practiced correctly, the Tow Hsing will develop tremendous balance in the practitioner and an ability to root on one leg. This then will become useful in numerous other ways such as reaping throws which require a one leg standing finish, kicking techniques, etc.

You will notice the rendering of Tow Hsing as Tortoise/ Alligator. This is simply because the name "Tow" has been rendered as either or both throughout Chinese history. The more recent attachment to the character is that of a Tortoise. But, if you go back far enough, certain texts render it as an Alligator. However, it would not be the same creature as the modern alligator according to the drawings in those same texts (the creature seems to be a sort of Alligator with a hard appearing "shell" on the back). For this reason, today's practitioners are hard pressed to decide what the original connotation should be. With that said, we will move on to the breakdown of the movements contained within Tow Hsing.

Tow Hsing has only three main phases of motion. In phase one, the lead leg inscribes an arcing step to a toe out position residing at a 45 degree angle from the starting position. The step itself will arc out, slightly forward and in front of the stationary foot before completing its arc, to the new position where it will form an angle that is slightly less than 90 degrees in relation to the general line of travel. This positioning is critical to protect the knee of the new support leg as the style change is completed. Simultaneously, the hand in the top position must "hook" at the wrist, rounding the arm, and begin to press down inside the opposite arm. For now, residing near the mid point of the body. At the same time, the hand that is in the bottom position must begin to shear up, giving strength to the radial side of the forearm. For now, reaching the mid point of the transition so that the fingers are residing near the height of the opposite shoulder with the elbow residing just above the opposite hand.

| Step at 45, shear top hand across centerline | Step to other side, change hands and transfer mass | Close to light foot and press rear hand down | Movement can also reverse, step back, keep mass forward | Transfer mass, close to light foot, change hands |

Phase two of the motion represents the timed release of the energy stored in the waist. The Dan Tien will rapidly motivate the force laterally and upward while the lead hand completes its shearing action, terminating its action to reside slightly above, and in line with, the same side shoulder. The rear hand continues to press downward residing at the level of lower Dan Tien with the elbow rounded outward. The intercostals of the rising/shearing hand will expand, while those related to the descending hand will close.

Phase three represents the completion of the change in Tow Hsing. The rear leg shall follow the lead leg to end its motion residing in the light foot position parallel to the floor and next to the medial malleolus of the support leg. The knee should be bent and extended slightly forward in relation to the support leg. This action will complete the closing of the intercostals on that side, thus stabilizing the body core.

Practiced correctly, the Tow Hsing will yield a very strong lateral shearing force. It will also impart a tremendous sense of central equilibrium and control of the root through the legs. If the mechanics of the change are performed inadequately, the practitioner will be unable to maintain balance. The proper performance of Tow Hsing will thus impart the qualities and skills listed above through repetitive practice. Given the context of the blending of the two forces that are belonging to Water and Earth within the form, a proper change will have the appearance of a powerful, transitional spiral of motion.

Tactically speaking, Tow Hsing is most effectively used in counter offensive strategies. But because of its strong lateral shearing quality, it can also be used as an effective and punishing arm bridge to open the opponent's center line. Its transitional shape allows for the usage of the upper arm to shear or strike, while the descending arm is used to elbow the centerline or the flank, in conjunction with a low line knee attack of the light foot to either the inner or outer thigh. Or, the descending arm can be used to hook, control or deflect creating opportunity for the shearing arm to attack in conjunction with low line foot or knee attacks.

As the classics say, it is "one of the most lively animals."

Note: *Movement can never be accurately portrayed in still form. For more information on both the movement structures and possible applications of the Tow Hsing (alligator form), please refer to our instructional DVD product "Hsing I Twelve Animals Vol. 3." This video can be found at hsing-i.com*

Gi Hsing

Rooster Form

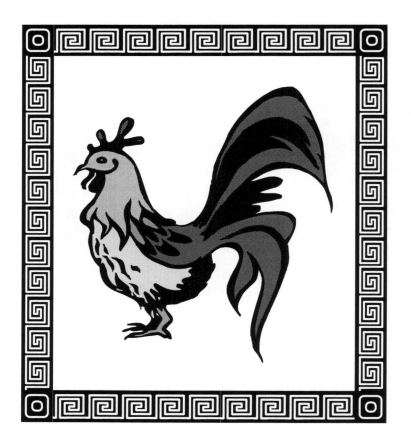

The theory and principle of the Gi (Rooster) Hsing (Form).

In the classics regarding Hsing I, the Rooster is defined in the following manner: *"It flies from the sky to the ground in a straight line to catch its prey and seldom changes direction. It is related to the liver. If the Hsing is practiced well, the Hypogastrium (Dan Tien) is filled with clear breathing to keep the body healthy and strong. Otherwise, the clear breathing will be obstructed resulting in illness."*

The first line of the reference quite ably denotes the overall aggressive nature of the Rooster form. If you have ever been chased by a Rooster, then you can well attest to their steadfast and linear tenacity in the effort to run you out of their territory. They can take on the appearance of a plump feathered arrow with rapidly kicking feet while moving along the ground. Even short flight oriented attacks from the top of the coupe tend to be on a direct trajectory.

The second line of the reference correlates practice of the Rooster form to the liver (wood element) of the body. This is self explanatory and in accordance with the principles of Chinese medicine. The Chicken form is influenced predominantly by the Wood Element which is composed of the liver (Yin) and the gall bladder (Yang). Therefore, "it is related to the liver."

The final part of the writing gives direct reference to the health benefits of employed Taoist breathing technique to mobilize internal energy. If the breath is utilized properly, the Dan Tien will become charged (full) with abundant energy which will help keep the body healthy and strong with circulation strongly motivated.

The Rooster Hsing is the seventh animal learned in the Hsing I system taught through my family. It is influenced predominantly by the Wood element with smaller influences from the Fire and Earth elements. The sinews of the body, especially those of the legs, will benefit greatly by proper practice of Rooster.

The Gi Hsing is unique in two ways as it is practiced in our family. First, it is the only animal form that does not begin with Pi Chuan. And second, it is the only animal form that does not repeat itself exactly in the second line. Still, there are only a few key concepts to be aware of while practicing Gi Hsing. In the opening series of the form (the five movements up to the

final settling into San Ti Shr), one must be sure to be mindful of core rotation in conjunction with bend, raise, open, close, stretch and withdraw. These qualities are conjoined and must not be separate. One should strive for a fluid linkage within all.

| Gi Hsing begins after the opening salutation | Sink, turn body left, move forearms across centerline | Sink, turn right, move forearms across center | Lift both arms upward, keeping elbows down | Turn right and pull both palms toward right rear |

While practicing the "pecking" series one must cultivate a Peng (penetrating) energy, not only within the finger and half fist strikes, but in the feet as well. Be light and quick while projecting the feet; cultivating knee, toe kick and stomp with each alternating step. Solidify the body and issue from the back upon executing the punch under arm posture at the end of the series.

| Step forward, shift mass and extend both palms outward | Shift mass rearward and settle into San Ti Shr | Step left to light foot and pierce right hand forward | Step right to light foot and strike left hand with half fist | Step and half step while punching right under left |

When moving into the turn, utilize the double bamboo step so as to time the closing of the body with the rear foot taking position in the center. Simultaneously, raise the lead knee and prepare for the opening phase. Then, energy is issued from the core in execution of both the low palm strike and in the front foot as it stomps downward.

| Double bamboo step forward and strike with left low palm | Shift mass forward, strike across centerline with right hammerfist | Pivot 180 degrees, strike with left hammerfist across center | Sweep right forearm upward, cross kick left | Crouch into cross stance, strike with right elbow |

The turn of the Gi form in our family is identical to the turn found in the Dou Gi form . The first hammer fist should both cross inward and project forward, creating a shearing effect.

Then, while performing the second hammer fist, a 180 degree pivot is required. One should take care that the right foot is positioned straight forward in relation to the new direction once the pivot occurs to protect the foot and knee during the next change. While performing the cross kicking technique, be sure to keep the frame small to avoid the opponent being able to penetrate the guard. Then, as the downward elbow shape is being formed, be sure to rotate the palm toward the body thus ensuring that proper position is achieved for the stroke. Also, be conscious of closing the front while the back expands in preparation for the final movement of the turn. In regards to the final movement, be sure that the body expands equilaterally with both feet moving up in a flat ascension as opposed to leaping up and then settling down. Be mindful that the last movement of the turn is composed of both forward and lateral energy.

| Full foot change, strike right forearm up, shear left downward | Step and half step into left San Ti Shr, left Pi Chuan Strike | Coil the body downward suppressing the legs | Step the front foot forward, toe out, while bringing right fist up | Step and half step to change styles to right side San Ti |

Upon completion of the turn, classic Pi Chuan is performed twice (see chapter on Pi Chuan). The movement immediately following is worthy of discussion on its own merit. When using the forearm, checking to the right, the intercostals should expand and the weight should shift slightly forward while the core rotates to the right in preparation for the withdrawal. As the front foot withdraws, the intercostals should close and the right forearm should spiral inward and downward in conjunction with the rotating core of the body. The right hand should then drift up through the centerline while the right foot becomes light in preparation for the foot change. Then as the foot change occurs the right hand should clamp downward and twist, pulling rapidly up to the floating ribs, while the left palm presses sharply downward in conjunction with the closing of the body. Classic Peng Chuan (see chapter on Peng Chuan), with a half step, is then delivered as a follow-up while the lead hand checks.

| Half step withdrawal, clamp right forearm | Half foot change, pull right hand, press left palm down | Step and half step while punching right under left | Double bamboo step forward and strike with left low palm | Shift mass forward, strike across centerline with right hammerfist |

The remaining movements of the line, through the completion of the turn, are all identical to those found in the first line. (See preceding paragraphs).

| Pivot 180 degrees, strike with left hammerfist across center | Sweep right forearm upward, cross kick left | Crouch into cross stance, strike with right elbow | Full foot change, strike right forearm upward, shear left arm down | Step and half step into left San Ti Shr, left Pi Chuan |

The final series of movements found in the Rooster form contain several nuances involving body connection. Initially, from left Pi (San Ti Shr) the lead foot will step back and plant through the heel establishing a strong ground path. In transition to this shape, the intercostals should close. As the foot plants, the energy should the thrust up from the rear foot issuing through the back while the intercostals expand and the right finger strike shoots forward.

| Step back, keeping weight to fore, pierce with two fingers forward | Toe in, turn body left, fold right elbow, left to armpit | Toe out, swing step keeping left post, pivot 180 degrees | Raise left knee, pierce forward with two fingers | Step and half step into left San Ti Shr, left Pi Chuan to finish |

As the spinning technique begins, the right hand should fold to touch the inner left shoulder while the right foot toes inward. The left foot immediately toes outward and the weight shifts onto it, setting up the swing step of the right foot 180 degrees behind the position of the last. While this spin is occurring, take care to keep the left foot weighted and close the intercostals in preparation (if not, the balance will be lost to the rear at high speeds). Thus braced into the right leg, the centrifugal force can now be channeled into a strong, whipping force with the intercostals first expanding and then slightly contracting on the right side to deliver the second finger strike. The series is then closed with classical Pi Chuan to finish the form.

Practiced correctly, the Gi Hsing yields a strong penetrative power in both the arms and legs. However, one should not neglect the role of the intercostals within these actions. Although, the opening and closing is performed in a minor fashion (using only the upper and middle thirds in narrow parameter), it is still vital to the overall flavor contained within the movements. Gi Hsing is primarily influenced by wood, and so should embody the proper characteristics of that element with punctuated bursts of kinetic energy.

Tactically speaking, Gi Hsing contains many offensive and counter offensive techniques. The low line kicking technique found in the pecking series is excellent both as a stop hit against a cautiously advancing opponent and/or a low line leading technique to scatter the opponent's mind. The "bait and switch" strategy found in the final series of the form illustrates the Hsing I concept of "even when I defend, I attack" quite nicely with its spinning barrage of elbow and finger strikes. And the use of Heng Chuan (crossing), within the turns of the form, of inward hammer fists is worth studying all on its own merit, with or without the use of the foot change illustrated in the middle of the form. Looking as a whole within the entire form and its given technical aspects, there is an apparent focus on high/low and low/high tactics.

As the classics say "it flies from the sky to the ground."

Note: *Movement can never be accurately portrayed in still form. For more information on both the movement structures and possible applications of the Gi Hsing (rooster form), please refer to our instructional DVD product "Hsing I Twelve Animals Vol. 6." This video can be found at hsing-i.com*

Tai Hsing

Phoenix Form

The theory and principle of the Tai (Phoenix) Hsing (Form).

The classic songs of Hsing I define the Phoenix as follows: *"A fierce bird of prey, possessing sharp claws and good eyesight. It sees and swoops, catching with its sharp claws. It is positive outside and negative inside. Practice properly, the positive breath in the kidney will rise, resulting in the full operation of both the "Ren" and "Du" pulses, as well as a good operation of other pulses and the Hypogastrium for a good life."*

The first two lines of the reference summarize the primary aspects found within the Phoenix form. The first statement regards the nature as that of a fierce predator indicating an aggressive stalking attitude. The summation of the key points found in the first two lines paint an easily understood picture. The picture is a coalition of the following attributes: aggressive (fierce), accuracy (good eyesight/sees and swoops), and a reduced striking surface (possessing sharp claws/catching with its sharp claws).

The third line references "positive outside and negative inside." This denotes a Yang exterior (surface tension) and a Yin interior (flexible core). This statement is true of all Hsing I, but is perhaps more apparent in such movements as found in the Tai Hsing. The motion construct has a strong emphasis placed on the qualities of "T'un" (literally to suck in) and "T'u" (literally to spit out). These two principles combined illustrate Yin (negative/contracting) and Yang (positive/expanding) kinetic energy use respectively.

The final line of the text again refers to the correlations of the practice of Hsing I and traditional Chinese medical principles. In this case, a correlation is drawn between the proper practice of the Tai Hsing and a positive energetic benefit to the kidneys (the kidneys play an especially important role in the theory of classical Chinese medicine). There is then an assertion made that this will in turn benefit the two primary pulses in the body, namely the "Ren" (conception) and "Du" (governing) pulses. There is a classical and well known statement found in the theory of traditional Chinese medicine that says: "If the Du (governor) is healthy, then all other pulses will eventually follow." Thus, the above text has drawn a linear correlation regarding three conceptual principles found in traditional Chinese medicine.

The Phoenix Hsing is the eighth animal learned in the Hsing I system taught through my family. It is soundly anchored in both the metal (splitting force) and water (drilling force) elements. As with all the animal Hsings, it carries with it several unique components to impart specific skills. The combination of the two elements, contained in its core strength, create some very powerful and utilitarian spiraling movement structures.

When practicing the Tai (Phoenix) form, there are several distinct components of which to be aware. The opening three fists/movements of the form exemplify the nature of the form in general. As the left fist moves, its trajectory is that of a lateral spiral (much like looking at one and one half coils of a spring lying on its side), moving downward then upward and forward while simultaneously moving inward throughout. These actions are controlled through rotation of Dan Tien and opening/closing of the intercostals to drive the limb. The left foot should parallel the movement of the left hand, coiling with the body as the foot circles and withdraws, and timing the release of kinetic potential as the foot places.

The right fist then moves in the same fashion as the left. However, since the right foot is both stepping through and forward in the second movement, the coiling of the body must take place in the transition (as the right foot comes next to the left). The release of kinetic energy will still be timed with the placement of the foot. In both of these actions, the practitioner should strive to open the intercostals as the fist reaches out and then close the intercostals as the body coils in the transition phase in preparation for release.

| Spiral the left across, down, inward and forward, step left | Spiral the right fist in the same manner, step right | Turn left to tiger foot, arc right fist over and through | Sweep left foot and both forearms up and across | Step into cross stance. Wrap, grab, pull left while punch right |

The third fist represents a slight variant on the theme presented in the first two. In this fist, the body will open on both sides as both fists drift away from center. And then the body will rapidly close as the left fist traps and the right delivers a strike over the top of the frame. The core rotates rapidly to the left to facilitate the release of power while the left foot takes position in the center in order to stabilize the frame.

The second major part of the form dwells on a kind of wrapping energy and the movement is repeated three times for emphasis. Although the movement represents one kind of technique or idea in sequence, it is important to view the movement in two parts mechanically. In the first action, the entire body rotates from the core toward the inside of the leading leg. Simultaneously, both forearms rotate with the action (so that the palms are facing the body) and the intercostals close and ground the body in preparation for the sweeping action to come. As the sweeping action is performed, the intercostals open to motivate the arms upward while the Kua (inguinal muscles) close to give power to the sweeping leg. Done properly, this will then stabilize the transitional frame while the body is on one leg. At this point, the second phase of

| Sweep right foot and both forearms up and across | Step into cross stance. Wrap, grab, pull right while punch left | Withdraw to tiger foot, right backfist downward | Step right foot back, hook left fist across centerline | Withdraw to tiger foot, hook right fist across |

the motion begins. The entire body will wrap forward and downward while the intercostals close. The leading hand will snap forward, followed quickly by the leading leg projecting/ stepping downward forcefully. And the rear hand will then complete the wrapping action, by both projecting forward and downward, as the body settles into the crouching cross stance.

| Raise left leg to crane stance, jab left forward | Step left forward at 30 degrees, lunge left hand to centerline | Step right forward 30 degrees, lunge right hand to centerline | Leap and pivot 180 degrees catching with left forearm | Shift mass forward and punch with right hand |

The third main component in the form is the reversal sequence. This component presents some challenges to the practitioner. It is essentially a large scale manifestation of T'un (suck in) and T'u (spit out) within a retreating wave of force. The sequence begins with a simple trapping mechanism as the body core turns to the left and the right forearm moves downward, closing the intercostals, while the left hand moves into trapping position underneath the right elbow. The weight then shifts forward and the core of the body turns to the right while the right arm sweeps upward, expanding the intercostals, leading with the right elbow and unfolding into a right back fist (splitting force). Both feet then spring away in a half step to the rear while the motion of the back fist continues downward (with the intercostals now closing) and ending up residing just outside the right knee with the body resting in a crouching, tiger foot position.

The sequence then continues with the right foot stepping back into a mid basin San Ti stance while the core of the body rotates to the right and the left arm is brought through the middle in the classic bended arm position of the Phoenix form. The right arm covers the center line of the body near the heart level and the intercostals begin to open partially. Next, as the left foot withdraws to a tiger foot position, continue expanding the intercostals and bring the right arm down in front of the face the through the center line while the left hand withdraws to the left side of the body residing palm up near the floating ribs. The culmination of this series is a rapid and profound closing of the intercostals projecting the left Phoenix fist forward at the face level. Simultaneously, the right hand comes to reside just next to the left elbow while the left knee raises to form an "Iron wall" posture, stabilizing on the right leg for release of the force.

The fourth primary component of the Phoenix form encompasses the "lunging" fists. These two movements are fairly simplistic mechanically, but there are a few points to address. The movements should be performed so that the front foot steps at 30 degrees off the center line of travel while the striking fist is aligned with the rear foot, effectively creating the ability to slip a linear attack and then simultaneously counter attack. The intercostals will first close, in the transition, and then open upon release of each fist in succession. When the form is transitioning from the first to the second lunging movement, the stepping foot should first move close to the support foot and then move back outward to the 30 degree position.

The final component would be the turn sequence and this also creates some unique challenges in and of itself. Initially, the front foot will toe out while the right hand prepares to grab. The left hand will form the hooked Phoenix shape and the intercostals will open in readiness for the leaping action of the turn. As the leap is performed, the core of the body will rapidly twist to the right while in mid air. The right hand will overturn, pulling toward the waist, and the left hand will not vary its already existent shape. As the body lands on the ground, the intercostals will close to solidify the frame with the weight mostly residing on the rear (right) leg. The final strike within the turn will simply be a rapid rotation of the core to the left, while the weight shifts to the forward leg, and the intercostals of the right side body rapidly open then close.

Practiced correctly, the Tai Hsing yields a power that is a study of combined prevalent concepts in the art of Hsing I, placing a heavy emphasis on T'un (suck in) and T'u (spit out). It is soundly anchored in the combined elements of Pi (splitting) and Tsuan (drilling) and should be practiced with these qualities in mind.

Tactically speaking, Tai Hsing presents a myriad of possible of uses. It is equally suitable for both attack and counter offense. The "S" hooked shape of the fist in Tai Hsing is easily utilized to trap, redirect and control the opponents limbs while creating opportunity to breach the guard. This "S" configuration also makes it difficult for an opponent to properly assess the effective distance of the attacking limb making the Phoenix form aptly suited for stop hit interruptions of the opponents movement.

As the classics say, it is "a fierce bird of prey."

Note: *Movement can never be accurately portrayed in still form. For more information on both the movement structures and possible applications of the Tai Hsing (phoenix form), please refer to our instructional DVD product "Hsing I Twelve Animals Vol. 5." This video can be found at hsing-i.com*

Yen Hsing

Swallow Form

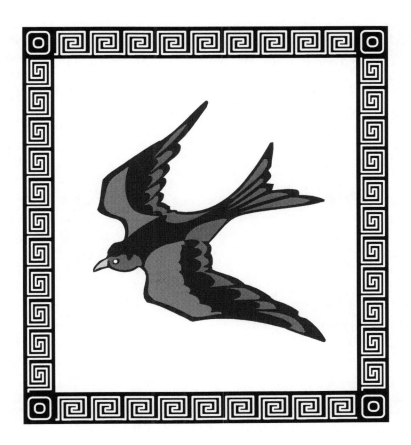

The theory and principle of the Yen (Swallow) Hsing (Form).

With regard to Swallow, the classic writings of Hsing I have the following to say: *"A bird very small in shape, but with long and powerful wings. It is considered the lightest and most agile bird. It can glide and fly at high speeds. A man with good acrobatic ability is a Swallow man. If the Hsing is practiced properly, people will feel comfortable in body and muscles. Otherwise, actions will be clumsy."*

This is perhaps one of the most easy of the songs to understand and needs very little explanation. The first line references the apparent dichotomy found in a Swallow form. When first viewed, especially by the untrained eye, the form may appear to be lacking in strength. This is certainly not true if the body mechanics of the practice are correct. And in fact, the "wing beating" sequence can deliver a most punishing series of palm strikes in the hands of an expert. Hence the reference to "long and powerful wings."

The second and third lines refer to both the speed and agility found within the Swallow form movements. And the fourth line emphasizes this fact by linking acrobatic ability directly to the form characteristics. The Swallow form is indeed all of these things and this, at least, can be seen by even the untrained eye.

The final line of the reference is straight forward enough. The proper practice of Yen Hsing will yield a graceful and effortless movement. The structure of the form is fluid and elongated. It is a study in one of the main conceptual ideas of the Internal Martial Arts, which is to learn to utilize the body in a non-antagonistic fashion, preventing the protagonist and antagonist muscle groups of the body from working against one another. If the practitioner attempts the form with localized tension oriented movement, then the form will feel awkward indeed.

The Swallow Hsing is the ninth animal learned in the Hsing I system taught through my family. It is influenced predominantly by the Fire (pounding) and Water (drilling) elements. The unique structure of Swallow provides the opportunity to crystallize numerous important skills. Like all of the animals, the lessons which are imparted through the practice are indispensable and cannot be gleaned elsewhere in the system.

Being one of the bird forms a Hsing I, Yen Hsing is rather long and complex in its movement structure as compared to many of the "lower case" or more simplistic repetitive structures found in the twelve animals. Still, we can break the form into several main components for purpose of discussion. The first sequence would be that of the turn. From the San Ti Shr position, the core of the body will motivate to the right and turn the frame 180 degrees. As this occurs, the weight will shift predominantly to the right leg (the new rear left leg, however, will still carry substantial weight). The intercostals will expand while the left hand overturns to a palm up position in this first stroke. Immediately thereafter, the right leg will withdraw to Tiger foot position while the right hand pierces upward and forward underneath the left arm continuing the expansion of the intercostals. This completes stage one of the turn.

| Begin in San Ti Shr stance | Pivot 180 degrees, withdraw, pierce the right hand forward | Double bamboo step forward while rolling palms into extended palm strike | Toe left foot, change and dive downward. Left along leg, right stays high to rear |

Continuing with the turn sequence, the practitioner next advances with a double bamboo foot work (essentially a skipping shuffle). While the right foot steps forward, the intercostals close and the right arm drops downward. Then, as the left foot shuffles up next to the right, the right arm rises upward as the intercostals expand and the spine bows backward slightly. In the final phase of the frame, the core will project forward and outward (creating what we call a "spinal whip"), the intercostals will rapidly close and then open again as the right foot steps into a front bow stance. As this happens, the left arm and palm will slide outside of the right arm to trap upward while the right palm rolls inward and then projects forward and outward.

The entire body frame will now drop several inches downward as the left foot repositions itself approximately four to six inches to the rear. Simultaneously, the right arm will lift upward while the left palm presses downward in readiness for the pivot contained in the turn. As the movement continues, the left foot will pivot so that the toes point to the rear. The body will turn with the foot and the left hand will shoot to the rear aligning itself with the left foot having the fingertips pointed in the direction of the left toes. The left palm will be facing the foot.

Staying in this low basin frame, the weight will now shift into the left leg and the left hand will twist to a palm up position motivated by the core mass of the body. When the weight shift is

| Shift mass forward, lift left palm while pushing right arm downward | Step to cross stance, pierce right hand under left palm | Rise, lift left knee and right arm, push left down | Condense whole body and cross arms in center | Release stored force. Both palms and left side kick exploding outward |

complete, the right foot will step through in front of the left into a classic low basin cross stance (so that the right foot will be toe out and carrying most of the weight and the left foot will be on the ball of the foot with the shin parallel to the ground). Simultaneously with this step the right hand will pierce, palm upward, underneath the left arm. The left palm will now be residing at the crook of the right elbow and the right palm will reside palm up and forward.

Without any interruption in movement, the body will now rise up onto the right leg with the knee of the left leg thrusting upward to reside in a crane stance. Simultaneously, the right arm will shoot straight upward with the intercostals expanding while the left arm hooks inward and then presses downward with intercostals closing. This action completes the turn sequence.

The next movement structure is the Swallow kicking technique. As the practitioner prepares to kick, the right arm will descend and the left arm will ascend to touch one another, with palms flaring outward, at the center line of the body near the solar plexus height. Simultaneously, the body will close in front while opening the back slightly. As the kick is executed, the body will rapidly expand, delivering this stored energy. Both arms will extend outward, with palms held in lateral position, at a height just below the shoulder level. The kick itself will extend to reside in line with, and just under, the left palm. It is important to remember not to pivot the support foot while executing this kick. Otherwise the recovery from the kick will be slowed, the center will be compromised, and this will present an opportunity for the opponent. Done correctly, the kick can be performed with substantial power and still allow immediate center line recovery.

| Step left down, strike right palm low, check high left | Step to cross stance, circle both palms a half circle to lateral | Raise left knee and forearm, thrusting the knee forward | Stomp the left foot down while grabbing left, mass forward | Stomp right foot a half step forward, pierce right in/up |

We now move into the "wing beating" sequence of the form. This structure is an exercise in opening and closing the body while motivating both the stepping and the striking/trapping movements from the core of the body. The real challenge of this sequence is to step with both agility and quickness while motivating power throughout the structure. There are a total of two movements repeated twice each. In the first, the left foot steps forward and the left palm fans across the body to reside just outside and at the level of the right shoulder. Simultaneously, the core rotates to the left, the intercostals close, and the right palm swings through under the left arm to strike at the bladder/groin level. The second movement seamlessly flows from the first with the right hand now sweeping upward and to the rear with the palm outward, while the left palm swings downward and then forward/upward. Simultaneously, the core of the body rotates to the right, the intercostals expand, and the right foot steps through to end up in a cross stance. When done properly, the core of the body combined with the expression of the intercostals will provide power to both limbs throughout the double change of the hands.

As the "wing beating" sequence ends, there is a smooth transition into the rising knee strike. As the intercostals of the left side of the body reach maximum expansion the knee is drawn up smoothly afterward and the left hand/arm rotates so that the wrist is leading the interception. Both the core of the body and the supporting right leg aid in thrusting the left knee forward and upward. Done properly, this movement should naturally lead the body into the downward stomping of the left foot in conjunction with the grasping of the left hand. The intercostals will rapidly close here to magnify the downward force. Immediately thereafter, the rear foot will half step up and stomp as the right hand pierces upward and forward with the right intercostals and core motivating the strike. This then will coil the body in readiness for the half fisted strike to follow. The left foot will now lead this action with the right foot performing the half step follow-up. The intercostals will open in a minor way and then close (wood/peng) as the blow is delivered and the right hand will pull back sharply for balance in the technique.

Step and half step while striking left half fist, pulling right back	Step left toe out, circle left counter clockwise and then pierce forward	Pierce the right forward while front toe kick hits the floor	Double bamboo step forward while rolling palms into extended palm strike

The final two movements of the line are piercing palms. The first is performed with the left hand which is now residing in the half fisted posture. This movement is an embodiment of the T'un/T'u (suck in/spit out) principle in that it is a rapid, re-directive circle to gain entry to the center line. The intercostals on the left side of the body should open then close then open again, as the hand circles outward, downward and then forward and upward in its piercing attack. The left foot will move forward a few inches and toe out as the strike is committed but should not move during the redirecting phase. As soon as this movement is complete, the right foot then steps up to a tiger foot position, in front of the left, and the right hand simultaneously pierces forward and upward sliding underneath the left. This last action will be motivated by both the expansion of the right intercostals and the rotation of the core of the body and should power not only the piercing right hand but also the toe of the right foot as it presses strongly into the ground. This last position then equals the position that occurs just before the turn sequence, and the form will now repeat itself on the return line.

Practiced correctly, the Yen Hsing will yield a loose, whipping and expansive energy combined with quick and agile movement of the body. The form is heavily influenced by fire (pounding) energy with minor influence from water (drilling) and so should be practiced accordingly.

Tactically speaking, Yen Hsing specializes in the combative

concepts of evasion, trapping and piercing. Combining these three concepts appropriately can cause the enemy to feel rather like they have walked into a living buzz saw.

The up and down movement contained in the turning sequences can be used to wrap or entrap the arms of the opponent for striking, or the legs for throwing.

The wing beating sequence allows easy opportunity to move either up the center line of the opponent or to the flank while trapping and evading, all the while punishing high to low or low to high target zones. The end sequence

of the form can be used to easily dominate the center line, first redirecting and then piercing vital points with blazing speed, making it quite difficult to counter on the part of the opponent.

As the classics say, "a man with good acrobatic ability is a swallow man." Indeed!

Note: *Movement can never be accurately portrayed in still form. For more information on both the movement structures and possible applications of the Yen Hsing (swallow form), please refer to our instructional DVD product "Hsing I Twelve Animals Vol. 5." This video can be found at hsing-i.com*

Hou Hsing

Monkey Form

The theory and principle of the Hou (Monkey) Hsing (Form).

The classic of Hsing I define Monkey as the following: *"It is lively, active, and intelligent. It has the capability of climbing the mountain and jumping among the branches. It belongs to the heart. Practiced properly, people will feel calm and serene both in the mind and the spirit. Otherwise, they will feel restless and uneasy."*

The first two lines of the reference give insights into the proper practice and/or possible utilities found within the Monkey form. Watching a performance of the Monkey form, the adjectives of lively and active are an easy relationship to make. The movements are light, quick and seemingly playful. My teacher used to say, "to apply the Monkey form you must be smart." The first line verifies his statement describing the Monkey as "intelligent."

The images of "climbing the mountain and jumping among the branches" conjure up the ideas of quickness and agility. But it also references the skills fostered in actual practice of the Monkey form... That of rapid fire low line kicking tactics to the legs combined with light and agile attachments to the limbs to control and neutralize.

The final three lines of the reference are all tied together. The Monkey form truly does belong to the seat of emotions (the heart) and as a result, if practiced properly, it will tend to bring peace and balance to the mind and Spirit. Improper practice can yield the opposite effect.

The Monkey Hsing is the tenth animal learned in the Hsing I system taught through my family. It is heavily influenced by the fire element and has additional influence from the water and earth elements. The unique "gathering" (Yin) energy of the defensive actions found in Monkey are seen nowhere else within the Hsing I system. Regular and correct practice of the Monkey form will yield a type of energy that is extremely useful for oblique, and practically untraceable attacks and counter attacks.

When practicing the Hou (Monkey) form, one must be cognizant of the different phases of receptive and aggressive motion. The first action within the form is a pull down tactic. It is required that both feet half step to the rear from the San Ti Shr position. To accomplish this without exposing the head to attack, will require a movement of the core backward to motivate

| Half step, withdrawing to tiger foot while pulling down | Step forward, toe out and arc left fist over left shoulder | Swing step, pivot 180 degrees and strike with two knuckles | Step back, mass forward, rotate left while striking right palm | Shift mass to rear leg, rotate right while striking left palm |

the foot change. The tendency will be to shift the weight forward before springing backward with a half step. This is an error.

Once the entire core has moved backward, the body must hinge rapidly from the waist with the intercostals closing and the front foot withdrawing to accommodate the change of position. Done properly, this will provide power to the pull down structure and also place the body in a stored position for the rising elbow which follows. As the elbow stroke is delivered the front foot should step forward into a toe out position and the weight should be committed forward. Simultaneously, the intercostals will expand and the left elbow will rise upward sharply with the right fist trailing to guard the heart cavity residing at the elbow of the left arm.

The right foot will now perform a swing step in preparation for the 180 degree turn leading into the Monkey fist. As the step is performed, the core will turn toward the left and the intercostals will close drawing in the elbows. As the strike is performed, the left intercostals will open and then close quickly in conjunction with the left foot withdrawing into Tiger foot position. The issuing should proceed from the back and the intention of the fist should reside in the first two half knuckles of the projected fist.

Now the withdrawing phase of Monkey begins. The left foot will step away as the right hand passes through the center with the weight still forward into the right leg. The core of the body will be rotating left as the intercostals first open and then close to motivate strength in the right hand. Then, with only a weight shift to the rear and no step, the left hand will perform the same action with the core of the body rotating to the right. The right leg will now step back and the right hand will once again perform a duplicate maneuver. The weight will remain forward on the left leg as this occurs.

Then, in the final movement of the withdrawal series, the left arm will cut into the center with the palm upward and the elbow aligned with the bodies center. The body will now be rotated approximately 30 degrees to the right. The right hand will reside palm downward just inside the left elbow. Simultaneously, the left knee will raise so that the left foot places itself on the right shin just below the knee. The left knee will also be angled at about 30 degrees to match the rest of the body angle. Done properly, this movement should create a coiled spring feeling with readiness to move forward with alacrity.

The advancing phase of the form now begins. In the first action, the core of the body motivates both the stepping of the left foot as well as the projection of the left hand. It will turn first to the

| Step back, mass forward, rotate left while striking right palm | Raise knee to crane stance, bring left elbow in and down | Step forward, circle left palm to strike across centerline | Step forward, toe out, strike right palm angling in/down | Step forward, low line toe kick and pierce two fingers to eyes |

left and then back to the right, as the left hand and arm circle outward and then inward, while the intercostals open and close in accordance.

The core will then rotate back to the left motivating the right hand and arm to sheer forward and downward in a lateral "Splitting" movement with the intercostals first opening and then closing in conjunction. Simultaneously, the right foot will step forward into a toe out position and the left hand will reside just inside the right elbow.

In the final movement of the advancing series, the core of the body will again rotate to the right and the left intercostals will expand to motivate the thrusting of the left handed, two finger strike. Likewise, the left low line toe kick will be performed at the same time.

These two structures of withdrawal and advance are performed three times in a "T" pattern with no deviation other than angle. And in the final series a substitution of the Pi (Splitting) palm for the two fingered strike.

Practiced correctly, the Hou Hsing yields a light, agile advancing step and a heavily grounded withdrawing (Yin) energy that makes good use of a rapidly rotating core. The form has strong influences from water (drilling), earth (crossing) and fire (pounding) energies and so creates a unique structure that blends the three into one.

Tactically speaking, Hou Hsing is extremely useful as a rapid cover-up against a flurry of high line attacks from an opponent. The oblique nature of its power allows for an easy "bait and switch" tactic to be employed by first attacking the center line, and then when parried,

to move quickly and powerfully to the outside. The utility of the Monkey hands can be devastating if focused in this manner to the side and back brain of the opponent. The advancing sequence provides a nearly unstoppable blend of rapid trapping hands in conjunction with equally rapid low line kicks which divide the opponent's mind and defenses. As is said, "it has the capability of climbing the mountain and jumping among the branches."

Note: *Movement can never be accurately portrayed in still form. For more information on both the movement structures and possible applications of the Hou Hsing (monkey form), please refer to our instructional DVD product "Hsing I Twelve Animals Vol. 4." This video can be found at hsing-i.com*

Fhu Hsing

Tiger Form

The theory and principle of the Fhu (Tiger) Hsing (Form).

The classic writings of Hsing I define Tiger as the following: *"Considered a king of all animals. The Hsing represents a kind of strength which issues from the back of the hip. It belongs to the 'Du' pulse. If the Du is well, all are well. The Hsing is characterized by its fierce appearance externally but softness internally. The Fhu and Pao movements are very alike in steps, but differ in hand movement. If the Hsing is properly practiced, the clean breathing filled in the Dan Tien will go upward for people's advantage. If not, the unclean breathing will stop at exhalation, resulting in a blockage and finally sickness."*

The first line reference is a direct indication of how important this animal is to the system. I once asked my teacher, Hsu Hong Chi, how I should best train power in Hsing I. He replied immediately, "practice Tiger." In our family, Tiger is unique amongst the twelve animals in that it contains all five energies/forces within the same form. In addition to this, the Tiger form in our system contains a unique half step pattern that my teacher simply called "pouncing step" whenever referencing this step. Because of these two unique qualities, the Fhu Hsing serves as more than a worthy extension in practice of the five forces.

The second line in the reference calls attention to the need for the body to solidify upon issuing energy. The lower spine must lock while the hips roll forward, tightening the Kua, to create the linkage needed upon delivery. This is a somewhat vague, but nevertheless direct, reference to relationship existent between Ming Men (Du 4) and Chi Hai (Ren 6). Between these two points within the body cavity exists the physical space we call lower Dan Tien. The motions practiced in Tiger create a circle moving back, up, forward and down in Dan Tien which when done properly literally feels as if it "issues from the back of the hip."

The next two lines refer to the health relationship of the practice of Tiger. The first of the two lines relates the practice of Tiger to the Du pulse, meaning that proper practice of the form will strengthen the circulation of the governor vessel. The second of the two lines quotes an old Chinese medical saying "if the Du is well, all are well" which is self explanatory given the context of the statement and the relationship to the central nervous system. This relationship is further affirmed in the final two lines of the quote; "if the Hsing is properly practiced, the clean breathing filled in the Dan Tien will go upward for people's advantage. If not, the unclean breathing will stop at exhalation, resulting in a blockage and finally sickness."

The next line goes on to talk about the characteristic of a "fierce appearance externally but softness internally." This is simply explained as an attempt to point the practitioner in a direction of exhibiting an outwardly aggressive (yang) energy while remaining relaxed in the core of the body (yin) to allow a reflexive readiness to adapt.

The sixth line then, makes a simple reference to the stepping pattern of Tiger comparing it to the practice of Pao Chuan (pounding fist). This statement should drive the point home of utilizing angular, 45 degree stepping to accomplish the goal of first evading by moving to the flank and then inserting to counter attack.

The Tiger Hsing is the eleventh animal learned in the Hsing I system taught through my family. In our method, it contains all five forces of Splitting, Drilling, Piercing/Crushing, Pounding and Crossing. This makes it a natural choice to expand ones power parameters within the art.

When practicing Tiger form, one must be mindful of the following attributes. In the transition phase existent between each of the five main hand postures, the core of the body makes two complete rotations to give power to each of the hands in turn. To view this transition as a simple double deflection is an error. This part of the form relates to the Crossing (Heng) energy and should be practiced accordingly. It is also important to note that although each of the main five hand changes relate to one of the other four energies of Hsing I, they do have a common ground. Each of the strokes, upon release, should contain a rapid expansion of the hands away from one another which creates a "tearing" of soft tissues upon impact. This is accomplished

Begin from San Ti Shr left	Step 45 degrees, circle right across center, pierce left	Move to Tiger foot, turn and separate both palms	Bring both fists together in the centerline, coiling	Step and half step, separate both palms forward /down
Step 45 degrees, circle left across center, pierce right	Move to Tiger foot, turn and separate both palms	Bring both fists together in the centerline, coiling	Step and half step, separate both palms forward /down	Step 45 degrees, circle right across center, pierce left
Move to Tiger foot, turn and separate both palms	Step and half step, thrust both palms forward and separate	Step 45 degrees, circle left across center, pierce right	Move to Tiger foot, turn and separate both palms	Step and half step, thrust both palms forward and separate

by using the natural elasticity of the body tissues upon issuing (fah jing). There should be no attempt to utilize localized muscle to create this separation. Rather, the technique is to simply position the palms together in a relaxed frame and then allow the actual issuing of the

| Step 45 degrees, circle right across center, pierce left | Move to Tiger foot, turn and separate both palms | Step and half step, thrust both palms forward and separate | Raise left knee, pull both arms apart, keep rounded | Step and half step, thrust both palms forward and separate |

| Step 45 degrees, circle left across center, pierce right | Move to Tiger foot, turn and separate both palms | Step and half step, thrust both palms forward and separate | Raise right knee, pull both arms apart, keep rounded | Step and half step, thrust both palms forward and separate |

| Step 45 degrees, circle right across center, pierce left | Move to Tiger foot, turn and separate both palms | Thrust two fingers from each hand foward | Step and half step while tearing both hands across centerline | Step 45 degrees, circle left across center, pierce right |

| Move to Tiger foot, turn and separate both palms | Thrust two fingers from each hand foward | Step 45 degrees, circle right across center, pierce left | Move to Tiger foot, turn and separate both palms | Step and half step, thrust both palms lateral and down |

| Step 45 degrees, circle left across center, pierce right | Move to Tiger foot, turn and separate both palms | Step and half step, thrust both palms lateral and down |

kinetic energy to facilitate this separation. In relation to our method, posture one is related to Pi (Splitting), postures two and three are related to Pao (Pounding), posture four is related to Tsuan (Drilling) and posture five relates to Peng (Crushing/Penetrating).

Practiced correctly, the Fhu Hsing will yield tremendous center line power driven from the core of the body aided and abetted by costal expression and thrusting from the legs. As always, the reference to the core of the body correlates to the usage of lower Dan Tien as the engine to drive all action. Since the different postures of Fhu Hsing relate separately to the five forces, each shape should be practiced accordingly.

Tactically speaking, Fhu Hsing represents quite eloquently the concept that we refer to as "Pyan" which means to adjust your angle in relation to your opponents attack so as to attain flank position. As a result, proper practice will yield substantial evasive skills. Additionally, the Tiger form embodies one of the concepts of "double attack" in that both hands are utilized simultaneously to penetrate the opponents guard. Utilized properly and with precise timing the techniques become virtually unstoppable in that the opponents mind is usually led to intercept one hand while the other hand slips through guard

not noticed until it is entirely too late. The Tiger form hand shapes make for excellent follow-up maneuvers to lead bridging gambits. Or, they can serve as excellent stand-alone counters to the opponents initial attempt to grapple.

As is stated, Tiger is considered "a King of all animals."

Note: *Movement can never be accurately portrayed in still form. For more information on both the movement structures and possible applications of the Fhu Hsing (tiger form), please refer to our instructional DVD product "Hsing I Twelve Animals Vol. 2." Found at hsing-i.com*

Lung Hsing

Dragon Form

The theory and principle of the Lung (Dragon) Hsing (Form).

Our same texts of Hsing I reference Dragon in the following manner: *"Lung Hsing heads the list among the twelve. It is one of the first animals to appear in ancient legends. With powerful strength, wings and sharp claws, it is capable of destroying most things in the world. Considered to be descended from heaven, it is a symbol of Emperors and Kings. If the Hsing is properly practiced, the Fire inside the body will be lowered or reduced to minimum. Incorrect practice will cause the Fire to come up."*

The first part of the reference seems to confirm that the Dragon is based on a mythical creature. For the most part, there is a consensus of agreement on this point. However, this does not preclude the possibility that the form is based either on some extinct yet real animal, or possibly one of such an animal's ancestors.

What can be said with certainty, is that the Dragon form is perhaps one of the most physically demanding in the Hsing I system in terms of performance. And it also provides a cross body strength through training that is quite useful across the board in terms of overall ability. This is reflected in the statement; "it is capable of destroying most things in the world."

The Dragon is often called the pinnacle of all Hsing I skill, and it will literally take the average practitioner years to perfect. This perspective is reflected in the fourth line of the reference; "Considered to be descended from heaven, it is a symbol of Emperors and Kings."

The final two lines of the reference once again denote the health benefits/detriments found in the practice of the Dragon form. To be more specific here, the "Fire inside the body" that is denoted is commonly called "Fire in the brain" in Internal Martial Arts and/or Chinese Medical circles. This is a condition that is formed due to excess Yang energy rising up the spine and then becoming trapped with nowhere to go or dissipate. The passage denotes that the condition will be alleviated by proper practice of the Dragon form. The consequence of the improper practice is exacerbation of this same condition.

The Dragon Hsing is the twelfth animal learned in the Hsing I system taught through my family. It is the final animal learned simply because the demands of the physical structure are extraordinary and the body cannot easily begin to perform the Dragon properly prior to this juncture. The practice of the form is an extreme "plyometric" exercise all to itself. Although sometimes, we do teach what we call "Dragon walking" to strengthen the legs of a student with weakness in this area. The Dragon exemplifies the elements of Metal (splitting) and Fire (pounding) which will become quite obvious upon viewing this remarkable form.

When practicing the Dragon form there are only a few main components of which to be mindful during performance. The opening sequence of the form is a quick turning to the right and then back to the left, while the left forearm first drops down to the right and then circles up and to the left creating two rapid center line parries. Simultaneously, as the left forearm drops down and to the right, the left leg is withdrawn into a classic iron wall position. Immediately after the left arm intercepts, circling up and to the left, the right hand will shoot forward in the Pi palm position while the left foot also shoots forward into a toe out cross kick position. As this is happening, the entire core of the body will motivate power downward and forward into the classic crouching Dragon shape. The intercostals will close and the weight will be primarily settled on the rear leg.

| Begin from San Ti Shr left | Raise left knee, sweep left forearm down and across | Drop to deep dragon stance, strike right forward, left back | Thrust right fist upward, preparing to leap and kick | Kick right (normally done in the air while jumping) |

The first leaping sequence now begins, and within each leaping change there are several points to be aware of regarding the performance. The primary point of concern should be the control of the legs while leaping/kicking in each change. In the beginning shape (crouching Dragon) the weight is resting predominantly on the rear leg with the front leg also substantial. Both legs provide the thrust to catapult the body into the air to deliver the kick. Once the legs have extended to launch the body skyward, they must contract before expanding into the kicking change. When the kick has been performed, the natural recoil of energy after the kick will cause an additional contraction of the legs. As the body begins its descent toward the ground, the legs must again extend so that they can then be rapidly contracted under control as the change is completed and the body once again forms the crouching Dragon shape. When done properly, the landing of the feet on the ground at completion should cause little or no noise.

The second main consideration in performing the leaping change is the timing of the hands as they change from the Splitting fist on the ascent to the palm on descent. This statement summarizes the timing specifically in that the fist must be held in position until the pinnacle of the jump has been achieved. The intercostals will have expanded to motivate the power of the fist and will now rapidly close to motivate the power of the palm as the body descends.

| Drop to deep dragon stance, strike right forward, pull right hand back | Thrust left fist upward, preparing to leap and kick | Kick left (normally done in the air while jumping) | Drop to deep dragon stance, strike right forward, pull left hand back |

The final component worthy of discussion is the transition from the crouching Dragon position into the Peng (crushing/penetrating) fists within each line of the form. As this transition is performed each time, the left hand will inscribe a counter clockwise circle... starting low, then moving up and to the right, then to the left and down as the foot steps through. It is important to note that the circle is core driven and results from both the movements of the stepping pattern and the opening and closing of the intercostals and not the limb by itself. Done properly, it represents a combination of Drilling and Splitting energies in minor shape.

The remaining portions of Dragon are straight usage of the Peng (crushing/penetrating) fists and should be practiced accordingly (see the chapter on Peng Chuan).

The Dragon form is certainly the most physically demanding of the twelve animals hsings. Frequent practice will promote tremendous strength and endurance. It is based soundly in the elements of Metal (splitting) and Fire (pounding) and should be practiced accordingly. The opening and closing of the body should be expressed fully.

Tactically speaking, the Dragon is counter offensive. It can be used to simultaneously neutralize both the attacking hand and forward leg of the opponent creating an opportunity to immediately punish the center line by utilizing either a leaping change to kick or a straight crushing/penetrating fist as follow-up. It can also be utilized to surprise and confuse the opponent upon initial bridging attempt by performing a low to high change to first evade and then counter attack.

As the classics say, "it is capable of destroying most things in the world."

Note: *Movement can never be accurately portrayed in still form. For more information on both the movement structures and possible applications of the Lung Hsing (dragon form), please refer to our instructional DVD product "Hsing I Twelve Animals Vol. 6." Found at hsing-i.com*

Practical Practice - Training Parameters

On the practice of form:

Form sequences in the traditional Chinese arts serve many purposes, including maintaining a living record of the system in question. Form in a traditional Chinese art is a living text book. It is a construct for the development of kinetic potential, a source of theory and tactical overlay perspective *and* a means of cultivating fitness/endurance in the body. It is also a means of evaluation of performance and skill capabilities. I.E.. if your balance falls apart at high speed on this or that movement, you either have work left to do or you have a mistaken perspective of that particular mechanic and it needs to be corrected.

From form we learn integration. Form gives us the "end frame" of motion for body kinetic alignment upon delivery of force. From form we also develop transitional strength. Form is VERY important. But not at the expense of other training. I.E. Comprehensive and appropriate "layered" drills to develop certain essential skill sets, resistance training, percussion training, strength training and endurance training. To focus on form alone is futile. But to remove form entirely (which I will say is impossible in a moment with an anecdote) is equally futile.

It is not important whether one utilizes any or all of the technique contained in a form. The essence of form is to train proper mechanics and/or kinetics. So that ultimately even waving the hand is powerful, connected and grounded. Only teachers really need become expert at all sequences as they are the ones to carry the living record forward for others to learn from.

All Arts have form, although I have often been told by my own students who have formerly studied boxing or kick boxing that they have not studied form.

At a seminar for MMA folks, a Muay Thai based fellow asked me about the practice of form and received a similar response as above. Whereupon he then said words to the effect of "I don't believe in forms at all." I asked him to assist me in a little demo and brought him out onto the floor. I extended my hand with a pad and asked him to kick it with his best round kick. He did so after a few misgivings. I then said to him; "Now, describe to me how you just now performed that kick as if I were completely ignorant." After a few questions for clarification of what I wanted him to do, he began to tell me in detail about when and how he stepped his front foot, when and how he rotated his waist, when and how he counterbalanced his rotational force, etc. When done, I said to him.. "*That* is form. You object to what you call form as overly long organized patterns of movement. But all movement, to be performed properly, has a form. You're just used to doing small forms revolving around one or two movements." Just because a boxer or kick boxer does not practice long sequences of movement in a standardized pattern does not mean that they do not practice form. They most certainly do.

In classic arts, the progression of forms training generally becomes gradually more complex and challenging in movement structure. If not challenging, then the mind will tend to wander, preventing the achievement of true harmony of mind and body.

The Internal Arts classics expound upon the premise of achieving "whole body power" in all motion. I submit to you on a purely logical level that one cannot possibly have whole body power without first cultivating whole body awareness. I mean, how would you even know? Graduated complexity of forms training forces exactly this methodology into the mind and body. There is simply no way to render a good performance of form without being aware.

On Training in General:
A common mistake in training by many practitioners is sequencing. Your self training sessions should always have two things firmly in place to guide them.

1) Train the most Yin to the most Yang in terms of sequence.
2) Train skills that require precision while still fresh and not fatigued.

Too often, I have students complain to me that they cannot calm themselves for meditation. Upon investigation, it is usually found that they are trying to meditate at the very end of their workout when their body and mind are too excited. Meditation should be in the beginning (or at another time entirely) to avoid this mistake. If you set out to do a sequence of; Meditation, Chi Kung, Moving Form, Some Paired Drills and some Heavy Bag Work... then that should be the order of appearance in your sequencing. This follows the most Yin to most Yang rule and your body will be more productive this way.

An equally easy mistake to commit is that of training "gross" strength methods prior to precision methods. E.G. doing some weight training prior to working combinations on the heavy bag. This is a mistake because the body will be both tired and tight before beginning the precision work on combinations, translating to poor muscle memory being ingrained during the workout. It is vital to remember that good and bad habits form equally quickly in terms of the body's muscle memory. And, as a result, we wish our bodies to not be fatigued when trying to ingrain key skill sets. It is also important to remember that you should end your precision trainings on a "good" repetition. This insures that the most positive muscle memory is carried forward from session to session, raising your skill level.

On Paired Drilling:
Too often when students go through fixed paired drills, they practice in an empty manner. When you practice a drill it must be as real as possible to you both in mind and body. The drill must be practiced "in the moment" as if you do not know what movement is coming next.

Initially, you should go through the movements slowly and methodically in order to learn the mechanical structure of each technique contained within the drill. Once this is achieved, the intention behind the technique must be understood and coupled with the physical movements. When both of these have been achieved, it is necessary to escalate the interaction to a level of reality that approximates free fighting. By this, I mean that each movement must be done full out in terms of speed and power. Too often, at this stage, it is entirely too easy to throw effective power out the window in an effort to gain greater speed and fluidity of motion. This is a grave error. If the drill is not practiced at a level of reality in terms of effective power, the practice is ultimately pointless.

Body Banging Drills - such as the two drills depicted here first, are for conditioning. Striking each other builds resistance to impact. The mind and body begin to relax regarding the notion of being struck. The body will read the stress as weakness and strengthen the bones and sinew.

1a. *Shift left, rotate your waist and strike your right forearm against your partner. Twist your forearm upon impact to the ulnar side.*

1b. *Shift right, rotate your waist and strike your left forearm against your partner. Again, twist your forearm upon impact to the ulnar side.*

1c. *Shift left, rotate your waist and strike your right forearm against your partner. Twist your forearm upon impact from radial to center.*

1d. *Shift right, rotate your waist, strike your left forearm against your partner. Again, twist your forearm upon impact from radial to center.*

1e. *Arc the right foot across center. Strike your right forearm against your partner twisting upon impact from center to radial.*

1f. *Corkscrew the right forearm downward, again impacting your partner's arm as you twist the arm the other way to the ulnar side.*

1g. *Pivot to your back side and strike your left forearm against your partner, again twisting upon impact. (picture angles for clarity)*

1h. *Corkscrew the left forearm downward, again impacting your partner's arm as you twist the arm the other way. (angled for clarity)*

1i. *Step the left foot back to a squared position and begin the drill as before. All strikes should be twisting upon impact, dissipating force.*

It is also extremely important to limit the scope and time spent in practice in relation to each drill to prevent fatigue and the ingraining of bad habits.

Long ago I held the notion that if ten repetitions of a movement was good, then one hundred repetitions would be better. The problem with doing one hundred repetitions of anything arises in two categories. The first is the mind; it tends to wander. The second is founded in the body via fatigue. Both of these qualities added together create sloppy movement combined with poor focus. Since bad habits form just as quickly as good habits in terms of body/mind memory, this approach to practice can be extremely detrimental over the long-term.

It is far wiser to limit the scope of the drill so that both mental focus and body integrity can be maintained throughout the practice. This insures that each session will ingrain the best possible

2a. *Hook your right wrist and then strike against your partner with a downward and inward pulling stroke toward yourself.*

2b. *Now hook your left wrist and strike against your partner with a downward and inward pulling stroke toward yourself.*

2c. *Twist and drill your right arm up against your partner, meeting in the center of the forearm and twisting to the radial side.*

2d. *Twist and drill your left arm up against your partner, meeting in the center of the forearm and twisting to the radial side.*

2e. *Fold your right elbow in an upward arcing motion, shift forward and strike your partners forearm.*

2f. *Step forward and crash your right inner shoulder and pectoral area into your partner. Be sure to brace the body properly as you do.*

2g. *Perform a foot change. Fold your left elbow in an upward arcing motion, shift forward and strike your partners forearm.*

2h. *Step forward and crash your left inner shoulder and pectoral area into your partner. Be sure to brace the body properly as you do.*

body/mind memory regarding each drill structure. I recommend if training a paired drill, that the time of practice be limited to 1-2 minutes each side in an effort to retain both qualities fully. If training a singular individual drill, a good guideline is to practice execution of ten "perfect"

2i. Perform a leftward fade step and position your body at a 45 degree angle to your partner.

2j. Step your right foot toward your opponent, brace the body and strike your right outer shoulder into your partner.

2k. Perform a rightward fade step and position your body at a 45 degree angle to your partner.

2l. Step your left foot toward your opponent, brace the body and strike your right outer shoulder into your partner.

repetitions and then stop that drill for that session (note that "perfect" is an individual standard based on experience level). And do not count the repetitions that are deemed "imperfect." You should always finish the drill with a "perfect" repetition to again ingrain the best possible body/mind memory for that session.

Skill-based Drills - The purpose of such drills is to imbed and practice a certain type of skill set with regard the governing principles found within the respective art form.

Skill-based drills need not be complex, but rather they should focus on one or two key concepts in a repetitive and live manner. It is important in skill-based drills that the practitioners spend time to first learn and hone the proper movement structures under cooperation. And then, once a certain comfort level has been achieved, the drill tempo and intensity should be gradually ramped up to simulate the property being practiced in an uncooperative environment. Such drills need to remain as live and true as possible. Meaning accurate targeting, good structure, proper force parameters, etc. If the drill is allowed to become rote routine, it will never really accomplish the goal of imbuing that particular skill set.

1a. *Shift left and rotate your waist while twisting your right forearm into your partner's arm, medial to ulnar sides.*

1b. *Shift right and deliver a low palm strike toward your partner's hip, impacting the ulnar side of your forearm against your partner.*

1c. *Shift left and softly snake your right arm around your partner's arm to touch lightly on the right shoulder. Keep the elbow down.*

1d. *Shift right and rotate your waist while twisting your left forearm into your partner's arm, medial to ulnar sides.*

1e. *Shift right and deliver a low palm strike toward your partner's hip, impacting the ulnar side of your forearm against your partner.*

1f. Shift right and softly snake your left arm around your partner's arm to touch lightly on the left shoulder. Keep the elbow down.

Skill-based drills, such as the one above (which focuses on shifting the mass) and those in the following pages, can also be a useful way to correct negative tendencies in a still developing practitioner. Sometimes limiting the scope can correct a consistently present error.

2a. *As your partner uppercuts toward your head, shift back and adhere to the arm redirecting it past you at a narrow tangent angle.*

2b. *Perform a foot change and angle outside the lead leg while simultaneously seizing and lifting the arm with your left palm.*

2c. *Circle your right arm around, shift forward and punch with a right vertical fist to the ribcage.*

2d. *Your partner should now shift back, hollowing the body, and knife his hand down across your radial nerve.*

2e. *Your partner now performs a foot change, angling off cenerline and simultaneously suppresses your forearm with the left hand.*

2f. *Your partner now shifts forward and uppercuts right to your head. This time, the left foot is forward. You again yield and redirect.*

Practitioners need to be aware of the necessity to focus on the details of each drill as they are practicing and to not become complacent in the "act" of a drill. This takes a shift of mind as it is important to stay in the moment even though you know what is coming next.

2g. *Perform a foot change, this time into the center line of your partner and simultaneously control the limb with your left palm.*

2h. *Shift forward, again delivering a vertical right fist to your partner. The partner will again knife down across the radial nerve.*

2i. *Your partner again performs a foot change, this time taking the position of centerline, while simultaneously suppressing your limb.*

2j. *Your partner then starts the cycle again, directing an uppercut to your head, while you shift back adhering and redirecting.*

2k. *Again, simultaneously perform a foot change and angle outside the lead leg while seizing and lifting the arm with your left palm.*

2j. *The drill continues repetitively onward. And of course the two practitioners should switch sides to work the left side also.*

Skill-based drills can be conformed to address pretty much any parameter. The drill simply needs to revolve around whatever skill set is the desired goal. The drill depicted in this and the preceding page revolves around a simple isolate trapping method employed with a foot change.

3a. *Half step your rear followed by front foot as you angle off center to flank position, redirecting your partner's right punch.*

3b. *Now, half step your front followed by rear foot as you angle off center to flank position, redirecting your partner's left punch.*

3c. *Apply a direct trap with your left hand, suppressing your partner's arm just below the elbow in preparation for entry.*

3d. *Enter with a half step, punching right. Your partner now half steps to flank position, assuming your role from "3a" and redirecting.*

3e. *Offset your centerline to pursue your partner with your left punch. Your partner assumes your role from "3b" flanking to the other side.*

3f. *Your partner now applies a direct trap in preparation for entry which will return you to the starting position found in "3a".*

Since Hsing I is fond of exploiting flanking angles, the drill above is a simple construct to imbed that ideology into the practitioner's mind and body. Repetitive practice will create the "habit" of looking to get to the flank of the opponent in combat.

The concept of "sticking" is also prevalent in this art, as is the concept of "uprooting." Sticking means literally to follow the opponent's limb or limbs as they are moved into your sphere of influence (the immediate surrounding space of your body). And the concept of uprooting is the method used to break the opponent's connection to the ground, thus making it easier to control their body center.

The simple drill depicted on this page allows for the initial rudimentary practice of both of these concepts in a live and resistant environment using each other's body mass in a Yin and Yang exchange.

4a. *As your partner half steps forward and chops at your neck, you will half step to the rear and redirect at a narrow vector past your center.*

4b. *You will now step forward and attempt to strike your partner in the chest while your partner half steps to the rear and deflects outward.*

4c. *Your partner now steps into you and attempts to strike your ribs. You withdraw your front foot only and redirect the attack to the side.*

4d. *Continuing your redirection from "4c", you will now trap and control your partner's limbs in preparation for entry.*

4e. *You now step forward into your partner and perform an uprooting push, displacing your partner's body completely (result not shown).*

As both practitioners gain in skill and ability, both the strength used and the pace of the drill should gradually be increased, adding more and more resistance on the part of the opponent to attempt to stop the uproot from completion.

What we call "triangle stepping" and a standard half foot change are combined in the simple drill found on this page to promote agility in footwork.

Triangle stepping is utilized as a tactical draw in our system and is discussed on that merit elsewhere in this work in the RSPCT section.

A foot change is a method we employ in a variety of circumstances, also tactically, to either evade or achieve rapid acceleration into the opponent's space. This is also discussed in more detail elsewhere in this work. Here, only the drill is presented.

5a. *Both practitioners step left at a 45 degree angle, keeping the right foot light, and simultaneously slap each other's left palm.*

5b. *Both practitioners step right laterally to the other flank, keeping the left foot light, and simultaneously slap each other's right palm.*

5c. *Both practitioners now fade the left foot backward to the original starting position on the floor in preparation for a foot change.*

5d. *Both practitioners now perform the foot change (shown in the transitional phase) in readiness to move back to the first flank.*

5e. *The drill now repeats with both practitioners returning to the first 45 degree flank position and simultaneously slapping left palms.*

The practitioners should attempt to maintain good balance and structure at all times. The footwork should be both agile and light but remain connected to the ground. This will then translate to agility and poise while engaging the opponent in free form scenarios.

On the practice of Mirror Boxing:

Perhaps one of the more difficult aspects of ingraining good combat habit is honing the ability to see a developing "hole" in the opponent's defenses and then to move in swiftly enough to capitalize on the opportunity presented. We've all been there. You see the hole develop but by the time you try to move, it has already closed and the possible opportunity has been lost. Certainly, by developing greater reflexive speed, this dilemma can be at least partially solved. However, by choosing to also develop perception, we can attack the problem from two sides of being.

This practice is designed to teach a fundamental and critical skill required for true combative ability. The practitioners stands in front of a mirror. The reflection seen is the representative opponent. As your position changes, so will the "opponent's" position. And you must seek to quickly move to the next target of opportunity presented as the image shifts by using the most expedient weapon available. Just as if this reflection were a live individual standing before you.

It is important to understand that you do not attempt to interpret defensive parameters to your attack executions. You simply flow with the positional change seen in your mirrored reflection and constantly re-target the openings presented within the reflection. This is true within actual combat also. One should not worry about the opponent's defensive actions, but rather read the changes in posture as new opportunities of attack. Any defensive action taken on the part of the practitioner is incidental and part of the overall scheme of continual attack.

Mirror boxing presents an overall perspective of seeing the developing shifts in position. And given that you are fighting your own reflection, the faster you move the faster "he/she" moves.

On the practice of Slow Speed Sparring:

This is a good avenue for exploration of possible technical perspectives. But the method does require complete cooperation on the part of both partners while engaging in the exercise. One of the most difficult aspects of learning how to apply any Martial Art within the context of live combat is that of being able to translate movements learned into opportunities presented. By slowing the sparring practice down several notches, the mind is allowed the luxury of time to think. This will begin to create a link between the trained movements and the opportunity to utilize the same. Over time, the speed can gradually be brought up one notch at a time, allowing the methodic integration of perception and training to manifest in full-scale live combat.

1a. *As Brandon leads, I step to the side and wait. He will, by necessity, need to turn his center to find a good line of attack.*

Initial stages should be limited to more simplistic

1b. As Brandon turns to realign his center, providing a good line of attack, I side step again and move to his flank while suppressing.

1c. I then enter by stepping my right foot into him immediately after the flanking step thereby achieving a dominant position.

structures and concepts. For example, one might start with just simple hand strikes alone. Then, as the combatants develop greater control and cognizance of potential attributes, then kicking techniques can be integrated. Followed by takedowns and throwing concepts and then finally to include ground based methods.

In addition, any perceived weakness in a particular area of combat can be addressed using this same approach by limiting the exchange to that particular area throughout the exercise.

The practice of utilizing a slow speed can take the pressure of rapid decision making off the combatants in favor of developing better perception of possible options. This in turn can lead to a much greater understanding of tactical overlay in given situations as opposed to simply defaulting to the same "go to" responses in presented circumstances.

2a. As Brandon jabs left, I rotate slightly, keeping my frame and check off the jab while waiting for his secondary attack.

2b. As Brandon then lunges long into his secondary, I deflect with my forearm by angling my elbow upward and across the centerline.

2c. I then suppress his limb with my elbow while immediately stepping into him and striking with my right palm to the head.

On the practice of Animal Sparring:
This is an exercise designed to strengthen the practitioners ability to utilize animal movements from the Hsing I system and to bring about a gradually broader, contextual grasp of possible application of movements already understood. In this exercise each combatant is assigned one of the twelve animals at random by a referee and then required to stay within the confines of that movement structure while engaged in the combat. Initially, I highly recommend that the practitioners stay solely within that particular form and not allow any other outside additions. However, as more familiarity with the exercise is gained, other qualities can be added to the exercise (i.e. kicking techniques that are not found in that respective form) to further broaden their experience. Oftentimes this exercise can be combined with the practice of "Slow Speed Sparring" (from the prior page) to effectively integrate proper technique from the animal forms into the mainstream combative vocabulary.

A good place to start in this interplay is by looking at the "antagonistic" animal relationships found in nature. I.E. Horse vs. Snake or Monkey vs. Tiger. These by no means are the ONLY relationships worth studying. They are merely suggested as starting points.

1a. *Alex opens with a direct trap to Brandon's lead hand while simultaneously delivering a Monkey style eye gouge attempt.*

1b. *Brandon counters with by stepping to Alex's flank and deflecting with his right limb setting up his counter move.*

1c. *Brandon enters with the second Tiger posture to Alex's flank to attempt a double strike to the head and ribcage.*

1d. *Alex utilizes a repealing, arcing step from the Monkey style again to contain and redirect Brandon's attack.*

This same method can be applied to the study of technical usage of the five fists/forces. The natural antagonists following the destructive cycle is again a good beginning point.

On the practice of Nine Palace Boxing:

Although nine Palace boxing is probably more commonly known in relation to the practice of the art of Pa Kua Chang, the practice can also be applied to Hsing I to enhance knowledge of spatial dimension and angle of attack in relation to multiple opponents. The practice of Nine Palace boxing contains several phases of development. And for best results, these phases should be practiced in their logical sequence with sufficient time spent in each phase to develop realistic skills.

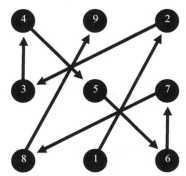

The first phase should consist of simple memorization of each gate and its assigned location. This is most easily achieved by simply moving around each gate in sequential order, changing from left to right side of the body using any familiar posture, throughout the pattern. With sufficient repetition the pattern will become indelibly etched in the mind and then it's on to phase two.

The second phase should consist of again moving from gate to gate in sequential order but this time varying the interaction with each gate utilizing either the five fists or the twelve animals chosen at random in the mind as the gate is approached and circled.

The third phase should introduce (wherever possible) multiple practitioners on the pattern grid simultaneously. Each new practitioner should be introduced to the grid as the previous practitioner passes from gate No. 2 to gate No. 3 respectively. As more people come onto the grid, this will inevitably cause close interaction amongst individuals as they stay the course of the pattern itself. This then creates an opportunity to practice "presence of enemy" while closely passing each fellow individual on the grid. As this process becomes more comfortable, the practitioners can exchange briefly while engaged in the process of staying the course of the pattern. These exchanges should only be allowed "on-the-fly" and should not be allowed to interrupt the overall flow of the pattern practice. In this way, each practitioner will learn to adapt and change in relation to an enemy while preserving the actual flow of motion regarding the Nine Palace pattern. This will eventually translate to great skill in terms of sizing up and overcoming the chaos of a multiple scenario with succinct agility.

The fourth, fifth and sixth phases are interchangeable games/scenarios that can be played as time and personnel permit to promote overall skills of combat. The first is a solo practice wherein each post becomes a tangible opponent with the goal being free fluid interaction on a tactical level with each respective post as you move through the pattern. This is primarily a freestyle solo combative practice to train distance, angle of insertion and precision. It can be practiced with smooth posts or posts that have had arms attached. However, the posts all need to be solidly anchored.

The second game requires at least two people to play. One person in the role of the practitioner while the other plays the role of the "caller." The caller's job is to verbally reference a given form while standing outside the pattern and then the practitioner must now quickly choose a movement structure from the form reference that fits the distance and scope of the next change within the pattern. This practice will promote quickness of mind in terms of decision-making of technical utility of the style within the changing scope of combat.

The third scenario requires a minimum of three to four people. In this structure, one of the practitioners is designated as the receiver and the others are designated as the attackers. The receiver will begin at position No. 1 while the attackers are allowed to position themselves anywhere within or outside the grid. The practice is a freestyle one and all players will move simultaneously. The receiver will move through the pattern grid in sequential order and interact with the attackers as they encroach upon his/her position. The attackers will simply begin to move toward the receiver in the most direct manner possible. This practice will teach the receiver how to utilize the grid in a multiple combat scenario. In the beginning stages of this game, I recommend that all players move one step at a time. Later, as more skill is acquired, the posts can be removed from the playing field. The players can then step up the pace and the receiver can begin to adjust the grid in his mind's eye at will to fit the scenario as is required.

On Multi-Man Training:
We have three graduated levels of drill structures that we use to develop Multi-Man capabilities for combat. These three levels are overlays that can be utilized with virtually any other type of training parameter from the unarmed methods to use of weaponry. In example, let us consider knife disarmament tactics. Once the student has been trained in various techniques for knife disarmament with a partner, and practiced those same techniques to a reasonable level of competency, it is time to test those abilities under pressure. This is a necessary step to ensure that the newfound abilities are actually practical and applicable to a real world environment.

The level one scenario begins with the receiver standing in the center of multiple opponents (as many as possible), all of which possess a knife, with the receiver being unarmed. The knife wielding opponents then begin to attack, one by one, utilizing *one* strong stroke with the knife directed at the receiver. The receiver should respond, attempting to disarm the attacker, and then disengage within three seconds. If the receiver fails to do so, then the next attacker can come randomly from any direction when the time of three seconds expires. If the receiver is successful in disarming the knife wielding attacker within the prescribed time limit, then the receiver is permitted to use the knife taken from the attacker against the next opponent (after use, the receiver must then drop the knife and proceed with the remainder of the drill).

The level two scenario allows two knife wielding opponents to attack at any given time with the subsequent opponents coming in at three second intervals. In the level two scenario, the knife wielding assailants are allowed to utilize one strong stroke plus follow up with the weapons.

The level three scenario is an "anything goes" construct. The opponents are allowed to attack en masse with no restrictions. The receiver attempts to survive utilizing any means possible.

This escalating scenario drill for Multi-Man combat can be utilized to train virtually any Martial skill. If a practitioner feels deficient in the seizing or locking skills department, the drill can be modified to train those attributes only. The same structure can be utilized to train throwing technique, leg technique, hand technique or any other specific skill. Any limitations to be set are up to the individuals involved.

Although there are many ways to play each scenario in a multiple encounter, there exist a few hard and fast rules that should be observed.

Perhaps the most important thing to remember is to work the perimeter. To stay within the midst of multiple opponents is an obvious folly. Correctly working the perimeter will allow you to engage the opponents one at a time for the most part and utilize selected adversaries as temporary shields against the others creating opportunity to engage a more level playing field. Increased awareness of this parameter will also permit temporary "stacking" or "herding" of such multiple opponents so that they interfere more with one another and have less chance en masse to get to the defender.

It is important to learn to view the "multiple" as a whole organism as opposed to individuals. This will allow you to move "with the flow" of the multiple adversary scenario and prevent you from remaining in a "tunnel vision" state of engagement with one adversary for too long.

Under no circumstances should you go to the ground in a multiple encounter. This will get you severely damaged, if not worse. If you find yourself taken to the ground against your will, then adopt a philosophy of hit first and get up quickly. Submission fighting has absolutely no place in a multiple encounter. And be advised, in a street fight there is usually no such thing as a one on one scenario even if it does start out that way. You must be ready to disengage without any hesitation. Therefore it is unwise to tie yourself up with any one adversary for long.

If the attackers are unarmed, another possible strategy is to utilize "the corner theory." If you place your back in a corner, then in theory the maximum amount of attackers that can engage simultaneously will be two. And the exposure of your body to the assailants is minimized to the frontal angles of attack. Simply put, at a 90 degree angle with each opponent occupying forty five degrees of space, they already tend to interfere with one another to some extent. And even more attackers will simply cause the frontal two to be pressured forward by the people behind affording them very little room to maneuver and making them fairly easy marks for counter attack. It should be duly noted however, that this theory should be applied sparingly, and for short durations of time only, to create opportunities of escape and/or greater mobility.

On Push Hands Skills

Push hands develops many different skill sets. Some exercises focus on only the maintenance of rooting, ground path expression and mechanical principles of neutralization and redirection. To achieve this, many fixed step methods are employed. Some focus on lateral circles of redirection. Others focus more on the vertical aspects. Some focus on sticking through the fore arms, elbows and hands. Others focus on qualities of T'un (sucking in) and T'u (spitting out). We have so very many patterns to develop such isolate skills. But we utilize what is called freestyle push hands more frequently than any other structure. Freestyle push hands, in our tradition, is a contest

Freestyle push hands ready position. Your lead hand is outside your opponent's rear hand and your rear hand is inside your opponent's.

with very few restrictions. The only initial rules are as follows below:

1) No kicking
2) No striking the face (at least not for a very long time, see below).
3) No fisted attacks, open hand only (this is to both encourage relaxed movement and to keep a relative safety measure in place but still allow the practice to be "spirited").

Everything else is allowed. We allow hooking the neck as the second "primary control." The other two controls being hooking the arm at the bicep/tricep area and hooking the waist. Hooks are common entries to "Shuai" (throwing) methods. We also allow elbows, knees, shoulder strokes, grappling, throwing, sweeping and ground submission.

1a. *Creating an opportunity to breach with an elbow stroke by pushing the opponent's hand down and to the outside. See "1b" below.*

In our tradition, what we call freestyle push hands is a practice method designed to be a "relatively safe" simulation of the clinch after the initial bridging engagement.

On "Specialized" Push Hands:

Freestyle push hands is an excellent way to cultivate close quarters combat tactics. However, the practice is also extremely useful if used as a remedial effort to correct deficient technical abilities. I.E, suppose a practitioner feels that their shoulder crashing techniques need to be improved. In this instance the push hands practice can be tailored to allow only shoulder crashing tactics to be employed in the scope of the practice as attack, while also allowing

any type defense in terms

1b. *Stepping in and breaching with an elbow stroke after creating the space to do so in "1a" above. Note the line from elbow to rear heal.*

of body repositioning through turning, twisting and/or stepping. Such specialized practice does require a willing and cooperative partner as a matter of course or the session may be less than profitable. Providing a suitable practice partner is available, this method can be applied to virtually any deficiency of technique. The seizing and locking aspects of the art can be isolated in this manner for practice, as can throwing skills, sweeping skills and any manner of specialized striking techniques. At upper levels we also will sometimes put on headgear and allow head

An example of breaching with a shoulder crash after controlling the opponent's limbs through grabbing. Again, note the line of the strike.

shots in freestyle push hands. But not until what we consider proper structure and grounding/ rooting/balance issues have been ingrained. Prior to that, the allowance of head shots contributes to bad postural balance and positioning.

An example of breaching with a shoulder bar by slipping under and outside. Note the simultaneous control of the opposite limb.

An example of sweeping the lead leg of the opponent to compromise the stance while simultaneously grabbing and pressuring the body.

On the practice of Accuracy (rattan frame):
Practitioners of the Martial arts often pay minimal attention to the development of accuracy. Many are content with their ability to hit a heavy bag "near the center each time" or to strike a more mobile target, such as a rhythm bag, "most of the time." In my opinion, this perspective is insufficient. A practitioner should strive for the utmost in control and accuracy of all striking motions. One of the "tools" that my teacher, Hsu Hong Chi, had me construct was a rattan wand grid. This grid was set in a two by four frame, approximately two feet in height by three feet in width. The rattan wands inserted were less than one inch in diameter. Some of the wands were cut to fit the height of the frame and others to fit the width. Grooves were then cut into the frame, in an offset manner for the vertical and horizontal, so as to allow the rattan wands to slide in creating an adjustable grid. I was then instructed to practice full power and full speed piercing movements with my fingertips into the boxes created on the grid. As my skills increased, additional wands were added to the grid causing the target boxes to gradually shrink in size. The tool is invaluable in sharpening one's accuracy to a very high level indeed. As a caveat, I would strongly recommend that any practitioner who would endeavor to practice this skill should wear gloves (strong leather ones) in the first month or two of practice. This will save wear and tear on the digits themselves and especially the "emergency" acupuncture points on and near the tips of the fingers.

On the development of the Grip Strength (bamboo bundle, etc.):
One of the most often overlooked skills in the Martial arts is grip strength. Grip strength is an attribute that it is easily developed and requires no special skills to be honed in the process of such development. Yet, grip strength is the foundation of all successful grappling, locking, throwing and submission techniques. There is also something truly scary about an opponent who has the ability to inflict pain via seizing the vital spots on the anatomy with a viselike grip. There are many simple tasks that can be done daily to develop grip strength and the following

117

are some of my personal favorites. Some of the exercises will require you to build or purchase some simple equipment:

Bamboo bundle: construct a bundle of bamboo or rattan wands (approximately 50 to the bundle, tied in the center). Then practice twisting the bundle, working one hand/wrist against the other. Twist inward and/or outward while holding the bundle vertically. And also twist to and fro while holding the bundle horizontally. Integrate stance and footwork as desired.

Paper/Leather Working: on a hardwood surface, *with palms staying flush to the surface* and the material being worked. Start with one sheet of newspaper (working up to 10) and while using the fingers only, first crinkle up the paper toward you and then smooth the paper away from you repetitively until tired. When 10 sheets of newspaper becomes easy, you may graduate to a piece of buckskin (dry initially and then damp when the dry becomes easy) and practice the same procedure until tired.

Catching Blocks of Stone: with a piece of stone broad enough that you can just barely catch the edge of it utilizing the final phalanges of your fingers and thumb. Grasp the stone in front of you while standing in a horse stance. Then lift the stone up to chest height and while dropping it to the ground, clap your hands and then catch the stone before it hits the ground. When this becomes easy, then clap twice or three times and perform the same procedure. Or, you may increase the weight of the stone to further your training. Stone key practice is also a very good alternative to this but requires a special piece of equipment (think concrete kettlebell).

Bath Towel Pull-ups: take two long bath towels and roll them up lengthwise. Then loop them over a beam in your garage and tape the ends. Practice doing pull-ups (for added challenge you may do them in a jackknife position), first using the entire hand. Then, as you become more comfortable, delete one finger at a time until you can do them with just the thumb and index finger holding the towels.

Fingertip Push-ups: make sure that you splay the fingers out and position yourself on the pads (not the tips) of the fingers properly. Passively grip the floor with your fingers. Then work with five, four, three and then finally just the thumb and index fingers.

V-Grip Exerciser: find a hollow ended v-grip exerciser and then practice placing your thumb in one end and then opposing it with a single finger (train them all) in the other end until tired.

Pole Wrist Exercise: use a pole that has sufficient weight to challenge you. Then daily practice lifting and turning the pole both clockwise and counter clockwise (while keeping the elbow of the arm being worked firmly against your side) to strengthen the wrist. Practice until tired and then change hands.

Exercise Balls: for best results, solid balls are the only way to go. These are difficult to find nowadays as the hollow ones have become more common. But without sufficient weight, you do not train the grip properly. Find and start with 2 to 2 1/2 inch diameter balls. Then practice circling them quickly in your one hand both ways until tired. Go up in the diameter of the balls as circling them both ways in your hand smoothly becomes easy for you.

On bag training:

As mentioned earlier, when much younger, I ascribed to the "more must be better" mentality. If practicing 10 sidekicks is good, then 100 must be better, right? Wrong. Both the body and mind will fatigue and once this happens, you are no longer doing your best.

Many people look at heavy bag training as an aerobic exercise. Although I will certainly agree that a heavy bag can be used in this manner, this is not the way to develop superior skill in the Martial Arts. You should not work to the bag for the sake of "working the bag." You should rather strive to deliver picture perfect and precise strikes and/or combinations. In this approach, if your goal is to do "10" repetitions of any one strike or combination, then the goal should be ten "perfect" executions. And most importantly, you must make the ending repetition as one of the perfect. This approach will then leave the best "body memory" from today's practice to carry over into tomorrow. In addition to this philosophy, I recommend that the duration of each exercise on a heavy bag be limited in scope and time to prevent fatigue of both body and mind. Physical skills requiring precision of motion should not be practiced while the mind and body are tired or you run the risk of imbuing false muscle memory. Therefore, the duration of each exercise is appropriately set at only one minute. When the minute is expired, it is best to move on to a new activity thus keeping the mind fresh in as you change from exercise to exercise. Both anaerobic an aerobic conditioning levels can be increased by simply adding new exercises in the sequence of training.

Again, the reader is cautioned to be mindful of fatigue. When fatigue sets in, you will become sloppy in your movements. And bad muscle memory ingrains just as quickly as does good. If you wish to develop more endurance, there are plenty of ways to accomplish that goal without the risk of denigrating your technical performance attributes. Body mass conditioning exercises can be done to promote endurance without the risk of denigrating refined muscle memory.

On redirected parrying:

In three words, MOVE THE BODY! The positional change is ALWAYS primary; the parry, redirection or control is incidental and secondary to position. The most common mistake a fledgling practitioner makes in relation to combat is to attempt to redirect the opponents limb to gain advantage for counter attack. Exercising this strategy will keep you in the line of fire, contesting the opponents strength and continuous attack directly. It is far wiser to think in terms of changing your position in relation to the opponents angle of attack, thereby escaping the line of attack altogether and positioning yourself for a flank counter attack. As you become more efficient in this tactic, you will find that oftentimes you do not need to parry at all.

Here I have angled off centerline in response to Alex's attack, making the parry incidental and allowing concentration of energy in the strike.

119

On training against edged weapons:

A disarm should be either accidental or incidental. Most high caliber Martial artists will agree with the preceding statement. Still, I felt that this statement should be included as I often see what I consider to be a mistaken perception in dealing with a weapon while unarmed. Twice yearly, when I teach my own students unarmed defensive tactics against weapons, I start the statement with the following comments: "The first, most important thing you must understand when dealing with a weapon wielding assailant is the proper distance. The proper distance is approximately two hundred feet away holding a high-powered rifle with a scope." Although I make these comments in jest, I am trying to make one strong point. Namely, if you find that you are unarmed yet you must deal with an armed opponent, it is best that you don't. You should flee if you can.

With that said, at some point in your life you may find yourself dealing with that situation. I personally have done so twice. The study of unarmed tactics against an armed attacker can and will save your life if you hold the proper attitude. The proper attitude is composed of a few specific qualities:

(1) Have a healthy respect for the weapon.
(2) Seek to injure the opponent in the most expeditious way possible. A direct attack is best.
(3) When entering, try to enter on the backward slash/swing as opposed to the inward. The opponents anatomical strength is less in this position and there are fewer options for a renewed attack from this position.
(4) A disarmament tactic should only be attempted when the opponent is (a) either severely weakened or (b) because of providence.

Again, to be redundant (which I believe to be extremely appropriate in this case), "A disarm should be either accidental or incidental."

On the three basin theory:

In going to the ground, always think strike first and primary. Grappling and submission should be adjunctive and secondary. With all the recent popularity of "no holds barred" competitions, newcomers to the arts are beginning to get an idea that grappling and submission is king in terms of fighting style. Nothing could be further from the truth.

1a. *As my opponent enters in the high basin attempting to grapple, I twine my left hand inside to grab and my right hand outside and over.*

1b. *I then step inside for a hip throw, pulling his right arm tightly inward, simultaneously levering his left shoulder with wheel method.*

1a. *As my opponent lunges, I slide into a mid basin position under his attack and simultaneously position my body and limbs for throw.*

1b. *Here I complete the throwing technique by pressuring into him with my body and simultaneously lifting his leg with wheel method.*

First of all, one must understand that so-called "no holds barred" structures do indeed forbid key techniques that are normally employed to defeat grappling attempts. Heading the top of the list would be gouging or piercing techniques to the eyes, throat, groin and other equally vital areas of the body. One must remember that in the street there are no rules and that all tactics, techniques and strategies are fair game. The worst possible thing that you can do in the street is go to the ground and stay there. However, it must also be understood that within any fight it is

1a. *Here, the opponent attempts a shoot at the low basin. I step my left foot back and brace, inserting my right hand inside his left arm.*

1b. *I then again use the wheel method to take his inertia past me at a narrow vector while leveraging his head downward, forcing a roll.*

certainly possible that you may end up on the ground. Therefore, you must have a reasonable strategy in place to deal with such a situation.

The art of Hsing I Chuan preaches what is called a "three basin" theory. Simply put, this means that all techniques are applicable in a standup, partially down or fully grounded position. The same strikes, locks and neutralizing techniques are applicable with only slight variation and/or modification. Striking is especially effective against submission tactics when it can be employed in the form of a quick gouge or

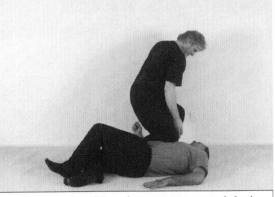

1c. *I follow with a knee drop to Alex's now supine position before he can recover or counter. Done correctly, this is one motion in sequence.*

piercing technique to vital areas. This can be especially effective when the opponent is busy with their hands attempting to restrain, lock or choke you as a gouging technique can often simply be "slid" into position in such circumstances. Since the arts derive power equally from the core, costals and legs, being deprived of only one avenue of power generation does not negate the other two. Consequently, when forced to the ground, the strategy should again be one of strike first and grapple only adjunctively and when absolutely necessary.

Two good exercises to practice this philosophy are what we call "downed sparring" and the "one down -- one up" drill.

In the downed sparring drill, both combatants get on the ground in various positions with one another in different contexts and/or angles so that they may "mock" what might become an initial guard, side or downed position. The combat begins with the emphasis being on exchanging blows while trying to stand upright as quickly as possible. Combatants are trying to accomplish two objectives: the first being to stand up themselves, and the second being to stop the opponent from standing up. All manners and methods are utilized to accomplish both objectives. In this exercise, the winner of the combat is declared when both objectives are met.

Performing a level change while diving under an attempted grab, preparing to lever the knee with my shoulder for takedown.

In the one down one up drill, one combatant lies down on his or her back while the other combatant stays upright circling the opponent. The one objective of the upright combatant is to attempt a submission strategy on the downed opponent. The one objective of the downed combatant is to prevent this from occurring and to stand upright. The winner of the combat is declared when either player has achieved his or her respective goal.

There are, of course, other possible variables that can be thrown into this game to mimic any key element of what may happen. For example, including additional opponents, which is a very likely scenario in a street encounter.

1a. *Here, as the opponent steps toward me, I catch his ankle and knee in a scissor take down, collapsing him to the ground.*

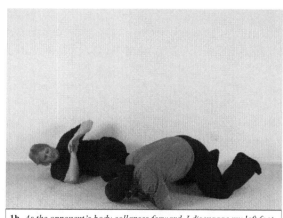

1b. *As the opponent's body collapses forward, I disengage my left foot from his ankle and follow with a round kick to the back brain.*

The High-Stakes vs. Low Stakes Poker Game.

Younger students have often lamented to me their inability to transfer their Martial skills to a first-time self-defense encounter. They wonder aloud why it is that during practice within the school they are able to manifest their skills and a level of competency that is quite satisfactory to them, yet, in attempting to apply the same skills in their first real-time encounter they fall far shy of that same mark of excellence that they have come to expect from themselves in practice. By the way, this is not at all uncommon across the board and certainly not limited to younger or less experienced practitioners. Seasoned practitioners may, on occasion, suffer the same issue.

In training full contact fighters for so many years, I came to refer to this same phenomenon in them as "the flail factor." Even a practitioner trained to fight, upon having their first real event, will tend to resort to simple head hunting under pressure. Skills go out the window in favor of just simply trying to pummel the opponent.

Hearing such statements from any student, I will usually deliver the following two lines with a facetious grin; "When faced with and pressured by a worthy adversary... rather than rise to your level of expectation, you will instead sink to your level of true ability." And then, once the confused and bemused look that I am after comes over their faces I proceed to elaborate.

Have you ever been in a low stakes poker game? I think we can all understand the mind state associated with penny ante poker. We will do things like draw to an inside straight, hold an Ace or King as a "kicker," try for a flush with only two cards held in that suit or any number of other foolish gambits that do not hold up in terms of the odds within the game. We do these things because in a penny ante poker game, the maximum projected loss per hand would be only a couple of dollars. And we feel safe as a result.

But, play in a high-stakes poker game, where the ante is one hundred dollars, and things will be quite different in terms of decision-making. Suddenly you will be not so likely to draw to an inside straight, hold an Ace or King as a "kicker" or try for a flush with only two cards held in that suit. In fact, you will more likely find yourself playing overly cautious. You will probably find yourself folding each hand if you do not start with at least a reasonably strong pair. So what has changed? It is not the game. The game is the same as it was. There are still 52 cards in the deck and there are still the same odds to make any true poker hand. The reality that you may lose hundreds, or even thousands, of dollars per hand has now entered your awareness. And this realization of has now made you skittish in terms of what you perceive the risk to be.

This same phenomenon is what tends to happen to all but the most seasoned practitioners in terms of street fighting, let alone the inexperienced novice. The practice of fighting within the school walls or even in an arena of some kind, no matter how reality based the combat, carries with it a feeling of safety and hence a much lower stress level. These factors will then translate into a relaxed, easy and almost playful mindset. This in turn will motivate a high performance quotient. The practitioner will begin to facilitate the learned technical aspects of the art in a most natural and uninhibited manner leading to greater and greater confidence on the sparring floor, or on the platform, or in the cage.

But, put this same practitioner into a street encounter and watch things fall apart. Suddenly, this same effortlessly skilled technician from the sparring floor or the competition platform cannot execute even one of their best techniques. What has changed?

Just as in the high-stakes low stakes poker game analogy, it is the mindset of the practitioner that has changed. There is now a perception of real danger present which was not at all in the picture within the safety of their known environment. The opponent now standing opposite is not a schoolmate or another competitive athlete. There is no referee present and no rules to govern the event about to take place. This opponent represents a completely unknown quantity and the knowledge of this will in turn elicit fear. Such fear can, and will, paralyze the mind and hinder physical performance. So, the question would be; how do we rectify this dilemma? How do we transfer the relaxed, casual mindset spawned within our comfort zone of training floor or competition arena to the street?

The first step is to recognize that all people have what I call the two great fears of fighting, whether they admit this or not. And these two fears will manifest themselves throughout the various stages of training in the life of the practitioner. The first is the fear of getting hurt. This is altogether natural as it stems from our base sense of self-preservation and is pretty much a given, which is present in most folks equally.

The second is the fear of hurting others. This one stems from compassion toward humankind and, in my experience, is not equal amongst all folks. And indeed, some may not need address this one at all. In case the reader DOES find that this fear exists in their being, I have found that one of the most effective cures is to attain what I call the middle ground of a good skill set. The middle ground would be the composite of the abilities such as locking, submission, pushing and throwing tactics which can be used to dissuade an attacker without serious injury. Attaining good skill in such abilities will give the practitioner confidence to go forward in the face of the enemy with compassion, if the circumstance warrants such compassion.

So, let us go back and address the first. We must understand that it's OK to have this fear. In fact, a little bit of this fear can be quite healthy as it will tend to promote caution in the face of an adversary or unknown circumstance. It is important to be able to differentiate what is true fear from what is the body's fight or flight response. The body's fight or flight response is your friend and you must come to know it accordingly to avoid confusing your mind and focus. The body goes through four stages of adrenal response. The first is a pre-event adrenal drip. The second is a full-scale adrenal dump as the event begins. The third is a second full-scale adrenal dump in the middle of the event (commonly called a second wind). The fourth and final is a post-event adrenal drip.

You must understand that the occluded vision, the racing heart, the shaking legs, all represent what your body is doing to prepare for either fight or flight. Once understanding the physical process, you will be more able to focus that energy appropriately. The simple fact is this; IF you allow yourself to begin to think those "symptoms" are fear, they soon will engage in exactly that manner and you will find yourself no longer in a proper state of mind to "fight."

THEORY AND PRINCIPLE:

The Nine Essences
(*My comments are in Italics*)

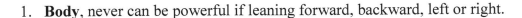

Theory and principle abound in the internal martial arts as one of the basic philosophies of training is essentially "limited scope of practice, infinite overlay or possibility." We strongly believe that having too much material to sort once the practitioner comes under pressure is counter-productive to skill in combat.

I will start with The Nine Essences as they are one of the more easy of the principle bodies to convey. The entire song pertains to the Spitting form, "Pi Chuan" posture (Metal Element), of Hsing I which also often doubles as a "guard" by advocates of the system when learning combat.

1. **Body**, never can be powerful if leaning forward, backward, left or right.

This means keep the head erect and the whole spine straight (not rigid). When you "drop" in posture, drop in the legs, don't bend your back or lean your spine and displace your center.

2. **Shoulders**, must be relaxed and dropping downward. Allow your shoulders to move along naturally with each other. It is through the shoulders that strength from the torso is transferred to the hands.

A common problem area for the novice is excess localized tension in and around the shoulders. This unnatural tension will both block the easy flow of the kinetic energy through the arms and isolate the limbs away from the core. This rule warns against the problem.

3. **Arms**, left arm stretched forward at chest level, right arm bent around right ribs. Embrace the space of the arm pits. Be bent but not flexed, stretched but not straight. Too bent cannot reach far; too straight cannot be powerful.

This references the classic Pi (splitting) hand position. The body is at its most efficient for distribution and reception of kinetic energy when postured in natural curves. The curve must be maintained through the whole limb. Do not "ground out" by closing the armpits. Maintain a golf ball size space. Otherwise, the opponent can use your limb to pressure your body center.

4. **Hands**, right hand to armpit and then to navel, left hand held as high as the chest. The latter relaxed, the former be strengthened also. Both hands palm side downward, strength be even.

The right hand will arc through the left armpit and come to reside at the navel as the posture is formed in change. The left hand is Yang and the right Yin. The Mind must be present in both hands equally as the shape is formed. Both must be tied to the core of the body.

5. **Fingers**, separated and curved as shallow hook, "Hu Kou" (Tiger's Mouth) rounded, taut but relaxed. Focus strength at fingers but never forcefully.

Here, strength means "Intention." Do not tense the muscles of the hand, simply stretch them moderately in the physical sense, and then allow your mind to come to reside outward through your fingers to infinity. You are also warned not to force this attitude. "Tiger's Mouth" is the space between tip of the index finger and the tip of the thumb.

6. **Legs**, left to front, right holding back. Be straight but not, be bow but straight, shape of a chicken's leg.

The word "holding" here refers to "rooting" through both legs. You must create a condition of passive flexion to realize a relaxed springiness in the ready position. The correct posture does actually resemble that of a chicken's bent leg.

7. **Feet**, all toes of front foot pointing forward, never to sides. Back foot will be close to 45 to 60 degrees sideward, following the lower leg. Separation is up to the individual. Toes be firm.

Stand natural for YOU in terms of separation in the feet. Gradually as leg strength improves you will adjust your stance appropriately. Hollow the "Bubbling Well" (Kidney 1) point by thinking of, and passively gripping, the ground with the whole foot. Do not overdue this effort. But, done properly, it will imbue the legs with a springiness that will be constantly at the ready for rapid movement. You need only pick either foot up to begin to unload the spring.

8. **Hips**, be tilted upward and forward so that "Chi" can be transferred to the limbs easily, or energy will be scattered.

Do not force, just passively bring the pelvis forward and align the lower lumbar region with the rest of the spine. This will create a unified core and transfer load to the ground as a result.

9. **Tongue**, "Chi" will be weak if tongue is not raised to the palate. Energy will sink to the Dan Tien if eyes staring. Hair standing, muscle on face be iron and inner organs are hardened.

I save the most difficult for last. Taoist teachings say that the tongue must be stuck to the palate just behind the teeth to connect the uninterrupted "circuit" of the Du (Governor) and the Ren (Conception) meridians. The tongue acts as a "fuse" and if this connection is not formed, your practice may lead to over accumulation of "Fire in the Brain" which is a Chinese Medical term referencing a specific condition of energetic imbalance. It is important to realize that you do not "Stare" AT anything. Rather, by diffusing your focus and relaxing the mind, the "Chi" will sink of its own accord. When this occurs, the "Chi" will circulate freely causing a sensation of your hair standing on end. Betray no emotion while practicing, as this will tend to draw the mind outside, removing vital energy circulation from the organs. Kept inside, the organs will be protected (hardened).

Pi Chuan is often called the heart and soul of Hsing I practice, so study this song well and often. It will be time spent that you will not regret in relation to your practice.

Theory of the Seven Stars

One of our more famous lineage ancestors, a man named Li Tsun I, was once quoted saying, "If you want mercy, best not raise your hand." It was furthermore said of Li that when challenged, "He put forth his hand, strode forward easily and achieved his objective."

In actual combat, the successful fighter needs three things, a calm mind, no hesitation, and a system that supports the kind of fluid energy necessary to win. True combat should be lucid, unbridled and succinct. "Stick like glue until conclusion." The opponent must be thought of as not a system of arms and legs but as one big target with unlimited points of attack.

Hsing I is well known for its rapid closing and punishingly powerful attacks. Anyone who has had the unpleasant experience of crossing arms with an adept of the Art will attest to this fact. They will probably also babble incoherently about the seeming impossibility that their nemesis seemed to have many more than just two arms and two feet. Blows seem to literally rain in from all angles and elevations, sometimes several at once.

One of the primary perspectives regarding my family style of Hsing I is found in the saying, "*Fold in, fold out, stick like glue until conclusion.*" Just how this is accomplished is the focus of this chapter. We show this to our opponents through use of the "Seven Stars" principles of Hsing I in fluid combination. These principles of striking hold that there are seven weapons of the body that can attack with devastating power. Following is a list of the specific tools found in the Seven Stars Song. The tool, and the part of the song pertaining to that tool, will be numbered and listed first with my comments following immediately thereafter.

1a. *As the opponent lunges right to the heart, I check downward and wait, deliberately exposing my head to his secondary attack.*

1. **Elbow hit.** "To strike is to be all out. To move hands and legs together. Fists as cannons, body as a dragon. Move as if you have flame all over in the face of an attacker."

The elbow can be an extremely damaging tool when utilized by someone who understands its usage. It is obvious that the bony tip of the elbow and/or the knife-like edge of the ulna can be quite destructive to various areas of the opponent's anatomy, even soft fleshy areas of the arms or legs. Its limitation being, of course, its range. You must work diligently on learning to "fold in" from a parried hand attack and, upon gaining control of the opponents center line, utilize quick stepping and angular footwork as a vehicle of delivery for sequential elbow attacks.

1b. *As the secondary attack is thrown to my exposed head, I shear it off with my right hand but remain in contact with his other limb also.*

Another excellent utility of the elbow is as a counter measure against rising knees in the clinch. A well timed elbow drop to the attacking thigh is a more than excellent deterrent in this situation.

2. Head hit. "The whole body moves as one. The feet take position in center."

The head is often unexpected in the clinch position when hands have been trapped or controlled and the elbows neutralized. If you strike quickly, you can control the situation adroitly. There exist numerous opportunities to strike virtually any time the opponent gets close and attempts to grapple. You must simply be alert to the possibility to take advantage.

3. Shoulder hit. "One is Yin (back) one is Yang (front). Hands are hidden. Right or left depends on the situation."

The shoulder can be a punishing weapon when used in the beginning of a clinch as a means of disrupting the opponent's balance (sometimes in conjunction with the head) or as an adjunct fold immediately after a successful elbow. The "bracing" posture must be utilized when using either the shoulder or head as a striking weapon. My teacher used to say "When you strike with the shoulder, you think 1,000 dollars stay ground. You must *GET!*" This perspective is simply to reinforce the need to "brace" (one line formed from the back of the head through the spine to the rear heel) rapidly to create the power needed.

4. Hand hit. "Moving from your chest, it is like a tiger catching a lamb. Strength put in hands should be instantly variable. Elbows are to be lower than armpits."

Proper Hsing I hand blows exemplify this principle. Keeping the elbows down allows proper kinetic alignment of the skeletal system for massive impact and alignment of the sinews for tremendous kinetic potential. If the elbow is raised, the flow of kinetic

1c. *I now drop a heavy handed palm strike into his back brain and then immediately clamp his neck with that same right hand.*

1d. *Continuing the momentum of the palm strike, the clamp now guides his head toward my shoulder as I deliver a shoulder stroke to the face.*

1e. *The flow continues as I now fold my elbow up under the opponent's jaw line, pressuring his throat as I do to lift and separate his body.*

power is diffused (localized strength) at the shoulder and cannot reach the hand. Adherence will also provide the means to avoid over extension of the limb thereby making it vulnerable to counter tactics. In addition to keeping an ability to strike immediately again with the same limb in quick succession if desired.

5. Hip hit. "Yin or Yang, left or right is up to the situation. Be natural while moving feet. Be quick as a sword while attacking."

The hip is the hardest of all the weapons to manifest power within as it is closest to the pivotal point of the waist. There is less distance for the wave of potential energy to travel and gain any momentum. The key here is as implied, you must be extremely quick with your issuing (*fah jing*). Try using the hip to displace the opponent's center upon entry by thrusting it into the opponent's hip. This will often facilitate a throwing (*shuai*) opportunity.

1f. I now hinge my right elbow and turn my core to deliver a right hammer fist strike to my opponent's pubic bone.

6. Knee hit. "Strike on vital points can be fatal. Hands up balancing body."

The knee is an excellent midrange tool if used in conjunction with the hands to immobilize and then attack. The knee must be snapped up from the strength of the abdominal muscle groups. It should not be swung up as a pendulum. The primary target should be the opponent's thighs (both inner and outer) to debilitate the opponent's legs and structure. Attacking the body with the knee should only be done in certain circumstances where the opponent's arms have been well controlled. And even then the knee is potentially subject to grab yielding a throw. So, with respect to that potential, the thigh is the number one target to destroy structure.

1g. I then hinge my right elbow again and drive a vertical elbow strike into the side throat, just under the jaw line of the opponent.

7. Feet hit. "Steps are firm. The strength comes from foot rooted to the ground, never let your attempt be known. Power of a tornado."

Too often the novice, in an attempt to gain more range or elevation in their kicking techniques, will violate the root from their support foot by coming up on the ball of the foot. It is imperative that there does exist a strong anchor from which to rebound the kinetic wave, or much of the energy potential

1h. The flow continues into an inverted clamp of the opponent's rear neck with my right hand while setting up for the knee strike to come.

will be scattered. Avoid "snap" kicks as they do more to irritate than to damage. Learn to bring the kick up in a flat arc from the ground to the target to avoid telegraphing the strike.

The reality of a proficiency in utilization of the Seven Stars principles in combat will rely quite strongly on the development of *Fah Jing* (issuing energy) skills to ensure that the very close range weapons of the shoulder, hip and head carry sufficient force to accomplish the goal. This is one of the main reasons this skill is so heavily emphasized in my family's Hsing I training curriculum.

1i. *The knee strike is now delivered while I simultaneously crank down on the opponent's neck and up on his right limb.*

Also, two person exercises in the San Shou (pushing hands) category will provide an excellent place to hone these skills in a relatively safe environment before putting them to the actual test in full contact training. Try occasionally limiting your push hands practice to doing *only* shoulder or *only* elbow strikes, (such as discussed previously in this work) or any other weapons or combinations of weapons where you feel deficient in skill. This "isolation" approach can work wonders in virtually any deficient area of skill. Start soft and slow and, as you develop more familiarity and confidence with the new techniques, gradually increase the speed for a more realistic experience of the true potential.

As a secondary step, try reduced speed sparring (also discussed previously in this work). This method will require cooperation on the part of both combatants. But if such cooperation is maintained, it can be an effective way to explore and ingrain new principles

1j. *This seven star sequence finishes by stepping down and across the center to deliver a downward elbow stroke to the back brain.*

and technical perspectives. The idea is to move at approximately one third to one half speed in a consistent manner, without suddenly speeding up to intercept or strike. If done properly, it will allow the time to think a bit during the evolution of combative flow, giving both participants a chance to grow in their appreciation of possible technique.

Learning the use of any new weapon simply requires a focused study of that particular weapon. It also requires a firm understanding of what is classically taught as "investing in loss." Any new technical perspective or new skill will require you to humble yourself during the learning curve. In other words you must expect to lose and frequently, while gaining that skill or ability, and this must be accepted to advance.

Learn the techniques of usage and then abide by the "three P's" which in older times were named as patience, perseverance and practice. This is still a good credo to keep in mind when attempting to develop new skills.

Of course, you can always just practice, practice, practice...

The Eight Fundamentals

The Eight fundamentals have many levels of interpretation. But at their root, they are essentially guidance for creating and maintaining a balance in the body between protagonist and antagonist muscle masses. When this postural guidance is learned and performed correctly, it will yield a type of unified strength that goes far deeper into the core structures of the body including the deep layer connective tissues.

This state of balance or ease within the body will then, in turn, promote a like ease of circulation yielding a greater sense of health and well being. And so, for the practitioner, these principles are important for both sides of the discipline. They promote an ease of motion and integrated strength which is useful for fighting ability. But they also promote an ease of stasis balance in the body which translates to reduced stress and greater health.

I shall list the eight fundamentals and make a very brief comment on the key phrase of each (which is in italics) immediately thereafter. The rest will become clear, little by little, as the student progresses. They should be re-read occasionally, pondered a bit, and then put away until later. In this way, these principles will become ingrained in the practice.

Let us start with one simple example of the Protagonist vs. Antagonist concept found within the body of these principles. Place your palm against a partner's chest. You will be utilizing just one of the three suppresses, "suppress your hands with upper arms but be natural." Relax your elbow downward and, while maintaining contact with your palm to your partners chest, have your partner attempt to bend your arm at the elbow with both of his hands while you resist. You'll find that this is relatively easy for him to do. Now, keeping everything else the same, add in just one of the concepts from the "three up thrusts," "up thrust your palms upward as if upholding objects." You will find that this minor adjustment of focus creates a modicum of tension in the antagonist groups of the arm. This is most easily felt through the upper arm. Now that you have established this, have your partner attempt to bend your arm once again. You will find a marked increase in overall strength of the limb.

For a further simple proof of the profundity of these guidelines, have a partner stand in San Ti Shr with a Pi Chuan pose. Now, conduct an experiment in body parameter strength using the principle; "Suppress your feet with waist and back but be closely linked" in the following way. First have your partner deliberately tilt his/her hips backward to magnify the curve of the lower spine. Then place one hand on the lower spine and the other hand on their extended palm and attempt to fold their body with pressure. You will find this fairly easy to accomplish. Now, have the partner exercise the principle by bringing the hips forward and using the waist and back to unify the pelvic floor by pushing down through the legs to the feet. This should effectively straighten the curve in the lower lumbar spine if done properly. Now, once again, attempt to fold their body with pressure. You will find this same person, with such a minor change of the body posture will now be able to keep not only your pressure, but likely that of two people, from folding them in the same way.

This entire body of principles is designed to impart relaxed, unified strength to the body in like mannerism across the board with regard to other key structures of the body. Translated below:

3 UP THRUSTS:
Up thrust your head as if up thrusting the roof.
Up thrust your tongue to the palate.
Up thrust your palms upward as if upholding objects.
Understanding the three up thrusts, strength is built to lift the trees.
Here, strength means unified strength of both Mind and Body.

3 SUPPRESSES:
Suppress downward your chin but gaze straight forward.
Suppress your hands with upper arms but be natural.
Suppress your feet with waist and back but be closely linked.
Understanding the three suppresses, Spirit and Mind are induced.
Taoism. By observing the three suppresses, the three gates of the spine (WeiLu, Ming Men, Yu Jen) will be allowed to open and energy will ascend the spine to the Crown point (Pai Hui).

3 CURVES:
Curve of the shoulders and back to be a hemisphere.
Chest curved, Chi is broadened.
Hu Kou (Tiger's Mouth) to be curved as a crescent moon.
Understanding the three curves, the secret is unveiled.
The "secret" here is Chi circulation as per Taoist teachings.

3 EMBRACES:
"Tan Tien" (Lower abdomen) to be embraced with Chi as the root.
Heart to be embraced with body as the basis.
Arms to be embraced with four limbs firmly still.
Understanding the three embraces, body is guarded.
Guarded against both illness as well as attack from an enemy.

3 SINKS:
With Chi sunk in Tan Tien, illness is excluded.
With upper arm sinking downward, deep meaning there hidden.
With elbows sinking downward, shoulders are the roots.
Understanding the three sinks, body is keen and shrewd.
Ready to issue energy with great speed and power from one's center point (body core).

3 CRESCENT MOONS:
Arms as bows like the crescent moon.
Wrists thrusting outward like the crescent moon.
Legs and Knees bent like the crescent moon.
Understanding the three crescent moons, posture is best oriented.
For ease of circulation AND usage for power. The body will be under constant, ready load.

3 STOPS:
Neck shortened and upward stopping, body is upstraight.
Body stop on four sides.
Legs and Knees downward stopping as roots of trees.
Understanding the three stops, Kung Fu is well rooted.
In Kung Fu, "Rooting" is a term which refers to a part physical, part mental "linkage" to the Earth under one's feet.

3 SENSITIVES:
Eyes sensitive.
Heart sensitive.
Hands sensitive.
Understanding the three sensitives, posture is invincible.
Here, the invincible is referencing fighting technique. The Eyes must watch for subtle change in the opponent. The Heart must feel for subtle changes of intensity in the opponent. And the Hands must stay light and alive, attaching to and guiding the opponent's flow of motion and energy of attack. Otherwise the response will be less than adequate.

As mentioned above, it is recommended that the reader contemplate and then practice. Once every few days or so, re-read the eight fundamentals and again reflect. Little by little, as you allow your body awareness to filter in while practicing, these principles will become clear.

Remember to relax. Antagonistic tension is the enemy here. As practitioners, we must learn to feel what is appropriate and what is not appropriate "linkage" of the structures needed in any given posture. To fail to grasp this is to reduce efficiency of movement. This in turn reduces speed which leads to reduction of power in usage.

To study the eight fundamentals is to study this relationship to a deep level of awareness in the body. Without such awareness, "whole body power" will simply elude you for as long as you are involved with the discipline.

Energy Release and Kinetic Potential

In this method of Hsing I Chuan, there exist three separate ways to release kinetic energy in terms of timing. It should be understood that this art form is based on sound physics principles and utilizes multiple applied vectors simultaneously within its force mechanics. Following are delineated the three possible timings of force "release" and a brief description of each:

Front release: This method consists of timing the release of force from the body at the moment the front foot hits the ground. This method is utilized most often in conditions where force is being applied with either a downward or forward vector such as in Pi Chuan or Peng Chuan. The reader should be cautioned, however, to avoid becoming over extended and off-balance as a result of becoming too zealous in this stomping of the front foot to release power. It is better to think in terms of causing the body to arrive at stasis balance at the moment of strike to avoid this condition.

Rear release: This method can concord the release of thrust energy with the rear foot striking the ground (i.e. the Hsing I half step) with the force vector of the arm as it shoots forward. This method is most appropriate in conditions where an entry has been achieved and the timing then provides for the opportunity of a follow up blow. This type is most often employed with upward forces such as Tsuan Chuan or Pao Chuan, but can also be utilized with straight blows such as Peng Chuan. This method allows more potential power to be transmitted through the body with the application of said unification. It should be duly noted, however, that for purposes of combat it is wise to get the enemy's attention before applying this method as it can be somewhat slower in delivery.

Conjoined release: This method is as it sounds. It is the idea of a concordance of more than one technique in a rapid string or sequence. And then timing the release of the first strike when the front foot hits the ground and the release of the second immediately thereafter with the rear foot hitting the ground. This method is more advanced and requires a longer term of practice before application is viable. Try developing a downward force, like Pi Chuan, on the front. And then following that with an upward force, like Tsuan Chuan, with the timing of the rear foot. This will also tend to utilize the closing and opening powers of the intercostal muscles in a more natural manner. Once learned, this conjoined method can be applied with double straight blows, like Peng Chuan, as well. Or virtually any other combination of the five fists and/or singular movements from the twelve animals.

Five Force (Element) Theory

The purpose of this chapter is not to detail the five element theory of cosmology. The reader should pick up a good Chinese medical text for such a purpose. This chapter will look at the five forces (elements) solely in terms of their Martial relationships and practice perspectives.

As a beginning point, notice that I have already made the stringent effort to name the five as "forces" rather than elements. This is specifically to emphasize that the element qualities are "associations" only and not the names of the five (a mistake made far too often in the West with regards to Hsing I). This is not to say that those same associations are unimportant.

Wu Hsing can be called the Heart and Soul of Hsing I practice. These five seemingly simple actions are loaded with subtleties and require years of practice to perform them with total Mind/ Body integration. Over the course of time they will teach the practitioner many things and can be directly related to many aspects of Five Element cosmology of traditional Chinese medicine.

In the martial art of Hsing I, just as in Chinese Medical thought, there are three "cycles" of the five that are considered and utilized in theory. The creative or generative cycle is as follows: Gold/Metal creates Water, Water creates Wood, Wood Creates Fire and Fire creates Earth. When younger, I was taught a sort of poem for remembrance. Gold/Metal, when molten, becomes liquid (water). Water nourishes wood (trees). Trees, when burned create fire. When fire is exhausted, you are left with ash (Earth). From Earth you mine gold/metal again.

The destructive cycle is as follows: Metal destroys Wood. Wood destroys Earth. Earth destroys Water. Water destroys Fire and Fire destroy Metal. Again, a similar poem was taught. The axe chops down the tree. The trees roots break through the ground. Earth mounded up can dam a river. The water from the river puts out a fire. Fire can melt the axe blade.

Neutrality is found in Metal overacting on Fire (fire not hot enough to melt metal). And Fire overacting on Water (not enough water to put out the fire). Water overacting on Earth (dam is too small to stop the flow) and Earth overacting on Wood (the soil is too hard for the roots to penetrate). Master Hsu used to joke and say; "Yes, true that Fire destroys Metal. But if you have only a candle flame against my axe blade, you no can endure."

Pi Chuan (Metal) teaches the force of Splitting. Its power association is the axe. It corresponds to the Lung and Large Intestine meridians.

Tsuan Chuan (Water) teaches the force of Drilling. Its power association is lightning/electricity. It corresponds to the Kidney and Urinary Bladder meridians.

Peng Chuan (Wood) teaches the force of crushing/penetrating. Its power association is the arrow. It corresponds to the Liver and Gall Bladder meridians.

Pao Chuan (Fire) teaches the force of Pounding. Its power association is the cannon. It corresponds to the Heart, Small Intestine, Pericardium and San Jiao (triple warmer) meridians (the latter two are termed "secondary fire" in Chinese medicine).

Heng Chuan (Earth) teaches the force of Crossing. Its power association is the Bullet (old style bullet from a sling, not modern). It corresponds to the Spleen and Stomach meridians.

These are not meant as idle associations. They are instead meant as keys to unlock the doors of Hsing I practice. For example to understand Heng Chuan (Earth); for technique, look to its force "Crossing." This means to cross your opponent's center forcing him to open it so that you may enter. For the method of practice, look first at its power association. Most people, when seeing that "bullet" is the power association to Heng will picture the modern day "bullet." This happens to work on the physics side of things, so let's go with that. What does a bullet do when it leaves a rifle barrel? What is its motion? It projects in a spiraling manner, does it not? So should your whole body and fist when you perform Heng Chuan (The original "bullet" denoted here was that of a projectile thrown from a sling. The physics of centrifugal spiral energy are the same, so either analogy will suffice. Still, I feel that the original association has a certain "charm" that the modern association lacks, so I include this for the reader's edification). Look second at its element, Earth. What is the first thing that comes to mind when you think of the ground, earth? Words like solid, firm, consistent, come to mind. Could we not say as a general quality that the "Earth" is consistently solid? So then, should the general quality of Heng Chuan be when properly performed. Each force/element of the Wu Hsing is unique and different in this respect. Hence the attitude of practice is also different in each action. Let us explore the others briefly as well.

Pi Chuan is associated with the force of "Splitting." This means to split the center line and unbalance the opponent. The power association is that of an Axe. In the western mind, when we hear the word axe we immediately think of chopping. This would be an error in regards to Pi Chuan. We must actually look to what the axe blade does as it impacts the wood, not what "we" do with the axe. An axe blade manifests a cleaving power upon impact. Another useful analogy might be that of a ship's prow cleaving through the water. The whole body must be involved. The elemental attribute is most often translated as Metal here in the West. But, the original connotation is that of Gold. Gold has specifically three primary qualities that are of use to us. It is quite dense, heavy and also malleable. So, get the perspective of a hard and rigid chopping action out of your mind for this is not truly Pi Chuan as intended.

Tsuan Chuan is associated with the force of "Drilling." This represents twisting or turning energy. The power association is that of Lightning, appearing and disappearing unexpectedly. The elemental attribute is water. And Tsuan mimics the energetic quality of a wave crashing on the surf, expanding and then rapidly condensing only to explode with expansive energy again upon impact. The turning/twisting aspect should begin in the core of the body, as the style changes, and move upward and outward through the fist in one continuous spiral.

Peng is associated with the force of "Crushing/Penetrating." The power association is that of an Arrow, swift and silent. It is utilized to pierce the gaps in the armor (guard) of the opponent. The elemental attribute is Wood. Like a tree root, it will take the path of least resistance and in so doing, it can fragment even the strongest stone.

Pao is associated with the force of "Pounding." The power association is that of the cannon. Its energy of delivery is that of a powerful broadside. And like its elemental attribute of fire, it is expansive and consuming. Like a flame licking up a tree branch, it attaches to the opponent's limb and then rapidly expands into the trunk and delivers a powerful expansive discharge.

Many people will ask why the meridian structures are associated with the Wu Hsing postures, and is this association simply a convenient tie-in to medicinal five element theory? The answer is a definitive no! The postures themselves, if practiced correctly, harmoniously align the body's meridian structures so that energy may flow uninhibited through the corresponding channels. There is also another, deeper reason for this correspondence.

Just as massage can stimulate energy flow, so can motion. The firing of the muscle/nerve structures that are inherent in each postural change combined with precise mental focus unite to course the body energy through the associated meridians.

To be successful with this approach, one must realize that there are three stages to Hsing I practice. First, the Mind teaches the Body. This is the stage of learning new movements (Hsing). Your teacher shows you what to do, and your mind tries to grasp the concepts and relays commands to the Body to form the postures. Then, later, comes the second stage; you must completely relax all unnecessary "parts" of the Mind and Body and *FEEL.....* In this way you will begin to slowly realize subtleties that your Mind missed during stage one. The Body is now teaching the mind. Patient, persevering and sensitive effort in stage two will eventually lead to stage three, a True Harmony of Mind AND Body.

As the practitioner begins to explore the combative applications of the five, look to the creative cycle found in the five element associations as a beginning point to link or string technical functions together. For example, with a little exploration it will be found that utilizing Splitting (Pi) successfully to the head will create an opportunity to use Drilling (Tsuan) as a follow-up to the jaw of the opponent. Or, as another example, if one applies Drilling (Tsuan) as an intercept of the opponent's limb while pulling down and attacking the face, drawing the opponent's other hand up to deflect, this will create an opportunity to follow with Crushing/Penetrating (Peng) to the now exposed center line while both of the opponent's hands are occupied.

It is also quite possible to relate *general* movement patterns to the philosophy of the five and then pick an appropriate *general* counter strategy according to the destructive cycle. For this approach to be viable, things must be pared down to their most base properties. In this line of thought, we consider the five forces in the following manner: Pi (Splitting) represents downward movement; Pao (Pounding) represents upward movement; Tsuan (Drilling) represents spiraling/turning movement; Heng (Crossing) represents lateral movement; and Peng (Crushing/Penetrating) represents linear movement. This would mean that an opponent who moves in mostly straight lines would be effectively countered with Pi (Splitting) as an overall general strategy. Whereas a fighter who moves with a great deal of lateral movement would be effectively countered with Peng (Crushing/Penetrating) as an overall general strategy.

These are general overlay strategies only. Again, the reader is reminded that it is most unwise to become so focused on one perspective during combat that all other input being received goes unacknowledged. No matter how much strategic or tactical knowledge a person may acquire, there is no substitute for intelligent adaptation given a specific opponent or circumstance.

The Five Keys of Hsing I application.

All Chinese Martial Arts systems contain sequential movement structures commonly called form (hsing). This goes without saying, but many people practice form in an empty manner without attempting to discover the underlying essence of what makes the form usable. This type of practice is of no value. The proper practice of form will yield a unity of mind and body eventually reaching a level of skill where mere idea will instantly create powerful movement. Still, without complete understanding of tactical principle this will be of little use.

Hsing I Chuan is a finite system. Its core movement structures are composed of only the five forces (elements) and the twelve animals. This makes mastery of the movement structures themselves attainable (by anyone with a strong work ethic) it about ten years, give or take a few years, depending on individual traits. But what makes the art combat efficient and translatable into true skill are the governing principles of tactical expression. These principles are what makes the art work in pragmatic terms. One of the most important sets of these principles is that of the five keywords.

The five keywords of Hsing I are named as follows: T'un (to suck in), T'u (to spit out), Yao (to shake), Guo (to wrap or bind) and T'swo (to cut). These are far more than just words. These words represent key perspectives in technical application of the art of Hsing I as is related to personal combat. The normal translation has been listed in parentheses immediately following each word above. These translations relate to the physical manifestation of that keyword only and we shall explore the connotation of that certainly. But, it is also important to understand that these keys carry with them far more than a simple physical expression. They also contain psycho/emotional relationships. And the context of these relationships should not be ignored, as they are equally applicable across the board whether to combat and/or interpersonal relationship and/or business strategies as well.

The principle of T'un (suck in) is a cornerstone of higher level strategy. A broad contextual application is found in the applied use of the concept as provocation. In other words, one should use a provoking strategy to elicit a response from the opponent and then follow-up with one of the other keyword strategies such as T'u (spit out), Yao (shake), Gwo (bind) or T'swo (cut). There are numerous ways to provoke and all good provoking strategies have one thing in common; they giveaway nothing to the opponent in the process of eliciting a response. A simple example would be a low line kick. The kick should angle in under the opponent's guard and be thrown with enough force to inflict pain but not so much force as to commit your center to the movement. Done skillfully, this will allow you to make potential opportunity out of the opponent's reaction to the threat. Another excellent provoking strategy is to simply stalk forward into the opponent, while maintaining your guard, forcing the opponent to react in either an evasive or aggressive manner. This again creates an opportunity to attack or counter attack. Although it should be noted that to apply this latter method of provocation requires above average skill and reaction time, as there is little margin for error.

The principles of T'un (to suck in) and T'u (to spit out) are often used together. T'u is a natural counterpart to T'un, rather like the Yang to T'un's Yin. The opponents energy of attack will be drawn forward (and sometimes even accelerated), then neutralized and expelled in one fluid movement. An example would be as the opponent's hand attacks your heart cavity, you might

Here, I hollow my chest against a centerline attack which both allows me to neutralize the force and bring my shoulders forward to counter.

Here, I recede the left side to gain an advantage of angle of insertion on the opponent's lead lunge, simultaneously attacking right.

hollow your chest cavity to the rear (T'un), effectively dissipating much of the incoming force of impact from the blow. Simultaneously, this same action has stored force for release in the back allowing the retaliation to be immediate and powerful (T'u). The epitome of these two principles in action would be found in the example of an "interrupt" (stop hit/counter strike). A properly executed interrupt maximizes the expression of both the opponent's force, which is moving forward into you, and also your counter force moving forward into the opponent.

Yao (to shake) is used to displace the opponent's center as he/she tries to attack. Generally, the principle expression is to attach to an opponent's limb upon attempted entry and then redirect their center to attain advantage for throw, lock or strike. This does not mean however then one cannot apply "shaking" to the body directly. The successful application of this principle will be dictated by the attachment point. If attached to the limb, then above the elbow nearer the shoulder is desirable. Regardless of where or how one attaches, it is necessary to understand

This is an example of using a warding force to turn the opponent's center as he attacks, providing access to his flank at the same time.

Here, I take the opponent's center as he attempts to grab and control me by stepping across and compromising his limb at the same time.

that the force must be expressed in the direction of least stability given the opponent's position at the time. An easy way to apply this principle is to utilize the tripod theory. One of the most stable geometric figures is that of the tripod. Since the opponent has only two legs, the point of least stability will be found in the direction of where a fictitious third leg (if constructing an equal lateral tripod) would be found.

Guo (to wrap or bind) is manifest pretty much as it sounds. This is Hsing I's principle of either seizing or hooking to control, lock or submit the opponent. The most common application of this principle generally utilizes one hand to seize and overturn an opponent's limb while the other hand pressures the elbow or shoulder in a hyper extensive lock, although it is also applied to wrap or bind the neck, torso or legs as well. It is important to understand that wrapping or binding do not necessarily have to come via the hands. But can be applied utilizing many parts of the body.

1a. As the opponent lunges in, I redirect while stepping to his flank creating the opportunity to move behind him.

1b. I now quickly step in with my right foot while going for the "second hook" of his neck with that same redirecting right limb for speed.

1c. Continuing the sequence, I step my left foot through and now complete my neck hold while securing my position behind him.

2a. As the opponent attempts to control me through a grab of my throat, I cover and simultaneously begin threading my left hand over.

2b. I complete my wrapping shoulder hold by continuing to snake my left hand in and under his armpit tightly behind his right shoulder.

All that is required is the ability to establish a lever and a fulcrum. For example if the opponent attacks your left side flank with his left arm, you might clamp the lower part of his arm to your flank using the pit of your left arm under the shoulder and then rotate toward the left causing a hyper extension of the opponent's limb against your torso. The application of such methods leave at least one hand free to attack with impunity. For purposes of hooking, we will consider the elbow/upper arm as the primary hook for control. With the neck and then the waist being the secondary and tertiary points of control. Hooked controls generally will precede a throwing/takedown strategy.

The final principle, T'swo (to cut) is perhaps one of the most important in the Hsing I system. For its connotation is that of cutting force and this is an extremely useful concept on a tactical level. There are numerous potential expressions of T'swo (to cut). A simple example; as the opponent attacks the high line with his right arm, you might rotate your body inside the arc of his blow and strike his frontal shoulder with your right edge palm, thus "cutting" his force and causing injury to his shoulder. Or, in another example; as the opponent begins to step forward in an attempt to attack, you might lower your basin and strike the inner hip of the advancing leg, thus causing the opponent to fall. A third example would be the case of an opponent trying to execute a hip throw whereby you place the palm of your free hand against the executing hip and press inward, thus neutralizing the opponent's attempt to exert leveraged force.

As the opponent performs a right round kick, I angle my body and cut his force by delivering a right palm strike just above his right knee.

As the opponent lunges left, I seize the limb while angling to his flank and simultaneously cut inward and downward across his elbow joint.

Although I have given a few specific martial examples of each principle listed above, this should by no means impose a limit on your perception or expression of the five keywords. In the physical realm alone there exist numerous other avenues of expression. The reader should be encouraged to use the examples listed as a template only and to explore the conceptual idea of each keyword further regarding martial utility.

As stated earlier, the five keywords have numerous contextual meanings and are by no means limited to physical expression alone (although this is the most common perspective). Following are a few other translations of the Five Keys to make this more clear:

Here are a few additional renderings of T'UN (to suck in):
"to swallow; to engulf; to gulp"
"to conquer and annex"
"trying to hide something while speaking"
"to swallow the prey"
"to suppress complaints or grudges"
"to store up; to hoard; stockpile"
"to station and army in the countryside and make it engage in farming"
"to hide one's hands in sleeves"

Here are a few additional renderings of T'U (to spit out):
"to escape fast"
"to erase; to blot out; obliterate"
"abrupt; sudden; unexpected"
"to offend; to go against"
"to break through (enemy encampment)"
"to project or jut out"
"and unexpected change"
"to advance by leaps and bounds; to progress rapidly"
"to attack suddenly, make a surprise attack; to raid"
"to encounter on the way; to meet en route"

Here are a few additional renderings of YAO (to shake):
"to insist (that someone did something)"
"to shake; to toss"
"to agitate; to incite; to annoy"
"to swing to and fro; to oscillate, oscillation; to vacillate- as a pendulum; vacillation"
"to change to another form at the twinkle of an eye"
"to spread out; disperse"
"to coerce; to force"
"to stop"
"to ambush midway; to intercept (an enemy)"
"to restrain"
"to spur the horse and level the spear; to take a challenging position"
"to move actively; to be in lively motion"
"to leap forward; to make rapid progress"
"to move and influence a person"

Here are a few additional renderings of GWO (to wrap or bind):
"to slap another on the face; to box"
"to whirl"
"to wrap or bind; things wrapped"
"to surround, and to encompass"
"to close in and force obedience"
"to force to join; to coerce; to impress"
"to pass; to pass through or by"

"to intentionally make it difficult for somebody"
"an intermediate stage; a transition"
"to pass by; in transit"
"to interfere with"

Here are a few additional renderings of T'SWO (to cut):
"to cut or engrave"
"to break; to damage"
"to humiliate; to treat harshly"
"to defeat the enemy, to give the enemy a bloody nose"
"to be caught unawares; to be taken by surprise"
"to rub hands; to rub between the hands"
"to select what is important; a synopsis"

Taken as a whole, the five keywords are eloquent expressions of the main principles involving tactical combat, interpersonal relationships and/or business strategies. Regardless of the specific venue, the application of each or any of these principles will cause a reaction on the part of the recipient. This reaction will provide opportunity to apply yet another strategy to achieve success. All such interactions can be pared down to a simple exchange of energy (Yin and Yang) and a constant state of flux within the exchange. A practitioner simply needs to be alert to this process and look for opportunity to achieve his/her goals within the exchange through application of strategy.

However, let me offer up the following caveat; it is unwise to be so focused on one's personal agenda that the real opportunities, upon being presented, are overlooked, disavowed or ignored in favor of trying to push the said agenda to the forefront of the mind during the exchange or encounter. A wise combatant understands that he/she cannot control another human being. Such a notion would be a complete delusion. The opponent is a free thinking, spirited, feeling individual. We cannot control them. We can seek only to coerce, merge with, neutralize and then take advantage of their expressed energy.

So when the opponent strikes us hard in the face with a good right hand, rather than get angry and foster the "need to retaliate," we must instead take a perspective of "let's not let that happen again" and re-evaluate our strategy. And we must do so in a calm and calculating manner.

To be successful, we must learn to approach combat with an emotional flat line. All facets of the exchange *must not* be taken personally. If anger, fear, or any other emotion is allowed to manifest within the combat, the combatant will cease being able to perform at optimal levels. Likewise, if the intellect is allowed to work overtime constructing strategy within the midst of the encounter, perception will again be occluded. Therefore, we must train to a level where we can remain detached throughout the encounter. The reality of the outcome will be dictated by the reality of our level of ingrained training. Otherwise, what will ensue is what I have come to call "the flail factor."

The flail factor = "When one is pressured by a worthy adversary, rather than rise to one's level of expectation, one will instead sink to their level of true ability."

Essential Knowledge

The 24 Stems

The 24 stems are based on a lifetime of experience as a professional martial artist. I have been a competitive fighter and, then later, a coach/trainer/teacher of others. When I first began to teach others, I needed a way to categorize what I considered essential knowledge for them to glean in development. So I created the 24 stems and 5 roots as you now see them in the following pages.

This is representative of combative "safe" distance. Even a long range kick technique from the rear foot will fall just short of the opponent.

In this illustration, both hands and both feet can hit the opponent with a mere shift of the body. This distance requires a response.

1. *"Distance should be such that when the combatant's hands are stretched outward, the fingers may interlace. When the wrists touch, attack!"* New martial practitioners often do not have a very good grasp of distance. A proper guard distance has to do with the utility and relative range of primary weapons of engagement. For empty hand fighting, the longest range weapon will be the leg. So initial guard distance should put you out of kicking range giving you a chance to interpret and respond to such an attack. You will find that in a condition with both you and your opponent's arm outstretched where only the fingers can interlace, you will be just beyond kick range. To get into kick range, a half pace step will be required with the lead foot. Hand range will require one full step to close. However, once the wrists can touch, a kicking technique is already in range and a hand technique will require only a small closing step to initiate. Therefore, if you find yourself within this range, you should either immediately attack. Or, if unprepared to do so, you should retreat strategically.

2. *"Observe the nine gates of attack and learn to utilize them in combination."* The nine gates of attack form a sort of tic-tac-toe grid on the opponent's body. They are offensive targeting zones designed to either cross, or separate, or coalesce the opponent's guard to one side. The zones are divided as follows; Draw a line vertically from each ear lobe straight down the body. Then draw two horizontal lines, one through the nipples. And one from the top of each hip, just where the pelvic bones crest. This will form a nine zone grid. Zone one is now the top left of this formed grid, incorporating the opponent's right side neck, shoulder well and right pectoral. Zone two is the top center, incorporating the head and throat. Zone three is now the top right of this formed grid, incorporating the opponent's left side neck, shoulder well and right pectoral. Zone four, center left, incorporates the right rib cage (especially the floating ribs). Zone five is

1a. The leg is attacked first to cause the opponent's attention to shift and the guard to lower a bit in preparation for breach.

1b. Zone three is attacked with a strong overhand right palm, forcing a panic response in the opponent of protecting with the left hand.

1c. With the opponent's guard now separated, a quick follow up to zone five with a right drilling fist is an easy choice.

the total center and contains the solar plexus, sternum and mid-abdomen. Zone six is the left rib cage. Zone seven, the frontal right hip and inguinal area. Zone eight, bottom center, contains the groin and pubic bone. And finally, zone nine is the frontal left hip and inguinal area.

By initiating attack sequences to the corners, one can expect to expose the center zones of the body to secondary and tertiary attacks. Attacking the corner zones will necessitate either a direct engagement on the part of the opponent or an evasive maneuver. Either of which should expose one of the center gates to attack. Sometimes, a skilled opponent must be attacked at two divergent corner zones with the primary and secondary attacks to expose a central zone for the tertiary attack.

3. *"Movement and stillness are one in the same; both are suitable defenses."* There can be no real advantage assigned to either staying in motion or guarding from stillness in a singular type of engagement. Different opponents require different tactical and strategic overlays. Depending on what type of opponent is being engaged, either a moving guard or a static guard may be suitably chosen. It depends a great deal on the strength of specific techniques as to which would be a better choice for any individual practitioner.

The one place where it can be clearly seen as a pro choice for motion is in a multiple encounter. In such a scenario, it is essential to move and move quickly, getting to the perimeter and using the adversarial pool against one another in terms of space and terrain. Stacking them so that they interfere with each other's ability to get to you, or temporarily using one of them as a shield for maneuvered safety. No matter what the tactic, moving in this situation is an absolute must. You simply cannot afford to be stationary for long.

4. *"Never more than two complete steps in any single direction. Do not chase. A smart fighter will time the third step and use it against you."* Fighting is a game of observation and timing. A good fighter will look for any pattern in the opponent that may be exploited. If you display any sort of a pattern, it can be used against you. Effectively, taking more than two steps in a single direction IS a pattern (and allows for momentum to be built up on the part of the opponent). This must be avoided in the context of combat. Therefore, in this system, we seek to employ angular changes of direction and foot changes to vary our patterns of both advance and retreat. This makes it much harder for the opponent to determine where we may be coming next.

5. *"There are four ranges of combat: foot, hand, trap and grapple. Know them well and be able to shift easily from one to another."* This statement is self explanatory. It is important to create a seamless amalgam of technique within each technical range. This will allow you to constantly pressure your opponent.

1a. *A quick low round kick is used at distal range to close on the opponent's position, creating opportunity for follow up.*

1b. *The opponent's lead hand is suppressed while a straight right to the face is employed to engage his secondary limb in defense.*

1c. *An indirect trap is now applied to his defending limb while a right elbow is simultaneously delivered to the high line.*

1d. *The trapping technique now flows into a grappling technique via a neck crank while still controlling the opponent's left limb.*

6. *"The best fighters always attack, even while defending. You must learn to exploit your opponent's habits."* Defense should be incorporated into a strategy revolving around attack and counter attack. To be in a defensive mindset is to be at a disadvantage. The attacker is required

only to see the hole as it opens and initiate an attack. As defender, you will first have to see the attack coming, then interpret its trajectory and finally move to intercept. You will always be a step behind your opponent. You must look to convert as quickly as possible.

7. *"When given a choice between inside and outside closing, always choose outside."* Outside closing simply means to achieve a flank position. In example, if your opponent is attacking with his right arm, the outside position would be to the right side of his body and the inside would be on the left side of his body. Closing inside will always put you at immediate risk to a secondary attack from the opposite limb. This should be avoided when possible. Outside closing positions will put you at a strategic advantage for the simple reason that you have a greater shear number of weapons available in relation to the opponent until he/she is able to rotate their centerline.

1a. *When the opponent engages my lead in a position that is too distal on my limb, I have an opportunity to fold inward on that same side.*

8. *"Fold from hand to elbow to shoulder and back again."* Folding is a principle of either being able to shift to the next range of weapon in your arsenal given a condition that the previous weapon has been neutralized. Or, to string a series of attacks together as each attack succeeds and moves the opponent to a different range either by breaking their structure or moving them away as a result of impact. A punch breeds an elbow. An elbow breeds a shoulder crash. A shoulder crash breeds a locking or throwing technique. One can both "fold" either inward or outward. As the opponent moves away from your elbow, use your hand. As your opponent moves away from your knee strike, use a kicking technique, etc.

1b. *Taking the opportunity that was handed me, I fold my elbow around his parry attempt, breaching the centerline with the attack.*

1c. *Playing off the success of my elbow fold, I continue the process and take advantage of the momentum to fold further into a shoulder crash.*

9. *"Once the closing is met, stick like glue until conclusion."* In a fight, bridging is the most dangerous part of the encounter. The bridge is when you are most vulnerable to a well timed counter attack. Therefore, once you have crossed the bridge and have closed with the opponent, you must press your position and/or advantage for as long as possible within the engagement. If

you separate before conclusion you will, by necessity, need to bridge again thereby opening yourself for yet another possible counter attack in the process.

1a. *As the opponent attempts to grab my shoulder, I clean his hand and grab while simultaneously delivering a palm heel strike to the face.*

1b. *I then stick and fold into an elbow with the secondary limb, keeping momentum on my side and the opponent off balance in defense.*

1c. *I flow immediately into a reverse neck hook and pull the opponent's body into a right knee strike to his inner thigh.*

1d. *I maintain the neck hook as I establish position and then let go at the very last instant to deliver a follow up left elbow to the back brain.*

10. *"The best time to kick is when the opponent is moving forward or back, immediately after a bridge has been attempted."* Kicking is risky. You break contact with the ground and become immobile in the face of the opponent until the kick is completed and the kicking foot touches the ground once again. Kicking at an opponent while they are in a comfortable guard is even more risky as they are able to receive the kicking attack with no other interference in their mind. Therefore kicking as the opponent attempts to bridge, when they are both focused on the respective offensive technique they are attempting and have forward momentum, is a good time to attempt a kicking technique. Similarly after a bridge has been attempted, and the opponent is separating away from you with rearward momentum and focused on recovering, also presents a less risky opportunity to kick.

11. *"The limbs are usually vulnerable."* The limbs are not considered part of the nine gates as they are constantly in motion, crossing zones. Therefore, we have a separate axiom governing the limbs. Most opponents think of their limbs as their defensive tools used to cover, block or

parry attacks away from their head and body. Thus they do not generally think of those same limbs as targets. Attacking the radial or ulnar nerves in the arms is an effective way to shift the opponent's guard creating opportunity for entry. Similarly, low line kicking attacks to the ankle joint or medial shin can be an effective way to shift the opponent's stance which again creates opportunity for other entries. Such attacks seldom cost much of anything on the part of the attacker and are difficult to defend against.

12. *"Pyan always at a 45-degree angle off the centerline of attack."* Pyan means literally to flank your opponent's centerline. The principle can be utilized both counter-offensively and offensively. The 45 degree angle is utilized counter-offensively to allow hand engagement and immediately smother the legs. In offensive utilization, the angle is more narrow at 30 degrees as anything larger will allow the opponent to step into your change. Distance is of primary concern in the utilization of Pyan, whether offense or counter-offense is being employed. Moving from too far out while applying angles stepping patterns will cause you to fall short of the target zone and fail in your technique.

1a. *I seize the opponent's lead hand and perform a drilling fist to his face, forcing him to engage my attack with his secondary limb.*

1b. *This sets up an opportunity for me to "pyan" to his left while now seizing his left hand and attacking his back brain with my right palm.*

13. *"Speed should be varied with purpose to lead the opponent's mind."* This is a fairly self-explanatory statement. A broken rhythm in terms of speed makes it more difficult for the opponent to track your movements. A deliberate variance of pace in technical exchange can allow you to penetrate the opponent's guard more readily. Sometimes, the act of revealing your true speed when it counts most can be an advantageous tactic.

1c. *Still in opportune position at 45 degrees off his flank, I then follow up with a left palm smash to his face.*

14. *"Never telegraph - strikes must be delivered from the present position."* This is huge and often overlooked by coaches and practitioners alike. The tendency to wind up or cock for the big strike is something that must be avoided at all costs. It is analogous to sending a telegram to the opponent saying "here I come" and must be systematically trained away. All movement must initiate

from the present position to avoid such telegraphs. A good fighter will read any slight type of telegraph easily, no matter how small, and turn it against you.

15. *"Look at the opponent's eyes (or throat) in a single match. In situations of multiple threat, look downward."* In a single match, you must see the entire body of the opponent, missing nothing. And you must never look at the opponent's limbs or look where you are considering targeting. This must all be done with a more peripheral gaze to avoid being read or feinted easily. In a multiple encounter, even with good peripheral vision, you have a blind spot that is nearly 180 degrees behind you. It is possible to reduce this blind spot to much less, approaching less than 90 degrees, by tilting the head downward about 45 degrees off of level. You will be able to see the feet of any adversary approaching from behind and this will warn you of their proximity. For the remaining blind spot, you should shuffle your feet back and forth in rotation to catch anything coming from that zone.

16. *"Strength used wisely is an asset, but be ever wary of the trap."* There is an old saying; "A good big man will beat a good small man on any given day." And this is a true statement which simply means that strength matters and should be cultivated. But the trap mentioned is that of a mindset that causes you to begin to believe that strength is all important and will always carry the day. This is untrue. Technical ability, tactical ability and cunning can all trump strength. This should always be remembered. Strength is but one of many tools available once it has been properly cultivated. But not at the expense of other tools.

17. *"Pain is an effective way to lead the opponent's mind."* We often refer to this tactic as an "interrupt" because of what it does to the opponent's awareness when inflicted. An interrupt can take many forms. It can be a painful control technique, pressure exerted in sensitive areas or a quick superficial strike to inflict pain (such as a quick flick to the nose). All these variations have one thing in common. They busy the opponent's mind with pain temporarily having the effect of scattering the awareness and making it more difficult to concentrate on the task at hand of defending continued attack.

18. *"When leading the body, be alert, sensitive, and maintain your sphere."* In our Hsing I methodology, leading the body is also employed frequently. The one instinctive response that is almost, if not impossible, to eradicate even through thorough training in a human being is the fear of falling. Human beings will go to great lengths to avoid loss of balance and falling. Therefore, it is wise to understand that this can be used against an opponent effectively. If I pull on you, you will tend to pull back. If I push on you, you will tend to pull back. If I float you, you will try to sink, etc. To be able to utilize this method, one must be constantly alert to the changes in pressure coming from the opponent's body as the attempts to correct failing balance are manifest. At the same time, within your own body you must make sure to maintain your structure and not be compromised yourself in the process.

19. *"While easier to employ, defense will not win the battle."* There is a reason that beginners are first taught defensive tactics and that offensive tactics are taught last. But for the practice of actual fighting, it must be understood that to remain defensive is to simply give the opponent chance after chance after chance to probe, discover and then exploit your defenses. Ultimately, a good offense truly is the best defense.

20. *"All true attacks initiate from the feet."* To deliver force from the guard position, meaning when crossing the bridge, a step must be made to initiate momentum toward the opponent. So it is wise to watch the footwork of the opponent and learn to see when a blow is a committed blow verses a non-committed blow. The reality of the difference will be found in the footwork. If an opponent does not commit his mass by stepping, the attack is of no consequence and should be studied, but not engaged.

21. *"Box a kicker, kick a boxer."* This, of course, translates across the board regarding any such strength in the enemy. One should never fight the fight of the opponent. Instead, one should try to force the opponent into less familiar territory. It is more likely that the opponent's method will fail if forced into an area that is not their expertise.

One of the most under-utilized techniques in all of martial arts is the front toe kick to the floating ribs against the opponent's lead.

22. *"Sweep a high stance, attack a low stance."* A high stance means more mobility, but by far less connection to the ground. Sweep the support leg as this opponent steps forward or immediately after initial engagement upon exiting. Conversely, a low stance means greater resistance to throw or sweep but less mobility in defensive motion. Strike the lead leg with low line kicks (their knee and below) as this opponent attempts to advance forward on your position, then follow up as opportunity presents itself.

1a. As Brandon leads right to my face, I shear the force of the attack off at a narrow vector and prepare to step inward.

1b. I then step and half step forward to deliver a tiger posture, utilizing both hands to simultaneously attack his high center and low oblique.

23. *"Study the double strike and the four methods of employment. It is unexpected."* Since most fighters utilize one limb and then another in combination, it can be useful to occasionally break the pattern by utilizing a doubled up strike. One hand used twice via circle to two different zones, one foot used to two different zone, two hands used simultaneously to two different zones or a hand and a foot used simultaneously to two different zones. All can be effective if used sparingly in variance of timing and speed with regular combination strings. Take note that I said "sparingly." Overuse of any tactic is ill advised. Such thinking goes to pattern once again.

24. *"Explore technique to grasp principle, holding principle, forget technique."* Oftentimes, fighters seek to acquire an arsenal of technique. This is a fundamental stepping stone, but should not be ultimately where you are headed. If you are reliant on an arsenal of technique, you are also reliant on a process of selecting such while under pressure. It is better to cultivate a deeper understanding of the whys and wherefores which govern technique at large. Understand the principles that govern power transmission and the tactical perspectives that govern combat. In this way, you free yourself from the selection process and your mind is freed during combat to simply observe in a detached way. This will translate to great speed in the face of a threat.

The Five Roots

1. Form - For unity and harmony of mind and body.
   - Slowly - For energy and circulation.
   - Moderate - For flow and linkage in motion.
   - Fast - For power in motion.
2. Meditation - Standing: For strength of mind.
   - Seated: For depth of mind.
3. Push Hands - To train perception.
4. Sparring - To train awareness.
5. Percussion - To gain understanding of physics and kinetics, yielding true power.

Form is of essential value in training. It is wholly necessary toward the purpose of training structure, balance and flow of motion. All of which translate to greater ease of force generation in combat. To neglect form is an egregious error.

Meditation improves performance. There are many modern studies to support this fact. And although the practical results of meditation are not so easily realized on a day to day basis, it is unwise not to invest daily time in this endeavor.

Push Hands is an internal martial arts tradition. Other styles have something similar but not the same in all aspects. From push hands we gain a greater understanding of the give and take of an exchange of kinetic energy from opponent to opponent, or should. Too often, push hands takes the form of entirely too much cooperation in the modern age. Isolate methods to develop key skills are fine. But it is necessary to take away the cooperative element at some point to realize any true benefit from the practice. Done properly, the benefits are worth the undertaking.

Sparring should be a no brainer need in any martial art. But frequently, sparring takes a much too limited form in many modern schools. In some, it is not done at all and this is truly tragic for the students of that discipline. Sparring should be done regularly and it should take many forms. From isolating certain technical perspectives to all out full contact, all phases should be addressed regularly in a systematic manner.

Percussion training is an absolute must. A practitioner must hit things, lots of things. We must gradually build our strength through the feedback of hitting objects harder than ourselves. To overlook or avoid this facet of training will yield a less than effective skill base. Striking a very resistant object is the only way to truly know if you understand structure and impact.

The Three Powers.

The so named "three powers" found within Hsing I are named as Ming Jing (obvious power), An Jing (subtle power) and Hua Jing (refined inner/mysterious power).

In the beginning stages of practice a student will move with a gross, obvious power. At once easily visible to the naked eye, even though untrained, but yet also obviously unrefined and harsh in its motion structure. This stage is labeled as Ming Jing (obvious power). It is present while the mind is still trying to teach the body how to move, how to position itself properly in terms of mechanics and how to stay structurally strong and balanced. It should be expected that a practitioner at this level of development will be utilizing a great deal of localized muscle in an effort to give force to each respective motion within the form.

In the second stage of development, An Jing (subtle power), the practitioner has developed a feel for the movement structures and is now *listening* to his/her body in terms of feedback on structural mechanics, fluid linkage and a balanced root in terms of the overall form. At this stage we would expect the practitioner to have a much more connected expression of power. It should appear smooth in motion and well balanced in a fluid structure. The practitioner who achieves this second level of development is quite powerful and a force to be reckoned with in combat. But the body mechanical attributes will still be quite easily visible to the untrained eye which will render many of the movements as too telegraphic in terms of combat.

In the final stage of development, the practitioner is able to truly harmonize the mind and body connection. This store and release phases are truly subtle and extremely difficult to see without exceptional levels of ability. We call this stage of development Hua Jing (a refined inner or mysterious power). The practitioner at this level is powerful in a way that is sometimes quite difficult to comprehend. The exhibition of power seems to appear suddenly and disappear as subtly as the wind on a breezy day. The movements of the body are small and refined and carry with them great force making this stage of development truly dangerous in the combative sense.

These stages are achieved naturally with time in practice. But the reason for attempting to get to the final stage should be fairly obvious as it translates to combat efficiency. Larger, more gross movement structures are not only telegraphic to the opponent but also very inefficient in terms of body energy which will cause the martial artist to tire too easily under the rigors of combat. Internal martial arts are all about efficiency of motion to prevent either of these two errors from occurring. And it should become clear that such perspectives are deeply ingrained in all aspects of the discipline.

Efficiency should be sought in all aspects of motion. The body should be trained to move in a fluid, non-antagonistic manner. There should be no overt and overall tension in the body at any time. Rather, the body should "pulse" the power transmission in a relaxed and synergistic way. Learning to move in this manner creates an effortless speed and unified body power. This is what is meant in the internal martial arts by "whole body power." First, train the components; "Power originates in the core, is rebounded through the feet, manifest in the torso, and exited through the fingertips." But, fight... by learning to lead with the fingertips. Trust that the long training is already imbued. Time this change of perspective carefully. Under a teacher is best.

Yin and Yang

The theory of Yin and Yang and is well-documented and it is not in the purpose of this chapter to reiterate that theory from the ground up in detail. But rather to discuss certain aspects of that duality that are immediately applicable to the Martial Arts.

If we label space that is occupied by a physical manifestation as "Yang," then we must also necessarily label the surrounding space that is devoid of that particular physical manifestation as "Yin." It is common for people to look at an object and decide that the presence of the object is the definition in and of itself. This is not true. An object is defined by both the "space" that it occupies and, just as importantly, the "no space" that surrounds and runs through itself and its perceived boundaries. These two quantities are juxtaposed and in a constant state of flux. We must look at both the "space" and the "no space" to see the whole. Seeing the whole, you can glimpse what is true reality. Not seeing the whole, your perception will be false.

In the science of fighting, it is important to learn not to look at the opponent's limbs (space). This can cause one to be easily feinted out of position. Instead, learn to look between the limbs (no space). This will in time allow one to easily perceive both the attacks and the target zones as they present themselves within the constant change of fighting.

It should be understood that when one side of the body is Yang then the other side of the body must be Yin at that given moment. And that it is anatomically impossible for the body to give resistant strength on one side while committing the other side to attack. To understand, try this simple experiment: Have your partner stand in a Martial stance, rooting him/herself firmly with the lead arm extended. Grasp the lead arm of your partner and pull with strength while your partner resists your attempt to do so and you will find that the resistance is quite feasible. Then, while still trying to resist your attempt to pull the lead arm, have your partner punch with force toward you with the rear arm. He/she will find it impossible to do both with substantial force. And you will find that you can easily pull your partner and control their center through their lead arm once the punch from the rear arm has been committed.

This concept is commonly referred to as "empty and full" and once understood can be infinitely useful in terms of tactical overlay. A small, re-directive tug can work wonders (if applied when the opponent is changing) to gain control of his/her center.

Furthermore, it should be understood that the duality of Yin and Yang is relevant and present in all aspects of motion and/or combat. In example, let us discuss "bridging" (to close the gap with the opponent). All fighters will readily understand that bridging with your opponent is the most important and critical phase of the encounter. To bridge successfully can spell success in the overall encounter. And to bridge unsuccessfully can just as easily spell defeat. It is the folly of most fighters to commit themselves completely upon attempting to bridge. For sake of discussion, this complete commitment can be quantified as Yang. It then becomes relatively easy to allow their extended Yang energy to reach its zenith while you become Yin and receive,

154

redirect and neutralize. It is far wiser to learn to employ the qualities of Yin and Yang toward your overall benefit in the encounter.

It is important to realize that because the duality of Yin and Yang is an ever present and real phenomenon within the construct of combat, the cycles of attack (Yang) and defense (Yin) will create a constant waxing and waning rhythm which is entirely natural. In other words, you hit the opponent and the opponent then hits you. It is therefore wise to understand that even the best laid strategic plans will begin to fall apart in the face of a thinking, reactive and constantly uncooperative opponent. Therefore, wisdom is found in constructing attack sequences in beats of three, adding fourth only in the event that the opponent becomes unstable and compromised in his/her ability to respond. Barring this event, after the third beat of the attack is attempted, it is intelligent to disengage and change position. Preferably to the opponent's immediate flank. Applied properly, this will allow a maximum benefit to be gleaned from the natural waxing and waning of offensive and counter offensive movement.

Ignorance of this constant state of flux within the construct of combat will certainly spell defeat against one who understands. There will be more discussion on this issue in the tactics chapter later on in this work.

1a. *This combination begins with a crossing fist entry from the outside crossing the centerline and drawing the opponent's lead to check.*

1b. *A second angular cutback is now performed to breach, attacking the exposed gate of the left lower ribs with a crushing/penetrating fist.*

1c. *Since the breach was successful, the advantage is pressed with a third angular step to obtain an elbow opportunity to the side head.*

1d. *At this point, if the opponent is not severely compromised, it would be wise to angle out in readiness to receive his impending counters.*

R.S.P.C.T. - (Realistically Structured Progressive Combat Training)

The concept of R.S.P.C.T. was born in the mid 1990's in response to fill a growing need. It evolved in several stages over the years and has gone through many revisions to get to the current point as it is taught today.

Initially, all my fighters that had gone into competition had been trained purely traditionally, like me before them. They learned all the traditional forms, drills, two person forms and exercises. They were taught, educated and practiced within the old ways of doing things. And they did this in all aspects of what was internal kungfu. The full contact fighting was in no way different. Nor was the preparation for same. But the traditional way takes time.

As the full contact teams gathered steam, more and more students that were in the younger ranks expressed interest in being involved with full contact competition. And they had not yet had the long years in the art as the seniors had before them. So there suddenly became this need to train a competent fighter in under a year's time in order to prepare them for the next cyclical contact events. And the beginnings of a program to achieve that goal were now in the works.

Initially, since they were still internal martial arts students albeit younger in the discipline, my focus was simply on creating drill constructs that would draw from what they had already been exposed to within the traditional arts. And then to take that exposure and teach them how to make it quickly combat effective. This endeavor formed the initial core of pad drills we now utilize in the training (although I am constantly evolving these still as I am never really idle).

By the time the mid 90's rolled around, we had trained so many successful champions for full contact kuoshu fighting that we now had people contacting us that wanted to learn just the fighting aspects of what the Internal Martial Arts had to offer. These people were not always internal martial arts students. These were just other fighters with other outside background that now wanted to learn whatever unique skill sets we had which they had seen demonstrated so often on the platforms. They did not want to learn the totality of internal martial arts. Often they were not at all interested in form or anything directly unrelated to the fighting aspects. So there became a need to further systemize the process of doing exactly that.

This is then what fueled the systemization of RSPCT as a stand alone program. The utility of such a program was obviously needed for such "fast track" individuals. But, being me, I chose to also make the program full blown from start to finish. Not just for competitive fighting, but for anyone who had a similar desire to learn the combative skill sets that internal martial arts has to offer without necessarily taking the time to learn the rest of the system. And after two years of construction and refinement, RSPCT finally came into being.

The program contains five tiers of training, with each tier broken into two segments, for a total of ten parts. The program is non traditional in that it does not utilize fixed singular form in training but rather a progressive series of drills and conceptual teaching to impart graduated fighting skill. RSPCT is a synthesis, a distillation of the Internal Martial Arts and their key concepts as applied strictly to fighting and fighting training.

Although the bulk of this book is dedicated to the Tang Shou Tao Hsing I system, I have chosen to include and discuss RSPCT training as well in this work. I made this decision based on the knowledge that all of my Hsing I students have profited immensely with involvement in RSPCT in addition to their traditional studies. And I feel the two compliment each other well. *The choice to include the structure of RSPCT in no way constitutes a license for any reader to infringe upon my copyright of creation. You do NOT have my permission to teach RSPCT.*

Within RSPCT training, most of the tactical and theoretical concepts are based in Hsing I and Pa Kua with the initial phases drawn almost exclusively from Hsing I. Though the principles of Tai Chi are also utilized within the structure, primarily in close quarters for neutralization prior to takedown.

RSPCT is divided into five broad categories of training; Reflexive, Structural, Perceptual, Conceptual and Tempering. The components of these five categories are being drawn from all three internal arts and then implemented based on relative utility. I shall endeavor to discuss each drill and/or concept in detail along with the accompanying photo illustrations so that the reader may better understand the scope of the training.

Throughout the discussion of RSPCT, I will refer to the "fighter" and the "handler" to denote the respective roles of the interplay within each drill. This again is not meant to imply that such training is useful only for the aspiring competitive fighter in any way. It is simply an easy label for the sake of description.

It should be duly noted that although RSPCT evolved from an initial need to train full contact fighters swiftly for the purpose of ring competition, it has evolved in design to prepare a trained practitioner for street survival as well. This will be shown more specifically in the final two tiers of the training method.

The RSPCT program is about efficiency in training key concepts and abilities of combat swiftly. It was never meant to be a substitute for traditional Hsing I or internal training. It is a compliment to such training from the combative side of things. But it does not address the non-combative or non-strategic aspects of traditional training.

I still do feel that traditional training is a better way to go if one is interested in a complete development entwined with holistic overtones for a balanced life approach. The exploration of Chi Kung, Meditation, Chinese Medicine and Philosophy are, to me, indispensible and should never be cast aside in favor of the pursuit of a combative expertise alone. Combative elements come out of what we do but combat is not the sole reason we train.

My teacher used to say; "To learn to fight is easy. To learn to heal oneself and others, that is true kungfu." I agree one hundred percent with him on this perspective.

R.S.P.C.T. Tier 1 - Reflexive Training

The reflexive training level consists of several progressively staged drills. Some are done with, and some done without, focus pads.

Protective gear is generally worn in training. And I highly advocate this practice. But we have excluded such gear here for clarity of the activities in the photo illustrations.

1a. *As Alex jabs right, I rotate my core slightly to my right to neutralize which both loads my right hand and mobilizes my left in potential.*

Working off the jab.

We begin by working off the jab. Most styles utilize the jab effectively as both probe and provocation. So a practitioner must become thoroughly comfortable with how to handle the jab effectively and efficiently or suffer the consequences.

We teach to check the jab though small rotations of our core. The fighter is trained to move cheek to cheek only, in terms of scope, utilizing the lead guard hand (which should sit squarely in front of the nose) for this measure of motion.

This degree of motion is adequate to check off the jab and the core rotation serves a dual purpose of both loading the body on the side of rotation and/or mobilizing the off side for counter potential. E.G. If checked to the outside, the check hand is loaded for

1b. *As Alex jabs right, I rotate my core slightly to my left to neutralize which both loads my right hand and left hands in potential.*

a counter jab or lunge while the left is mobilized forward for immediate counter stroke if available. If the jab is checked to the inside, the check hand is loaded for backhand strike and the rear hand becomes loaded for cross in terms of mechanical availability.

It is important to ingrain this core rotational philosophy into the practice of the drill as moving the arm only will not provide the same result. Core mechanics are one of the cornerstones of Internal Martial development and so we seek to seamlessly integrate this methodology into all that we do in training. All motion is core driven. No motion is performed with isolate muscle.

Understand that the jab is ignored at your own peril. But also understand that it is by and large a setup for things to come. As a result of this knowledge, a fighter must not "buy into" the jab no matter how well the adversary sells it in usage. To try and move forward immediately off the opponent's jab is to usually walk into something far worse as he/she is generally using the jab to gauge your responses. The jab should be studied.. not countered with authority.

The concept of "framing" (to maintain frame).

Your "frame" is like a picture frame. A rectangular area that spans from the crown of your head to your solar plexus in height and from inner shoulder to inner shoulder in width.

The concept of framing is a fairly simple one to understand but takes a fair amount of practice to ingrain into body habit. The notion is composed of three components:

1) Do not "block" in the conventional sense.
2) Divide the body into zones for purposes of cover.
3) Create opportunity while defending.

Let's take these one at a time and explore what is actually meant in relation to these components:

One; Do not Block. Internal martial arts impart a philosophy of combat that is based upon redirection of force as opposed to any attempt to stop force outright. Redirection can take many forms, but in relation to the framing concept it means to shear all attacks away from you through core rotation while always maintaining the integrity of your frame.

To block is to arrest motion and momentum in your own body. This then will require you to create new momentum to deliver any counter attacks which is far slower in utility.

Instead, we seek to create potential load in the body immediately by "shearing" the opponent's attack. We utilize the framing concept thus creating kinetic potential at the same moment we defend.

This approach allows us to seamlessly integrate defense and counter attack as one movement which translates to both great efficiency and great speed.

Two; Divide the body into zones. I wish here to distinguish that "tactic" and "habit" are two different things, or should be so. The defensive zone concept we utilize is taught and integrated as *habit*.

As Alex strikes left, I should rotate my core slightly and shear the blow back and to the rear keeping my forearm aligned with my shoulder.

As Alex strikes right, I should again rotate my core slightly, shearing back and to the rear keeping my forearm aligned with my shoulder.

As Alex strikes left low, I should rotate my core slightly, sinking and dropping my elbow to shear the attack back and to the rear.

159

A "habit" is an ingrained response that will keep you safe when the opponent has the jump on you and has compromised your space and your defenses. Such properly ingrained habits will allow you to convert bad situations into opportunity by being able to "weather" the metaphoric storm of a lousy position until such time to convert presents itself.

A "tactic" is a *decision* which is made during the engagement to *create* an opportunity. And such tactics are not bound by the zone defense, or any other perspective. We will discuss more on tactics later. For now, on with the zone perspective.

The *upper zone* is defined as the zone from the crown of the head to base of the sternum. Habitually, the hands and upper forearms should be used to defend this zone.

The *middle zone* is defined as the zone from the base of the sternum to the hip bone. Habitually, the elbows and lower forearms should be used to defend this zone.

The *lower zone* is defined as the legs themselves. And habitually, the legs should be used defend this zone. This can be done either through leg check as illustrated on the next page, or, through dynamic use of what we call a "foot change" which will be discussed in more detail later on in this work. Leg checks are more useful for kicking attacks that come in to the upper leg/thigh above the knee. Whereas foot changes are really the only effective way to deal with low line kicking attacks, that are delivered to the lower leg, at or below the knee.

Again, it must be emphasized that all defensive measures are to involve core movement and *active engagement* of the attacking limb, meaning to move upon contact. An active engagement of the attacking limb results in a redirect of motion on the part of the opponent's attack and *not* a block. This should be true in all contexts, including leg checks. The parry should not arrive ahead of the blow as this will result in a block and a cessation of momentum. Instead, the parry should engage the blow as it is still en route

As Alex strikes right low, I should again rotate my core slightly and sink while dropping my elbow to shear the attack back and to the rear.

As Alex kicks left, I should rotate my core slightly to the right, raising my leg upward at the same moment that his kick force is delivered.

As Alex kicks right, I should rotate my core slightly to the left, raising my leg upward at the same moment that his kick force is delivered.

and accelerate the already present momentum past you on a narrow angle off your centerline. This will both negate the opponent's attack and load your body for retaliatory counter. And this is the overall purpose of the method.

Three; Create opportunity. As previously mentioned, the act of redirected parrying creates an active engagement (as opposed to static) with the opponent's limb. When coupled with core rotation to accomplish such active engagement, the body will be forced to naturally load itself physiologically with stored kinetic potential on the receding side of the core rotation.

Simultaneously, the side that is now rotating to the fore of the core rotation is already in motion toward the opponent. This method creates opportunity to simultaneously defend and counter as opposed to first defending *and then* countering which is vastly less efficient in terms of speed.

In all instances, by using arcing, circular or spiraling returns, the resultant load of the redirected parry can be converted into kinetic potential by preserving the momentum in the body.

A framed, redirected parry on the left hand high line of attack lends itself to immediate counter with the right. A framed and redirected parry on the right hand high line of attack lends itself to immediate counter with the left. A framed, redirected parry with the right or left elbow in the midline of attack will coil that same side hand for immediate release and/or motivate the opposite side hand forward for immediate counter. A leg check, done properly, will load the body kinetically for immediate counter kick with that same leg and/or coil the body for a foot change to kick with the other leg.

This is all about getting your core involved. Core involvement allows the principle to work. If you move your body in a muscular, isolate way then these principles will not work for you. Such habits must be ingrained through constant, repetitive drilling of the body and mind.

The practice of "slipping."

The ability to slip a high line attack is an extremely important skill to cultivate. But it is often misunderstood in fight circles.

The two most important attributes of a properly performed slip are to (A) keep your body stable, especially including your neck/spine for balance and integrity so that you may absorb any impact that may come through because of less than stellar timing on your part. And (B) to yield to the angle of attack via utilization of a circular fade and return so that you may lessen or avoid impact altogether which is the primary goal.

The most common beginner's error is to attempt to dive forward and under the incoming attack. This is

Bringing the body forward and downward in an attempt to "dive" under the blow is the most common error and will add to the impact.

161

a mistake on two counts in that it will not only lessen the time factor you have to complete your evasion but it will also significantly add to the potential force of the impact should you fail or misjudge your timing.

Your body mass momentum will now be added to the opponent's mass and momentum behind the attack. The result is rather like two rams butting heads. Both fighter momentums crashing into one another equaling a very bad day for the defender.

Bringing the body straight downward is the second most common error and will also add to the impact although less your forward momentum.

The second most common error is to attempt to drop straight down. This would commonly be known as "ducking" the blow. This is better than diving, but still not ideal, as you again have less time to avoid the attack and you still have not yielded to any of the incoming force on the part of the opponent.

The target (your head) has remained at the same mean distance from the opponent and you will receive the full force of the impact if you should misjudge (Although it is true that sometimes the blow can be partially diminished by a poorly timed duck as a result of improper contact regarding the intended striking surface of the hand thrown).

A proper slip is performed in two stages as you see to the right:

1a. *The proper way to slip is to first yield to the angle of the blow so that any impact force can be lessened if your timing is a bit late.*

Stage one; the body yields away from the line of attack and then drops, making sure to keep integrity in the spine to preserve balance in the body. And also keeping integrity in the upper cervical spine to protect the head and neck in case of any impact.

Stage two; the body weaves/shifts to the other side, sliding under the attack, to achieve better position in relation to the enemy.

So you will see that by properly performing a slip via circular yield and return, you will once again kinetically load your body and preserve the use of momentum going into the evasion. The use of a circular return again creates this potential. The circle should be tight, just enough yield to create the load

1b. *After yielding the body will then shift and weave to the other side in an effort to achieve positional advantage. Notice the openings avail-*

and just enough weave to create the flank opportunity. Too large of a circle in performance of the slip will move you into the centerline and leave you vulnerable to the opponent's secondary. So this is to be avoided.

In the two illustrations at lower right on the prior page (1a & 1b respectively), you will see how the yield phase loads the right leg for thrust and also loads the core by rotating to the right. This gives potential for a strong midline strike (see at right) to the opponent's floating ribs at the same moment that those ribs are expanded into his attack as you slip underneath the blow. We often include this stroke when the handler has a body pad in various drills (Such a stroke can be worked with hand pads only but a body pad makes the drill more seamless in execution and practice).

Midline rib stroke taken upon slip of the right hook or cross from the opponent.

And once the weave has been completed, you will have achieved good flank position on the opponent allowing for a punishing counter to be delivered to the kidney or head.

A well performed and tight slip will also yield good position for a knee counter into the inner thigh of the opponent which can be a useful tool to destabilize his position. And often leaves good opportunity for an elbow stroke to the high line in follow up sequence.

Again, it must be emphasized that good structure must be maintained throughout any slipping maneuver to preserve integrity of the body for resistance to any impact. The most common mistake is to allow the head and neck to relax while slipping which leaves the cervical spine unsupported if any impact is sustained during the effort.

Elbow follow up to the high line after slip and weave have been completed.

Also remember that while the slip is being performed, you must simultaneously load the body core and legs for possible counter retaliation both within and when the movement is complete.

A sloppy slip, meaning too wide in the arc, will most often get you into trouble rather than into better position. This method must be practiced over and over again to yield the proper results in a live situation.

Slipping skills should be drilled repetitively and often until ingrained and perfect. Slipping is at once a necessary skill set for survival against a strong and agile opponent as well as a tactical skill set to gain positional advantage in close quarters.

Do not underestimate the value in such repetitive training.

Reflexive Drill #1 - Slip and Weave

The following drill is designed to practice basic integration of slipping skills with immediate, retaliatory counter striking.

The drill should be performed live, with no set rhythm on the part of the handler. Blows should be thrown at random times and from random sides. It is extremely important to not allow the fighter to "pattern" within the drill. The fighter must learn to read the attack as it happens in real time and not simply react according to the drill.

"Patterning" happens when the handler gets lazy about the timing of the attacks and makes them at regular intervals as opposed to a varied and non-rhythmic methodology. It is important that the handler move as much like a real opponent would as is possible while handling.

The fighter is to work on maintaining a good frame and structural alignment throughout the slipping phase and then countering quickly. We often use open hands in this drill to facilitate relaxation and speed on the part of the fighter.

1a. As the attack comes, the fighter should first yield to the angle of the blow, slipping away and down, maintaining good structure.

1b. After yielding the fighter will shift and weave to the other side as the blow passes overhead in an effort to achieve positional advantage.

1c. The fighter will then unload the kinetic potential from the properly performed slip in a first quick strike into the focus pads.

1d. The fighter will then quickly follow up with a secondary, attempting to torque the body back to the other side for power.

Since the focus of the drill is more on the structure of the slip and quickness in achieving a good retaliatory position, an open hand will help keep the limb and body from tensing up allowing the fighter to flow more easily.

The fighter should be cognizant of the following while performing the drill:

1) Good structure... Meaning no leaning, spinal integrity maintained throughout, especially that of the cervical spine in case of impact.
2) Body load... The legs should connect to the ground as the fighter sinks into the slip and weave and they should remain connected and stable upon release of counter strikes. The heels should never leave the ground and the knees should never straighten upon delivery.
3) The core should be actively engaged both in the effort of slipping (in case of a presented low line possibility for counter) and while motivating any counter strikes toward the targets as presented. A strike that is delivered from the isolated torso or shoulder alone is far less powerful and hence less effective.
4) The fighters hands should remain in "frame" while performing the slip and weave. And should return to frame immediately after any counter strike is thrown.

As the fighter progresses in skill, the handler's tempo should be increased. The handler's blows should be varied in terms of angle of attack and the cadence should also be varied. In example, for the beginning fighter, start with just one attack. Then as progress is achieved, go to 1,2's and then finally varied strokes with mixed rhythm and tempo.

The handler must also eventually vary the targets in terms of presentation. Both the elevation and the angle of target must be varied to encourage live response from the fighter. The fighter should not be allowed to pattern into anything like left/right over and over again.

The handler should also force the fighter to work at varied distances. The engagement range should be varied from distal, to close, to closer, to moderate and back again. The fighter should be forced to adjust on the fly, keeping proximal to the handler in terms of distance at all times by changing foot work.

The drill must remain alive to be a successful training tool. A patterned, rote drill is never effective. The fighter must learn to "read" the attack properly and this can only be achieved by varying the scenario frequently.

It is the handler's responsibility to bring these things out of the fighter. So the handler needs to be well schooled in both the drill construct and how to get the fighter to perform properly.

Reflexive Drill #2 - Frame and Go

Fighters often get into trouble when an opponent is faster and flurrying them. Or in an instance where a strong attack gets through with sufficient impact to scatter the mind temporarily. Such a circumstance can cause a fighter to lose focus and being to make mistakes unless he/she has been well trained to not allow their defenses to fall apart.

The frame and go drill is designed to promote the use of a quick "framing" in cover up against an opponent's one/two attack or a flurry situation. The idea is to promote the ability to stay calm, stay in frame, and look for the opportunity to retaliate while staying protected.

In this drill, the handler should mimic quick one/two attacks, one/two/three attack sequences or outright flurries to the high line at various speeds and sequencing. The types of strikes and the angles of attack should also be varied to simulate different combinations that may occur under pressure circumstances. During the course of the drill the handler should periodically, and quite randomly, present two targets to the fighter.

2a. *As the hander mimics a right lunge, the fighter maintains frame and rotates his core slightly, shearing the force off on a narrow vector.*

2b. *The hander now mimics a left cross. the fighter again maintains frame and rotates his core slightly, shearing off on a narrow vector.*

2c. *The fighter now feeds off the rotation of the core, stepping forward with the left foot into a lead counter with the left vertical fist.*

2d. *The fighter then quickly follows up with the rear hand while half stepping the rear foot resulting in a very quick and powerful one, two.*

166

The fighter should learn to see and respond to the targets as they are presented with the most expedient counter strike available. Then, as soon as the fighter has retaliated to the targets, the handler should press the fighter immediately with a fresh combination or two.

The fighter should seek to maintain the frame for as long as necessary and then to retaliate as quickly as possible once the targets are presented by the handler. The fighter should remain vigilant and agile and not allow the attacks to at any point become overwhelming.

The fighter should be cognizant of the following while performing the drill:

1) Maintaining a good frame throughout the drill, keeping the hands tight to the center, and return to frame after each counter sequence thrown.
2) Keep the elbows and shoulders down and relaxed both to keep the centerline guarded and to conserve energy while defending.
3) Keep the defensive hand movements to a minimum of motion when receiving the handler's blows. Redirect the attacks at narrow vectors through core rotation rather than give in to the urge to "bat" attacks away via blocking.
4) Keep the knees flexed and legs loaded for a quick and agile style of footwork (achieved via Hsing I half stepping) toward the targets when they are presented. And then again away from the handler once retaliation is completed each cycle.
5) Move through and from the core when motivating retaliatory strikes and concord stepping with such motivation to ensure mass potential is involved.
6) Keep a good center of balance throughout. Avoid leaning into counter strikes which can create an over-extended posture leaving you vulnerable to throws and takedowns.

Again, any "patterning" on the part of the handler should be avoided during the course of the drill to ensure that the fighter does not pattern their responses in return. Change things up frequently to keep in fresh and alive. The handler should vary the tempo and the volume, the intensity and eventually also the angles of the attacks.

The handler should push the fighter out of their comfort zones in terms of timing and distance, making them go long, then short, then long again for example. Various scenarios and ranges must be mimicked throughout the drill to give the fighter a chance to learn to adapt on the fly.

Reflexive Drill #3 - Dog Chase

One of the most difficult things in fighting is learning to stay proximal to the opponent. Too far away, and you cannot retaliate swiftly enough. The opponent always seems to be just out of reach. Too close, and you get pummeled seemingly never being able to get out of range quickly enough.

"Dog chase" is a concept of evasion and quick retaliation taught in our system. If you have ever played with a big dog, this concept will be fairly easy for you to understand intellectually through the following imagery.

When you play with a big dog, the dog will bring its toy to you to play. It will bring the toy very close to your hand and dare you to take it from him. When you try, he will pull the toy just out of your range

3a. *As the handler mimics a left lunge, the fighter fades a half step and sinks into the rear leg, loading it for return thrust energy.*

3b. *As the handler withdraws the target, the fighter pursues swiftly with a driving left vertical fist timed with the front foot landing.*

3c. *The fighter then quickly half steps the rear foot up and times a second vertical fist with the right hand as that foot hits the floor.*

3d. *As the handler now mimics a right hook, the fighter performs a slip and weave to the left (loading the left leg) in preparation for counter.*

3e. *The fighter now releases the load in the left leg, turning his core, and steps into a short range hook counter of his own.*

and then, when you withdraw having missed the grab attempt, follow your hand very closely with the toy as you pull your hand back toward yourself again. This is what is meant by the phrase "dog chase" in context of combat.

Besides integrating the dog chase concept in this drill, the idea is to incorporate quick retaliation against the lead followed by an evasive slip and counter against the hook. If the handler wears a belly pad (not shown), an uppercut can be added on the part of the fighter delivered as the slip and weave occur.

The fighter should be cognizant of the following while performing the drill:

1) The fighter should seek to stay agile, grounded and maintain a reasonable guard with hands up at all times upon beginning the engagement with the targets.
2) The fighter should seek to stay "proximal" at all times to the handler and targets. The effort should be to get just barely out of range and then immediately into counter attack distance.
3) The body should be loaded upon the retreat phase in two ways. One, the core should rotate *slightly* away from the lead side to prepare energy in the initial return lunge. And two, the body should sink into the rear leg, creating compression into the ground, in readiness for the return lead lunge.
4) The fighter should take care not to lean to the rear when retreating. Nor to lean to the fore when retaliating.
5) The initial return lunge should be a whole body effort. A conjoined spiral force off the rear leg thrust in conjunction with core driven rotation should be fed into the lead return lunge.
6) The lead foot should hit the ground in correspondence to the lead hand arriving at the target.
7) The rear foot should hit the ground in correspondence to the rear hand arriving at the target during the "1,2" initial return of lunge and follow up.
8) During the slipping phase, the lead foot must step slightly forward and outside to achieve angular advantage on the handler. And the fighter must "dig" into the ground with the stepping foot (meaning compress the leg as you step and load properly).
9) The body must commit by step, leg thrust and core rotation to complete the final blow of the counter series.

Again, the handler should vary the pace of this drill to avoid any patterning on the part of the fighter. Speed, rhythm and distance should all be randomly varied throughout.

This is especially important with regards to distance. The handler should sometimes push the fighter to extend longer than they normally reach to learn to control their balance under the pressure of attack. And then quickly force them back to withdrawal so they learn to respond to different timings of engagement.

Reflexive Drill #4 - Low Frame, High Frame

One of the cornerstones of Hsing I training is the methodology we use for force generation. And from our view, force is generated not only from the legs and waist, but also the intercostal muscles in the thorax are utilized in conjunction with the limbs themselves for power.

The low frame, high frame drill is a study in how to open and close the ribcage while simultaneously employing conjoined stepping for augmented force mechanics.

If the fighter allows the natural rhythm and flow of the strokes within the drill to take their natural shape, a feeling of easy, natural and powerful flow will manifest in performance.

4a. *As the handler mimics a front toe kick (or shovel punch) to the rib cage, the fighter drops his elbow down to meet the attack.*

4b. *The handler now hooks to the head. The fighter shears up and back, maintaining frame and loading the left side core and costals.*

4c. *The fighter steps the front foot forward timed with a left palm strike downward, releasing the load in the left side and loading the right.*

4d. *A rising uppercut is now timed with the rear half step, releasing the compression in the ribcage from the prior move in the process.*

4e. *The kinetic flow is continued by crunching the abdominal wall motivating the drive of the front toe kick before projecting forward.*

170

The upward rising defense of the second portion lends to the downward closing action of the palm strike, which then in turn lends to the upward rising action of the uppercut. This then lends itself to the natural contraction in both the abdomen and thorax to motivate the force of the front kick. The drill has been structured in a way to promote this flow so that the practice will imbed such key qualities into the fighter.

The fighter should be cognizant of the following while performing the drill:

1) When dropping the elbow for the low line check, sink the body but do not lean.
2) Shear the forearm straight up and back while checking the hook punch. Do not meet the force of the blow with a block. Redirect the attack past your ear by rotation.
3) Be sure that the forward step, core rotation and closing of the intercostal muscles are concordant upon delivery of the downward palm strike.
4) Be sure that the rear half step, core rotation and opening of the intercostal muscles are concordant upon delivery of the upturned fist.
5) Keep the hands in frame while contracting the abdominal wall upon motivation of the front kick forward and through delivery.
6) Strive to project the hips into the front thrust kick without unduly leaning to the rear so that a quick follow up is possible if available.
7) Recover while still in frame after the completion of the sequence each time. Do not allow the hands to drop through complacency while recovering.

Again, both pace and distance should be varied throughout the practice to force the fighter to adjust ranging and utility of the counter attack. Patterning should never be permitted.

The handler needs to vary the speed and curvature from the low line attack into the mock hook punch to force the fighter to adjust to varying tempos of such a sequence.

The handler also needs to vary the distances of both the high line retaliation targets and the front kick fading target to force the fighter to match his/her footwork to a changing situation with regards to different opponent reaches.

Reflexive Drill #5 - Angular Chasing

Sometimes, when there is an advantage to press, it is necessary to chase the opponent briefly in order to deliver a finishing strategy. The problem with chasing an opponent lies in the inherent nature of becoming too exposed in the rush to get into closing range. A smart opponent will still be looking to turn the tide even when in trouble and rapidly retreating to regroup. Therefore, for us, chasing the opponent is done only under caution and specific methodology.

The angular chasing drill is an amalgam of several key skills;

1) Dog chase once again makes an appearance here up front, this time in conjunction with a long counter lunge.

2) Angular chasing stepping is employed to both gain momentum and to make it more difficult for the enemy to counter as you move forward.

3) And the last component is again a slip and weave. But this time paired with a knee and elbow

5a. *As the handler mimics a left lunge, the fighter fades a half step and sinks into the rear leg, loading it for return thrust energy.*

5b. *As the handler withdraws the target, the fighter pursues swiftly with a driving left counter lunge timed with the front foot landing.*

5c. *The fighter now offsets his front foot in a pursuit angle and strikes with a downward vectored right palm, closing the intercostals.*

5d. *A second angled chasing step is now employed with the release of an uppercut, taking advantage of the kinetic load from the prior.*

5e. *As the handler now mimics a right hook, the fighter performs a slip and weave to the left, staying tight to the handler's position.*

5f. *A short, sharp rising knee is now performed as the fighter reaches the flank position. The handler should present a low, thigh high, target.*

5g. *The fighter now steps his right foot across the grain, pivots and engages his core for a downward, crossing elbow strike.*

combination in counter movement against a mock opponents hook to the head.

We have already discussed the dog chase concept a bit prior. But it is important to note once again, that although you do move away, you do not move away by much. You must remain proximal in terms of the distance yielded to have the ranging available for a swift return.

It is also necessary to remember to sink, thereby loading the rear leg for the rapid retaliation forward. If you do not sink, you will be slow in return.

Now let's look at the individual components:

A lunge in Hsing I is a bit different than in many systems in that we do not break contact with the ground by raising the rear heel as we extend. Rather, both feet are brought forward in a very long and quick half step with the impact being timed on the front foot and then with the rear foot following up swiftly so as to prepare to move forward immediately yet again. In other words, the rear leg must quickly shuffle up and re-load to the ground through the heel. Much like the way a fencer lunges.

Angular chasing is much like leaping side to side while moving forward but by far more controlled. The body steps, drops and loads the lead leg as you move to each side thus preparing thrust to move quickly laterally and forward the other way. Done correctly, the steps will build swift momentum. And the angle of motion makes it more difficult for the opponent to make a determination on your precise trajectory. This makes it much harder to intercept in practice than a linear chasing movement.

Angular chasing is employed commonly in Hsing I for this very reason. The key is to make the angles wide enough to confuse the enemy but yet narrow enough so as to not allow easy entry into your center while you advance. For this type of parameter, meaning either offensive or counter-offensive chasing, we utilize a 30 degree angle as a training parameter.

The angle stepping will then come forward again under the opponent's thrown hook to set up the knee. The step should be tight to the opponent to allow this range without reaching and overextending the knee strike.

The knee strikes in Hsing I are most often delivered to the leg of the opponent to denigrate structure. And in this drill, the handler should present a low target to practice this skill. The knee strike itself should be motivated as the body naturally rises from the floor so that the thrust from the leg, the shift of the body mass and the contraction of the abdominal wall may all simultaneously contribute to maximum power generation. The knee strike should never be thrown using isolate strength from the leg and hip flexors only. It is not strong enough in this circumstance and becomes too susceptible to being hooked by the opponent which will yield a throwing position immediately thereafter. The knee should be motivated by whole body power and brought upward and forward sharply. The mechanical force is almost like the physical action of doing an abdominal "crunch."

Elbow strikes in Hsing I take a wide variety based upon the five forces. The one illustrated in this drill is a crossing elbow and the angle of delivery is lateral and partly down as a result of closing the intercostal spaces upon the delivery. The impact is actually done with the upper part of the ulnar bone as it becomes the elbow proper. This is where the bone is strongest but still forms a knife-like edge for impact purposes. This type of elbow is generally utilized on target zones of the throat, side neck and back brain. In this drill, the stepping will take a lateral form, across the grain of the opponent's centerline to set up this elbow stroke.

It is important that the rear heel remain grounded throughout each phase of this drill. The heel is much stronger as an anchor to the ground than is the ball of the foot. The fighter should stay true to Hsing I footwork and principle to reap the maximum benefit from this drill structure.

The fighter should be cognizant of the following while performing the drill:

1) Maintaining an angular footwork of 30 degrees each step off the general line of travel.
2) Keeping a flow of technique, moving seamlessly from one movement to the next without any sort of "chambering" for subsequent strokes. Strokes should be delivered from frame and from the last position as the frame changes in motion.
3) Keeping the knees flexed for speed of step. And the feet grounded for solidity.
4) Maintaining a good balance throughout the chasing phase. Do not become over-extended.

Again, the handler should vary the speed, cadence and distances frequently in the drill to maximize the potential for the fighter to adequately develop the necessary skills of both reading the opponent and matching his/her footwork to an ever changing situation.

Reflexive Drill #6 - Interrupt

We've all seen comedic representations of an hysterical person being slapped to restore their normal cognitive function. And although this is often portrayed in comedy, it is also quite true on a psychological level. Such a slap can indeed, in effect, jar the mind and serve to reset the mental state of the recipient.

In combat, we utilize the antithesis of this phenomenon by attempting to jar the opponent's mind into a different state as well. However, in addition to affecting the mind, we also seek to affect the body in the same process.

In our tradition, an "interrupt" is a sharp, quick strike used to either scatter the opponent's mind or their attack rhythm and it can take many forms depending on the circumstances.

In the following drill, we are working the concept of an interrupt which is being performed in conjunction simultaneously with a shearing defense by the other hand against the handler's lead hook attack to the head.

6a. *As the handler mimics an wide arcing hook punch on lead, the fighter simultaneously shears off the force and strikes centerline.*

6b. *The fighter immediately follows with a rear palm strike, closing the intercostals in the process and taking advantage of the kinetic flow.*

6c. *As the handler now hooks left to the head, the fighter slips and weaves with a small right step to the outside, loading the right return.*

6d. *The loading of the right side is now released in a short, sharp overhand right. The fighter should be at flank position at conclusion.*

Our initial interrupt is followed quickly by a powerful palm strike (Pi) to the same target zone. And then a forward slip and weave is utilized against a secondary attack by the handler to achieve outside position for a crossing counter blow.

In this structure, the fighter should concentrate on feeling the natural rhythm of the opening into closing coming as a result of the first and second strikes respectively. The body will naturally "open" on the first as a result of the combination of shearing back with the parry hand while striking forward with the opposite side. And then a "closing" will naturally occur as the ribcage compresses into the palm strike of Pi from the rear side.

This downward closing will then naturally feed the forward and outside step conjoined with the roll of the body in slip and weave to create a powerful torque into the crossing blow.

The fighter should be cognizant of the following while performing the drill:

1) Stepping the front foot forward into the initial counter movement to ensure that body mass is involved in the interrupt effort.
2) Making a rapid one/two sequencing out of the first two movements by allowing the natural expansion and contractions of the thorax to feed both speed and power in the actions.
3) Ensuring that the shearing hand does indeed shear to redirect the handler's attack and not meet the blow in some form of block. Blocking will reduce both speed and power.
4) Feel how the forward and downward closing of the second blow naturally feeds the step as the slip is performed against the handler's secondary attack.
5) As the slip phase is performed, be sure to coil the core in readiness for retaliation. Also be sure to properly load the stepping leg for the coming thrust mechanic.
6) Keep a good frame throughout the entire drill and do not chamber. Work on non-telegraphic motion in all strokes.

Again, although said numerous times already, a varied pace and timing of the attacks on the part of the handler should be a given to avoid patterning on the part of the fighter.

It is always the handler's job to ensure that the fighter develops proper reading skills and does not treat any drill as a rote patterned exercise. It must be kept live.

Reflexive Drill #7 - Iron Wall and Go

Most styles teach to check kicks with the leg when delivered to thigh high targets. And we are no different as this is a very good practice. However, what is often not practiced is immediate counter retaliation with the check leg.

When done properly, a moving check leg also creates kinetic load in the core muscle structures of the body. This load can then be easily channeled into a retaliatory kick. And what could be a better time to deliver such a weapon than when the opponent's leg is still in the air in full or partial extension.

The iron wall and go drill is a drill designed to hone just such an ability to both perform a proper leg check and then utilize such stored potential in the body for an immediate counter kick with the checking leg.

Again, I wish to emphasize that in our system, a leg check is NOT a block. The proper utility is to raise the leg as the opponent's kick is being delivered and not prior. This method allows for

7a. *The handler attacks with a round kick to the inner thigh. The fighter moves to intercept, checking with an inside iron wall.*

7b. *The fighter then releases a side kick into the handler's presented target, taking advantage of the natural chambered position prior.*

7A. *The handler attacks with a round kick to the outer thigh. The fighter moves to intercept, checking with an outside iron wall.*

7B. *The fighter then releases a cross kick into the handler's presented target, taking advantage of the natural chambered position prior.*

the physics of your moving leg check's present momentum to, in part, dissipate the incoming force of the opponent's kicking technique.

If your leg arrives early in the check position, you will receive the full force of the opponent's kick into your checking leg. Also, since you have now effectively stopped in motion, your retaliation tactic will be slowed.

Done properly, the momentum of the check itself will create stored potential in the core of the body for immediate release in a counter kick technique. The movement of check and counter kick should be seamless when done correctly.

And even if this is not your intention, that same stored kinetic potential can be used to quickly propel the body forward without any hesitation via a foot change or similar stepping method. This will then allow for a more fluid exchange no matter what the tool of choice in counter.

The fighter should be cognizant of the following while performing the drill:

1) Maintain a good center of balance at all times whether checking or delivering a counter kick to the presented targets.
2) Ensure that the checking legs are indeed still in motion and redirecting the incoming kick. This will be readily felt when either correct or incorrect.
3) Be sure that retaliatory kicks are delivered from the core via stored kinetic potential and NOT simply a snap kick return from the leg.
4) Be mindful of both the timing of their leg checks and a natural return path for counter kick (such as in the two illustrations on the prior page). The return path should never be a forced effort or it will be non-viable in combat.
5) Keep the hands high and in a reasonable guard position while counter kicking. DO NOT use the hands for balance in kicking allowing them to fly willy nilly out of the centerline. Such improper hand positioning leaves you exposed and vulnerable. Form good habits.

The handler should endeavor to deliver randomly timed kicks of various types into the fighters inner and outer zones.

The handler's kicks should be delivered with the authority to simulate an actual attacking leg. Anything less will give the fighter a false sense of the forces necessary to properly check the attack and this mistake could affect the fighter's balance in a real situation.

It is recommended to start with single leg attacks until the fighter learns to perform well. And then the drill can be stepped up with multiple combinations of leg attacks to challenge the fighter further.

Again, remember, keep it live.

Reflexive Drills #8 & #9 - Evasive Practices

Evasive skills in a fighter are, of course, huge. And such training should never be neglected in favor of focusing on offensive skill sets. While, although true, the best defense is a good offense and defense alone will never win a fight we must still develop good evasive skill sets for when we find ourselves being pressured by a worthy adversary.

8a. *The fighter slips the opponent's hook, keeping eyes on the opponent and staying as proximal as possible for potential opportunity.*

8b. *The fighter then foot changes against the opponent's secondary, angling outside to flank position, turning the body to evade the blow.*

8c. *As the opponent realigns and releases his tertiary attack, the fighter again changes feet and flanks to the opposite side.*

We have two types of evasive drills. Both types are depicted on this and the following page. And both are fairly simple, yet important constructs, which get the desired results if practiced frequently. It is highly recommended that safety gear be worn on the part of the fighter while performing these drills (not shown). This will allow the drill to be gradually "ramped up" without undue injury.

In the first, depicted above, the fighter should simply try to stay proximal to the enemy while the adversary attempts to strike with all manner of attacks. The fighter is not allowed to parry or block but is instead to focus on movement and footwork to evade only.

Slipping, stepping patterns, dog chase and all evasive concepts should be employed during the course of the drill *without touching any* of the opponent's attacks with your limbs. The fighter may position their limbs during the drill in mock performance but the focus is completely on evasion.

1) The fighter should seek to stay agile, balanced and grounded throughout the drill.
2) The fighter should not lean or allow themselves to be forced back over their heels.
3) The fighter should seek to stay close enough for retaliation at all times.

It is about position... Position... Position...

Backing up is a common problem that must be addressed and modified early on in the fighter's training. A fighter that constantly backs up may escape the attack but does not properly position themselves for appropriate counter technique. Such a perspective is a losing proposition. And since we teach to interrupt the opponent's mind and kinetic flow as quickly as possible, staying proximal to the opponent is critical to our methodology.

The second drill depicted below focuses on side to side, lateral evasion. We do this drill against a wall to forbid the fighter to back up against the opponent's attacks.

9a. *Pinned against the wall, the fighter must attempt to angle to the flank of the attack each time an attack is thrown.*

9b. *The fighter should physically both step and shift the mass against each attack. This simulates flanking stepping in practice.*

This is a simple construct of a drill. The wall behind the fighter forces lateral movement since retreat is blocked by the wall itself.

1) The fighter should focus on keeping a lithe springiness in the legs to allow for quick lateral movement and return.
2) The fighter should learn to *move his/her feet* each time an attack is thrown and not simply cock the head from side to side or lean the torso. Cocking the head leaves the cervical spine of the neck very vulnerable to impact injury. And leaning the torso creates an out of balance disposition in the fighter's posture. Both mistakes are to be avoided.
3) The fighter should seek to take small lateral steps in both evasion and return.

The handler can start with simple straight line blows to the head (the fighter should wear a safety headcage) and then gradually progress to one, two combination attacks.

Once the fighter is capable of dealing with the linear assaults, then the handler can begin to incorporate non-linear attacks into the mix as well.

As always, variance is key to avoid any sort of patterning and to promote true reading skills in the development of the fighter.

Reflexive Drill #10 - "T'swo" Cutting

Hsing I's principles governing combat are time tested in some of the most extreme possible environments. And they adapt just as well to the modern age if you understand their usage.

The principle of cutting is one of the five keys of Hsing I training (discussed earlier in this work in detail). To cut an opponent's kinetic potential is an effective tool in combat.

When applied to the arm, cutting is delivered to the "shoulder well" (where the head of the humerus meets the clavicle) on a straight line attack. And cutting is delivered to the elbow on an oblique or arcing attack.

When applied to the leg, it is most often applied just above the knee to induce hyper-extension of the attacking leg while kicking. But cutting can also be applied to the frontal hip joint as the opponent steps to destroy his/her structure.

The drill below depicts a basic practice of cutting in a free flow drill. This drill allows the

10a. *As the opponent attacks right, the fighter shifts to his right moving away from the blow and jams the shoulder with his left palm.*

10b. *As the opponent attacks left, the fighter shifts to his left moving away from the blow and jams the shoulder with his right palm.*

10c. *As the opponent attacks right, the fighter shifts and rotates to his right, jamming the shoulder with his right palm.*

10d. *As the opponent attacks left, the fighter shifts and rotates to his left, jamming the shoulder with his left palm.*

fighter to manifest the cutting principle on either the same side or across the grain as is depicted below in illustration. The illustrations depict a starting point for drilling only as the possibilities are fairly unlimited once understood.

The handler should throw random blows toward the fighter at various, broken rhythm intervals. Starting with straight blows is advised until the construct is more familiar to the fighter. And then gradually, oblique attacks and eventually leg attacks may be added.

The fighter should seek to shift off centerline of the attack and then strike either the "shoulder well" or the elbow of the attack to neutralize its forward progress thereby also arresting the opponent's core movement.

If cutting is done properly, it will yield an opportunity to either counter attack immediately or, in the alternative, draw the opponent's secondary for available counter.

It is suggested to start with the simple structure depicted on the previous page so that the fighter may learn to properly read the attack before progressing to more difficult trainings. Once this has been accomplished, move the drill to more of a free form method, incorporating live footwork and variety of attacks within stepping configurations. As the fighter gains more experience with the method, leg attacks can be incorporated as well and all aspects of cutting may be explored and practiced.

The fighter should be cognizant of the following while performing the base drill:

1) Keep a strong, structured balance when applying force in cutting the handler's limbs. The cutting force you exude should in no way destabilize you as you meet the handler's attacks.
2) Focus on precision of impact. A sloppy cutting stroke will not accomplish the objective.
3) Relax. Pay attention to the signals from the handler's core in terms of reading which side is coming at you. Do not "guess."

The handler should work with the fighter in developing his/her reading skills initially by making the attacks more overt. Then gradually, less and less chambering/telegraphing should be introduced to hone the fighter's reading capabilities.

The handler should, of course, vary things as much as possible in the process. And as the drill progresses, the handler should act accordingly. With each introduction of new types of attacks, the handler should educate the fighter by dialing the pace back a bit and then ramping it up gradually once again as the fighter becomes more comfortable.

Reflexive Drill #11 - Foot Changing

Have you ever accidentally banged your shin into the edge of your coffee table? Most of us have at least once in our lifetimes.

Now think back to that incident and remember the level of pain, magnify by one hundred times and that is about how it feels to have a hard soled penny loafer or boot slammed into your shin in a street fight by someone who knows how to deliver such a technique. I've actually seen grown men sit down and weep from the pain of this type of impact.

11a. *In the midst of the foot change drill the fighter is staying proximal to the opponent, with attitude and weight disposition forward.*

Foot changing is realistically the only way quick enough to defend against relentless low line kicking

11b. *As the opponent cross kicks the lead leg, the fighter performs a foot change and angles to the side in the process, again staying close.*

11c. *As the opponent then tries a side kick to the newly placed lead leg, the fighter again performs a foot change and angles to the flank.*

attacks. This drill is meant to work the foot change over and over again against such attacks to allow development of this skill.

1) The fighter should remain stable at all times while performing each and every foot change, staying proximal to the enemy.
2) The fighter's attitude should remain somewhat forward in terms of weight distribution to avoid shifting to the rear in each change which slows the movement considerably.
3) The fighter should strive to not only change feet to get off-line of the attack but should also attempt to develop positive thrusting force off the changing leg in order to swiftly counter.

The handler should explore every possible low line option of leg attack in this drill. Quick and repetitive attacks to the knees and below should be brought into the drill in every conceivable way. This drill can then serve a dual purpose of sharpening such attacks in the handler's arsenal while training the fighter to evade same.

Reflexive Drill #12 - Kick Shearing

As a martial art, Hsing I is about two things; efficient use of kinetic energy combined with an aggressive domination of the opponent's space, body and being.

It has already been stated that instead of blocking, we seek to first preserve and then utilize the opponent's already existing momentum against them. This allows us to concentrate all of our energy on our attack strategies.

Kick shearing is a utility of simultaneously taking the force of a kick past you while stepping forward and upsetting the balance of the opponent. It can be employed with either a step to the fore or conjoined with a foot change. It embodies the ideology of preserving and capitalizing on the opponent's momentum while efficiently and simultaneously countering the attack.

12a. *Against a mid-line round kick, I shear the kicking force back with my left hand while simultaneously stepping forward to throw.*

12b. *A kick shear is performed against a skipping side kick in the same manner. The shear, step and leverage against the body must be as one.*

1) The fighter should attempt to seamlessly shear the kick away while turning the body and moving forward to pressure the handler's body upsetting the balance.
2) The fighter should concord the stepping though, and grounding of the rear foot, with impact of the lead arm on the opponent to maximize mass involvement in the effort.
3) The fighter should learn to adjust his/her footwork through foot change if necessary to match the opponent's penetration of attack.

The handler should explore various thrust kicks and round kicks to the fighter's body. It is suggested to start with single kicks to train the fighter in this tactic before progressing to any combination attacks.

All manner of kicks should be employed over time and the intensity gradually increased. Eventually the drill should expand to include hand techniques in order to simulate a live encounter and force the fighter to respond at appropriate timings.

R.S.P.C.T. Tier 2 - Structural Training

Tier Two Structural training builds upon the reflexive training already learned in Tier One and begins to hone better body mechanics, kinetic alignment, angles of insertion and the ability to maintain proximity to the opponent.

The drills found within this tier are designed to imbue a more refined understanding of how to move with a live opponent. The patterns are still fixed but they will contain enough variance because of changing footwork patterns and distances utilized by various partners to create a focus on developing applicable live skill sets.

It is important to work these drills meticulously at first to develop the proper angles of insertion, footwork and body alignments before escalating the speed and scope of the drills.

Although all drills are depicted without safety gear, it is highly recommended that such gear be worn while these structures are practiced. The gear will allow for a gradual escalation which approaches real time combative speeds and intensity with minimal risk of injury.

The fighters must focus on true targeting at all times. The notion of "cutting the partner a break" is counter-productive to complete development and often ingrains very bad habits.

Structural Drill #1 - Cutback Drill

Angular stepping is a major component of Hsing I's attack strategies although the art is more well known for controlling the centerline (which we also do well). The cutback drill is designed to teach the practitioner the basic ideology of how to capitalize on the opponent's position by using angular stepping for attack purposes.

The fighter should first provoke a response from the opponent in an effort to cover the flank. This can be done by either stepping strongly or idly moving toward the flank of the opponent until the opponent feels forced into turning his or her center to cover the now exposed flank position. Sometimes just simply box stepping over gradually to the flank or a quick gait to the outside of the opponent's guard.

The key, like in all attack strategies, is to make it an integrated effort in the overall scope of the combat. It should flow from the environment seamlessly and not appear contrived or it will likely be interpreted by the opponent.

Any number of various set ups may be used for this strategy, but they all involve getting the opponent to turn in an effort to cover the now exposed position.

1a. *I angle out against Alex's guard forcing him to rotate to protect his flank. The angle needs to be enough to force his response.*

1b. *As he responds by turning in the prior, I quickly angle step into his centerline and attack the high line, forcing a quick cover response.*

1c. *Alex's prior reaction creates an opportunity for me to quickly angle out and attack. High or low line will be determined by check position.*

Then the fighter should quickly step across the grain inside the guard of the opponent to draw a defensive movement. Once the defensive movement has been engaged, a rapid shift and step back to the flank should expose a target either high or low.

Various strokes should be practiced to learn proper timing and angle of insertion given the various responses of the opponent in live scenarios. Intensity should be increased as familiarity is achieved through the drill.

Once the fighter is comfortable with the basic scope of the drill, he/she should experiment with different guards, stepping and lead strokes to understand how different variables may influence the partner/opponent's responses.

The fighter should be cognizant of the following while performing the base drill:

1) Move to the opponent's flank until you actually provoke a cover response. If the opponent does not feel truly threatened on the flank, this strategy will likely fail.
2) Be sure to engage at a range that accounts for the geometry of an angular closing footwork. The most common mistake is to attempt to move from too far outside.
3) For attack purposes of angular stepping, a 30 degree angle is best. Going even as wide as a 45 degree angle will allow the opponent too much time between changes thereby giving rise to the opportunity to simply step into the center of the change of direction and neutralize.

To make the drill as progressively live as possible (once the fighter gets the basics wired) the partner/opponent should engage with many different defensive parameters and timings to force the fighter to adapt. Sometimes defending with right hand, sometimes with the left, sometimes with stepping or shifting, etc.

Structural Drill #2 - San Shou Pao (free hand pounding)

2a. *Both fighters start from a left San Ti Shr guard position, but with wrists already touching simulating the provocation range of attack.*

This is one of two orthodox Hsing I drills that I learned in Taiwan and chose to keep in RSPCT training unaltered because of the contained rapid shift from angular stepping to centerline breach via direct trapping.

This alternating format within the drill makes for a good mix of ranging skills and rapid positional shifts of both footwork and hand method.

This drill essentially employs two of the five fists in repetitive sequence, Heng (crossing) and Tsuan (drilling). These are incorporated with angular stepping and direct stepping with half step respectively.

2b. *One steps inside the guard and attacks with a highline crossing fist while two steps back, redirects and matches the angle of attack.*

2c. *One now direct traps with the left hand, breaches center with drilling fist. Two steps back and redirects looking for flank position.*

2d. *One makes a quick change, playing off the redirection and angles to the other side. Two repeats the matching angle and redirection.*

2e. *One repeats the direct trapping breach while two repeats the same flanking defense. And then two will now cross and one will defend.*

The drilling method is utilized via centerline direct trapping over the initial defensive hand after the bridge. And the Heng method is then used to pass the guard once the secondary is engaged.

The use of the Heng method in passing the guard of the opponent becomes especially useful if practiced regularly. The Tsuan fist uses a very standard direct trap to denigrate the guard upon stepping to centerline and the resultant movement is short, sharp and quick in entry.

This application can set up a panic response in the opponent making passing the guard with Heng very easy indeed.

The fighters should be cognizant of the following while performing the base drill:

1) Both the stepping and the proximity should be constrained to tight, streaming movement.
2) When performing the drilling action, the trap should be short, sharp and succinct. The blow should be driven by core rotation and projection through stepping. There should NOT be any sort of cocking/chambering of the fist in this transition. It should explode from the body core and not the limb.
3) In performance of the crossing action, the goal should be to literally slide off the secondary parry against drilling and slip effortlessly to the outside of the guard. In the drill construct, this movement is performed to the high line target. But you will find tactically that the same method will employ far better to the mid-line (floating ribs) in actual combat circumstances.
4) In receiving the crossing attack, each fighter should seek to half step to a proximal flank position on the opponent. A good way to test your positioning is to arbitrarily pause at this juncture and test to see if your non-parrying hand can easily touch the opponent's ribs. If not, you need to adjust your footwork accordingly.
5) In receiving the drilling attack, each fighter should position so that they are only one short step away from flank on the opponent. This position is also used to change roles within the drill, so that will serve at its own test. If you cannot reach the opponent's head with your crossing immediately, you need to re-evaluate your positioning accordingly.

This drill can be a very fast paced and adrenaline pumping exchange once you get the hang of its structure. When it begins to flow well, the two practitioners should begin changing roles at random timings. Change roles sometimes after three, two or even only one sequence and vary the right or left sides for change as well.

Vary the speed of the attacks to create natural broken rhythms as well.. Long, short, long, short, short, long, etc.

This will keep the drill fresh and alive by forcing both fighters to rapidly shift from offense to defense and back again.

Structural Drill #3 - Two Person Five Fists

This is the second of the orthodox Hsing I drills I learned on Taiwan that I chose to include

3a. Both fighters start from a left San Ti Shr guard position, but with wrists already touching simulating the provocation range of attack.

3b. Alex pushes my hand down and breaches with a Crushing fist. I yield, circle my hand around and strike his limb, half stepping back.

3c. Alex breaches again with a crushing fist to my face. I again yield a half step rearward, going to Tiger foot position and redirect his attack.

3d. I now start my foot change, attempting to seize Alex's wrist as my first foot hits the floor in preparation for my attack of Splitting.

3e. As Alex feels the pressure come onto his wrist from the attempted grab, he yields the front foot back, coils and withdraws his hand.

3f. I step my right foot forward and make my Splitting attack to his head while Alex simultaneously half steps into me with Pounding.

3g. *As Alex's Pounding fist progresses, I turn my body and deflect beginning to disengage for a foot change to gain better position.*

3h. *The foot change is now completed and I have angled over to Alex's flank while still suppressing his limb for control in the moment.*

3i. *I now deliver a Drilling fist. Alex half steps both feet, disengaging from my control and striking the radial nerve my attacking limb.*

3j. *Alex now counter attacks with a Crossing fist. I withdraw only my front foot and redirect his attacking limb past me at a narrow angle.*

3k. *Continuing my prior action's momentum, I wrap Alex's hand around to the other side, exposing his centerline in the process.*

3l. *I then half step both feet forward into a Crushing fist. Alex steps back and strikes my limb. The drill repeats, roles reversed from "3b".*

within RSPCT training. The incorporation of the five types of force as archetypes of the five fists is, of course, one of the main reasons. But this short little two person set is an effective study of the subtle interactive angles in footwork to achieve slight positional advantage.

It is also valuable as an excellent protocol for learning to stay proximal to the opponent and thereby smother all possible foot technique in the process.

It is suggested to do both this drill and the prior San Shou Pao drill while wearing protective gear, and at full contact, once learned. They will vastly improve your distance awareness.

The fighters should be cognizant of the following while performing the base drill:

1) Note that what may appear to be "blocks" are actually strikes to the limb in illustrations "3b," "3i," and "3l" respectively. In both "3b" and "3l," which are the same stroke, the idea is to strike the radial nerve at the transverse crease of the elbow with the palm heal. And the stroke depicted in "3i" is an impact to that same nerve pathway.

2) In "3c," note the narrow "threading" of the hands through the centerline. Any separation in this transition will allow the opponent entry by simply jamming his lead elbow upward and forward into your face.

3) As the hand overturns in "3d" and attempts to grab, the receiving side should already be withdrawing against the downward pressure of the overturn. If you find yourself constantly being grabbed here, you are not sensing the pressure change and are moving far too late.

4) The receiver in "3e" should withdraw only the lead foot to stay proximal. But should move both feet forward a half step in "3f" to crowd the opponent's space.

5) The receiver in "3g" should turn the body while checking the hand. And then as the change step is performed in "3h," he should angle slightly outside. The movement of the limb should be very small. The appearance of being larger is solely because of the core rotation combined with footwork.

6) The receiver in "3i" should move both feet back a small half step to allow for complete disengagement of both limbs, avoiding a controlling read on the part of the adversary. And then move both feet forward at a slight angle outside in "3h" to achieve flank position.

7) The receiver in "3j" and "3k" should withdraw only the front foot to stay proximal in order to smother the legs. He should also strongly engage the core in the twining action in the effort to open the centerline for Peng.

Over the performance of this exercise, both fighters must stay proximal at all times. Exercise the principle of dog chase to get just out of range but to stay close enough for immediate retaliation. This type of ranging also smothers most, if not all, leg technique which can yield advantage once trained properly.

Observe the small angles of change in relation to the footwork found in this exercise. Small angular degrees in footwork can be a huge advantage when employed at the proper timing within the context of the exchange.

And remember, in this system, NOTHING is isolated to the limb itself. All movements are core driven and in concordance with step. This ensures both maximal efficiency and kinetic potential within all frames.

Structural Training - Counter Sequencing utilizing the Five Fists

Once the five fists have been ingrained into natural movement by performing the previous two drills regularly, we introduce a free form structure of counter sequencing while utilizing the five in live environments.

There are many possible permutations of the five so sequencing is almost limitless. However, a couple of good beginning points for the process revolve around the "cycles" of the five. These same cycles are found in the five element cosmology and are talked about previously in this work. But in terms of counter sequencing, they simply provide convenient places to begin the exploration.

For example; you will find that stringing the fists together in motion following what is called the creative cycle to be extremely easy. If you begin with the downward, falling action of Pi (splitting) the action will tend to fairly spontaneously generate the proper mechanic for the rising spiral action of Tsuan (drilling). This then will tend to easily give the body the motivation to generate Peng (drilling). This sequence has been illustrated below as an example of a good starting point for this drill.

1a. As Brandon attacks with a right fist, I shear the blow off with the rising fist of Pi (splitting) wedging his attack and controlling center.

1b. I then seize Brandon's attacking hand and strike the head with the Splitting Palm, pulling him into the blow as I do so.

1c. The falling action of the Splitting Palm sets up a natural kinetic flow into the rising action of a Drilling Fist to the jaw line.

1d. Finally the rising action of Drilling in turn promotes the sinking action of Crushing, making for one very swift and powerful sequence.

You will find that this same sequence will work readily from a combative perspective as well. If you are able to breach and strike the opponent's head with Pi, the resultant reaction will allow a follow up of Tsuan to the now exposed jaw. If you are successful in impacting the jaw with Tsuan, the opponent will be now over his heels with his body expanded. Peng to the rib cage or solar plexus under or between the guard is a now natural choice.

The right/left/right or left/right/left utilization of these fists in sequence is a natural, fluid and powerful mechanical construct of the body in motion. This is classic teaching.

However, there exist many sequencing possibilities that do not follow any of the cycles and instead are oriented towards the natural rhythms and flow of combat.

Depending on whether or not you are in an offensive position, or a counter-offensive position, these sequences will vary and good choices are made on a variety of factors. But this drill stage is about counter-offense as that is easier to learn initially. And it is always possible to provoke the opponent into attack before your attacking skills are there.

For example; the sequence below illustrates a natural string against an opening hook punch when forced to stay inside the guard. Sometimes when caught inside the best strategy is a quick interrupt followed by a couple of swift, punishing blows.

The sequence below accomplishes this by first interrupting with Pao (pounding) which will both buckle the opponent's head forward and maintain your parry arm in close proximity for a very fast follow up with Pi (splitting) to the head. This will then drive the opponent back and allow easy follow up for Tsuan (drilling) to the jaw to end the sequence with a punishing impact.

2a. *As Brandon attacks with a high right hook punch, I step into his centerline and deliver Pao (pounding) as an easy counter.*

2b. *The expanding nature of Pounding gives a natural and very quick flow potential to the falling action of Pi (Splitting) as a secondary.*

2c. *And again, the falling action of Pi (splitting) gives a natural kinetic assist to the rising action of Tsuan (Drilling) for a swift tertiary attack.*

193

As stated earlier, there are a myriad of permutations given the nature of the five fists. These are but two simple illustrations to get you started within the drill.

The fighter should be cognizant of the following while performing the base drill:

1) Stay within the context of the five fists initially to explore their archetypical expressions before beginning variant expressions.
2) Seek to stay within the construct of a grouping of three. One to enter, one to follow up and one to finish.
3) Once comfortable within the construct, do not be afraid to mix and match footwork, angles of insertion and hand shapes with any or all of the five forces.
4) Move from a naturally framed position. Stay grounded but also agile.
5) Involve the core maximally and the limbs adjunctively.

While practicing the drill, the handler/opponent is encouraged to come to the fighter with all manner of hand attacks. When first beginning to train the drill, keep the attacks confined to one strong hand technique and allow the fighter to simply work on sequencing ideas.

Once the fighter is comfortable in the drill and has a few good working ideas, the handler/opponent should mix up the tempo by using combinations and rhythm changes forcing the fighter to read appropriately and try to work his/her ideas in a live situation.

When these ideas become workable in a live context, the drill can be dialed down again to work on new sequencing. If you continue to alternate the "working" phase of the drill with the "live" phase, you will develop several reliable sequences in a matter of months.

Once you have cycled several times between the "working" and "live" phases and developed a dozen or more reliable ideas, the drill construct can be evolved in an alternating venue of "attacker" and "counter attacker." A few months of this and a live sparring venue utilizing only the five forces will naturally present itself.

This is one of the best ways we have developed to truly integrate five force methodology into a freeform combative scenario. Take the same steps and it will manifest for you as a practitioner in the same way.

Again, although not shown, protective equipment is very much advocated for live practice.

Structural Drill #4 - Center Tied Drill

In my days in Taiwan, my teacher had simple ways of fixing almost any deficiency in us rather quickly. And many of these methodologies did involve the use of ties to get this or that point across. Tying our arms together to teach us to keep a frame and to keep our elbows in and down while attacking and defending for example.

The two fighters are tied together at the provocation range. This will ensure a pretty much constant state of engagement in the drill.

This drill is exactly what the name implies. The developing fighter often has difficulty staying proximal to the opponent. They back up too much. This method was my teacher's fix for such a problem in my day. And I have carried the drill into my teachings as well because it simply works.

The idea is to learn to work the flanking angles of insertion instead of backing up and to learn to keep both hands viable to the opponent.

Stepping and positioning for leg counter attacks as well as hand, elbow, knee and eventually grappling counters should be integrated.

It is recommended to start with hand technique only. Once the fighters are comfortable, then progress to include foot technique next. Then finally, as the drill becomes truly comfortable, include close quarters strikes of knees, elbows, shoulders.

There is never a need to integrate throwing into this drill. If you have learned to get close enough to throw, you have no need for this drill any longer.

The fighters should be cognizant of the following while performing the base drill:

1) Focus on stepping in harmony with your partner/opponent. Seek initially just to preserve the status quo. If he/she angles to the right, you match by going right. If he/she advances, you will retreat. If he/she retreats, you advance. By learning to preserve balance first, you will become gradually more astute at determining developing, positional change.

2) After you have spent some time doing what I suggested in "1," you can then begin learning to cut the opponent off. If he/she angles right, you angle to the left to intercept. If they attempt to circle you, then you step into the centerline.
3) In both these phases, rather than seek to retaliate immediately, instead learn to see. Develop your movement skills prior to countering. Focus on staying with your partner/opponent in all ways before this drill becomes adversarial. In other words, as I say it to my own fighters, learn to dance before you fight.

After all such structural drills have been practiced for awhile, what we call "limited sparring" and "slow speed sparring" are introduced as a means to further evolution of the skills acquired in Tiers One and Two.

We continue to do this as each new skill set is introduced, explored and understood. In this way, the fighter's ongoing development of mind is paired along side the development of body. We again designate such differences as "working" or "live" phases of development and these occur many, many times in cyclical form in a fighter's development within our way of doing things.

Slow speed sparring is exactly what it sounds like. Speed is reduced in a cooperative effort to allow the fighters to better mentally process and select the best methods in utilization given the changing scenario of combat.

A coach will supervise these matches for the purpose of giving advice on less than favorable choices made and why.

Limited sparring is again, what it sounds like. We will limit the scope of the encounters depending on where the fighter's skills reside at the time. It may take the shape of a limited exchange of hands for example;

1) One entry and a follow up and then one counter and a follow up.
2) Or one entry, a follow up and a finishing blow in sequence, etc.

As the fighter evolves further, the limitations may become range based, grappling based or throwing based. For example;

1) One entry move, a follow up then position for throw and execute.
2) Or start from clinch and work your way out via striking.
3) Or neutralize and throw while staying inside.

Again, a coach will oversee to ensure that good choices are being made and implemented for gradual improvement.

Even in limited or slow speed sparring, it is highly recommended that safety gear be worn while practicing. There is no sense to being injured unnecessarily in a practice environment.

Structural Training - Tan Twei (springy leg drills)

Tan Twei drills are designed to promote lithe, quick and responsive leg technique. We have

1a. *In all Tan Twei drills, both fighters will commence from a San Ti Shr guard position simulating bridge (shown in this first pic only).*

2a. *As Brandon delivers a front kick to my groin, I will check the kick off with an inward iron wall and wait.*

1b. *Brandon attacks my lead knee with a skipping low side kick. I foot change to escape the impact to my knee, staying proximal to him.*

2b. *Brandon then recoils and delivers a round kick from that same leg. I perform a foot change, angle away from the kick and jam his knee.*

1c. *Brandon recoils and delivers a high line side kick from the same leg. I drop, rotating 180 degrees and deliver a dragon tail sweep.*

2c. *I now deliver a low line round kick, taking out Brandon's support leg. Note the jam of the knee is not necessary if the angle is correct.*

four fixed springy leg drills that all fighters are taught initially as depicted on this and the prior page. Practiced regularly, Tan Twei training develops a control and precision in kicking that is not easily achieved in other ways.

3a. Brandon delivers a high Muay Thai style round kick to my head. I slip and weave underneath. Note the target of opportunity not taken.

4a. Brandon delivers a skipping hook kick to my lead knee. I quickly raise my attacked leg to avoid the impact.

3b. Brandon then recoils and delvers a side kick to my mid-line. I shift, bringing my right leg to my left and hang his leg with an underhook.

4b. As Brandon's leg misses and finishes its arc, he quickly assesses the situation, seeing the target under my guard.

3c. From my flank position advantage, I then deliver a low line side kick to Brandon's supporting knee, compromising his structure.

4c. He takes the target with a round kick coming back the other way. I simultaneously jam his kick and cross kick his support knee.

One of the most overlooked aspects of kicking training in general is that of recovery. A good kick should have a recovery pathway that is quick and *unavailable* to the opponent for an easy catch and throw.

The nature of springy leg training tends to imbue this recovery quality automatically if it is practiced regularly and correctly. In an effort to throw a double or triple kicking technique with force off the same leg, a full and speedy recovery becomes a necessary component of success.

Although the drills depicted here are combative choreography for initial practice, we will also train these same double kicks into focus pads to ensure that the mechanics are being properly developed within the fighter. Without hitting something, the fighter will never truly know if the kick is realizing its full potential.

The fighters should be cognizant of the following while performing the base drills:

1) The fighters should be encouraged to keep a reasonably active guard position while training to avoid ingraining the nasty habit of dropping the hands while kicking. The body can learn to counter-balance and still keep the guard.
2) The fighters should take care to deliver a full kick each time they attack utilizing double kick techniques. The most common mistake is to short the second kick by simply flipping the leg into position using momentum rather than true core mechanics. The fighters should focus on a complete "store phase" for each kick before release.
3) The fighters should learn initially to bring their foot back to the proximity of their own knee between kicks in the double kick sequences. This practice will tend to ensure a more active engagement of the core in the secondary attack.

Once these springy leg partner drills have been learned, the best practice is that of a rapid exchange with a swap of roles on every other repetition. Meaning that I attack and my partner defends and then my partner immediately attacks and I defend. This will better simulate live circumstances of attack and defense and force both fighters to recover their balance and center position quickly.

For an even further escalation of these drills... when you feel like you have them wired, try then randomly attacking with any one of the four double kick methods and forcing your partner to identify and respond with the appropriate counter sequence on the fly.

It is still a "fixed" drill but this change can add a whole new dimension to the exchange making it feel more alive and forcing each fighter to develop a higher level of reading skills in the process. Besides being just a lot of fun as well.

It is again, highly recommended when ramping up to the final levels that safety gear be worn when practicing. Kicking technique can really cause some damage if precautions are not met.

R.S.P.C.T. Tier 3 - Perceptual Training

Perception is a tricky thing. To learn to see what truly is, feel what truly is, without infusing or overlaying past experiences is no easy task.

Our minds, because of our past experiences, tend to do this automatically. We selectively pull from our past experiences to understand what is happening to us now. Moreover, we tend to ignore the vast majority of data that comes our way through all of our senses in favor of a predisposed perspective or perspectives of what is important vs. what is not so much.

I call this process "filtering" and it is a wholly normal process in all human beings. But it is not a good thing in a fighter. A fighter must never be caught thinking about what the opponent "may be doing" but instead needs to know what the opponent "is" doing.

Tier three will now focus on honing the fighters real time flow skills. The training structures are designed to now integrate the reflexive and structural parameters learned in tiers one and two into fluid combative training methods to further enhance real time reading perception within the moment. To learn to truly observe and become "proactive" as opposed to always "reactive."

The fighter will now focus on relaxing within the encounter and responding to both visual and sensory cues to make appropriate responses. In other words, the fighter will now be trying to *get out of his or her way* in terms of thinking and just simply be in the moment. Moment by moment, within the conflux of combat.

Perceptual Training #1 - Stop Hitting

Being able to convert the opponent's attack and force him/her to become immediately defensive is one of the internal martial arts credos. The more quickly you can convert the situation, the higher chance of success in any one encounter.

This drill is a relatively simple construct. To learn to stop any opponent's forward progress and/or momentum is the only goal. And to learn to do this in a direct manner is the methodology.

The fighter is looking to read the actual attack, in whatever form it may be, and then swiftly move to interrupt the opponent's forward momentum

The attacker attempts to punch me in the face with his lead hand. I half step both feet to the right, angling my body, and strike his shoulder.

and technical sequencing in the most expedient way possible. The fighter must learn to ignore the "noise" of combat and instead focus solely on the evolution of the encounter.

Done correctly, this will yield two advantages:

One; pain. The resultant forward impact potential of the fighter's strike will be added to the existing forward momentum of the opponent's body mass thereby magnifying the force.

And two; this same interrupting pattern will also affect the opponent's mind thereby creating a pause in thought processes which translates to opportunity for the fighter.

The attacker attempts a rear hand strike to my head. I angle my right hand inside the arc of his attack, cutting it off and striking his face.

The attacker lunges with his lead hand to my face. I shift my weight to my rear foot and deliver a side kick his frontal right rib cage.

It is suggested to start with single, focused attacks and then progress to combinations in this drill construct. Naturally, a broken rhythm and non adherence to pattern should be the goal of the opponent in training the fighter.

The fighter should be cognizant of the following while performing the base drills:

1) Try to be present.
2) Actually see and not merely think you see.
3) Do not guess.
4) Truly perceive by watching the opponent/handler. See the tell tale chambering of the shoulder. Watch the core rotation just before the limb comes. Look for the placement of the lead foot as the opponent/handler begins to set up each attack. See the eyes flash just prior.

As the fighter progresses, the drill should be ramped up gradually in scope. Single attacks should give way to more of a free form combination structure. But with the focus always on the goal. The opponent/handler must make only strong attacks at first. But once the fighter is more savvy, sometimes disguise the intention with "empty" probes so that the fighter can learn to distinguish the differences.

As always, safety gear is a must (not shown) for this drill.

Perceptual Training #2 - Trapping

One of the most difficult Hsing I concepts to employ within the context of combat is that of a "non resistance" to force. This goes against human nature and requires a great deal of training to "re-program" in terms of a natural response. Our natures are to resist force and/or attempts to control our limbs and bodies.

But this ideal is central to our philosophy of combat and goes hand in hand with the concept of applied trapping of the opponent's limbs upon reception of such force.

There are many kinds of trapping techniques and far too numerous to illustrate them all here. We categorize them into direct and indirect trapping according to the nature of the method employed.

A direct trapping technique is an offensive suppression of an opponent's limb which then will create an opportunity for our other limb to enter the space created. It is applied to either a static guard or as the opponent probes forward into your space.

1a. *In parameter one, my training partner uses an upward striking force against my extended limb.*

1b. *I yield to the force, chambering my core to the right as I do, and hinge my elbow into a low line palm to his ribs.*

2a. *In parameter two, my training partner uses a downward striking force against my extended limb.*

2b. *I again yield to the force, chambering my core to the left as I do, and hinge my elbow into a high line back hand to his face.*

An indirect trapping technique can be either offensive or counter-offensive. Indirect trapping also involves the suppression of a limb but occurs after the opponent has engaged a defensive measure and there is now momentum in his/her limb which can be capitalized upon.

3a. *In parameter three, my training partner uses an inside to outside, lateral striking force against my extended limb.*

4a. *In parameter three, my training partner uses an outside to inside, lateral striking force against my extended limb.*

3b. *I once again yield to the incoming force, twining my limb around in a clockwise direction and chambering my core to the left as I do so.*

4b. *I yield to the force, twining my limb around in a counter-clockwise direction and chambering my core to the right as I do so.*

3c. *I then continue hinging my elbow and tying the movement to the release of core energy in a knife hand attack to his side neck.*

4c. *I then continue hinging my elbow and tying the movement to the release of core energy in a palm strike to his side face.*

The drill represented on the previous two pages is designed to imbue only the latter quality and skill in the fighter, as once this has been learned, a direct trap is a very easy thing to employ.

The emphasis here should be to follow and yield to the force being exerted on your limb by the opponent and then flow into the gap created while you simultaneously employ a controlling trap to the opponent/handler's limb with your non-striking hand.

The fighter should seek to not resist the force given in any way while the opponent bridges against his/her limbs. Instead, the response should follow the incoming pressure and return to centerline via the most expedient circular pathway possible. Usually, this will involve hinging the elbow and rotating the shoulder in the direction of existing momentum. However, the fighter must take care to also involve proper core mechanics for power potential.

The fighter *must not utilize only localized muscle of the limb*. This will be counter-productive.

The fighter should be cognizant of the following while performing the base drills:

1) The fighter should cultivate true perception of whether the force/pressure is up, down, left or right. Or ultimately any combination thereof.
2) The fighter should create a firmly established base but maintain a flexible core strength feeding the limbs in motion.
3) The fighter should incorporate natural feeling footwork during the course of the drill. In most cases, a simple half step will suffice. But as skill and perception progress, certain responses may require angular stepping as well.

The handler/opponent should attempt to utilize a variety of force parameters in order to move the fighters limbs around but this should be done in a gradually progressive manner to train true perception in the fighter.

The handler/opponent should start with the four simple directions of up, down, left and right. Once the fighter gets a handle on these four basic movements, the handler should then gradually increase complexity within the drill. The suggested starting parameters for both the handler and the fighter are depicted on the previous two pages.

Over time, this type of engagement will become second nature to the fighter. He/she will learn to truly read incoming pressure and respond fluidly without resistance. This type of counter movement is extremely fast once trained as there is literally no break in momentum from the moment the opponent touches the fighter's limb to the conclusion of counter impact.

Perceptual Training #3 - Knee/Elbow San Shou (push hands)

One of the most difficult sets of weapons to hone to a natural utilization are the medium ranged knees and elbows. Most fighters will instinctively resort to hand strikes, even in this range. It takes time and effort to make knees and elbows a natural "go to" weapon under pressure.

Therefore, we find it useful to work knee and elbow combinations in an isolate form of push hands for training.

Since push hands starts at a range that is just before clinch, it is a natural fit for working such tools. Such training is not only useful for entering clinch range. It is also useful while caught in the clinch and then finally while escaping same.

3a. *The two combatants begin in a neutral position. Each has the lead hand outside while the rear hand resides inside that of their partner.*

3b. *As the practice commences, I push Brandon's left hand down and to the outside, creating a space for entry of my right elbow.*

3c. *As I enter with my right elbow stroke to Brandon's chest, he shifts back and sticks to my attacking elbow, pushing it across the mid-line.*

3d. *Continuing the flow, I take advantage of the new position of and move my right hand to a neck hook, still controlling his right hand.*

3e. *Once the neck hook is established, I pull Brandon forward while driving my right knee into his inner thigh. I still have his right hand.*

Although this is demonstrated in the photos on the previous page without safety gear, I don't want you to get the wrong idea. When we practice this method, we pad up and go with contact once the basic idea is ingrained.

The fighters should be cognizant of the following while performing this exercise:

1) The fighters should both stay light and sensitive to the ever changing pressures of the clinch and try to keep aware of all potential variables of attack angles.
2) The fighters should also attempt to remain solidly grounded upon striking with either weapon. To "float" while using a knee will likely end up in a takedown.
3) Elbows should be short and sharp. They should not be held distal from the body but instead should stay close for superior leverage and use of the entire core to power them. A good tip for beginners is to learn to bring the hand of the striking elbow in to touch the mid chest while employing. This will tend to encourage the proper utilization.
4) Knees should be delivered no higher than the thigh in almost all circumstances. If the body of the opponent has been completely controlled along with his limbs, then kneeing above this height may be acceptable. But a knee thrown this high will always be at risk to being hooked resulting in takedown.

Start slow and explore potential before increasing the tempo. It will take some time to enter and control the opponent skillfully.

Once the practice has evolved to the point where the fighters understand good basic utilization, the practice should be ramped up by utilizing safety gear.

A good variant to this exercise, once understood, is to start distally from one another and then move forward into clinch range and commence from there. This twist simulates bridging followed by clinch engagement.

Once either fighter is successful in gaining the upper hand in the exchange, separate and start again in the same manner. This can force the fighters to learn to more quickly adapt since the amount of time in "read" is severely reduced with this twist to the drill.

Perceptual Training #4 - Bump & Throw

Many clinches will end up in potential throwing opportunities *if* the fighter is alert to the possibility and grounds his/herself immediately. But the effort to throw needs to be instinctively ingrained for the window of opportunity is small.

The bump & throw drill is a simple construct designed to practice grounding and redirecting "clash" energy into a throwing technique.

4a. *Brandon tries rushing forward on my position with an attempt to tackle me using a bear hug.*

4b. *I shoot my right hand and shoulder in under his left armpit while simultaneously moving inside and seizing his right arm with my left.*

4c. *Stepping to the side at a narrow angle, I wrap my right arm over while pulling with my left. This will result in takedown (not shown).*

Throughout the course of the drill, the handler/opponent should simulate all different kinds of clashes randomly.

The handler should engage with clashes such as direct tackling of the torso (shown above), single and double leg shoots, over-hooking the shoulders, etc.

The fighter should seek to first stabilize by grounding and then, by redirection of the incoming momentum, create an opportunity to throw. Grounding in this context will in most cases simply mean to sink the mass and brace into the incoming force briefly.

And then as soon as there is the resultant recoil in the opponent from the "bump," to proceed with the most expedient path to "throw." This is generally a pathway along a narrow vector just past your position. Trying to move such momentum in a major way is not easily possible. But by mostly preserving the already existing pathway of momentum, it can become quite easy indeed to effectively redirect even the most strong with this method.

The timing is critical. Too long in position, you risk being overwhelmed by the momentum as it comes through you. Move too early and you risk disengagement.

207

Perceptual Training #5 - "Contact" Push Hands

Although this is non-traditional, this is as it sounds.. Taking push hands to the next logical level for fighting development. Safety gear is donned by both combatants (which is not shown), head shots are now incorporated, and clinch combat ending in throw followed by submission ensues.

Obviously, whatever isolate parameters the fighters may wish to focus on can be agreed upon as to scope prior to training. But generally by the time this is ready to be introduced, all isolate ground should have been covered fairly thoroughly and now it is time to test all of these acquired skills in a free form environment.

The fighters are encouraged to engage at all zones and level changes and to do so at will. They should be focusing on staying grounded, balanced and strong throughout each engagement. Learning to preserve center equilibrium is key here.

But still the modality should be relaxed, sensitive and quick in terms of sequencing. The goal is to string together quick inside strokes, takedowns and submissions in each engagement.

5a. *The two combatants begin in a neutral position. Each has the lead hand outside while the rear hand resides inside that of their partner.*

5b. *As the practice commences, I push Brandon's left hand down and to the outside, opening his centerline for possible attack.*

5c. *Brandon wisely yields to the pressure and immediately circles his left palm, trying to attack my right side head.*

5d. *I drop my center and utilize an elbow check to deflect his palm away from the intended target.*

5e. *Upon clearing his hand with my elbow, I seize his left hand with my left and simultaneously deliver a knife hand to his side neck.*

5f. *Brandon quickly ducks and engages his free right hand to push my attack up and over his head.*

5g. *His movement now opens an attack line to my side neck which he attempts to take with his own knife hand.*

5h. *I relinquish my hold on his left hand and drop my body while redirecting his left hand away with my left. And so on it will go.*

The fighters should be cognizant of the following while performing this exercise:

1) This is effectively a clinch and follow through simulation. So each fighter should be trying to work from touch into impact into control. And then into takedown and into submission IF the opportunity presents itself by either design or providence.
2) All manner of strikes, locks, throws and potential submissions should be explored and implemented in a fluid and spontaneous manner.
3) The fighters should not "strength" each other to make a failing technique work. They should instead learn to adapt and change strategies when a technical gambit gets to that point.

In the interest of both safety and exploration of sequencing, the fighters should stop the contest whenever either of them achieves complete control and restart from neutrality once again.

Because of the nature of this exchange, it is highly recommended appropriate safety gear be worn during engagement.

Perceptual Training #6 - Knife Sparring

We like to use knife sparring to further heighten and amalgamate the perceptual skills gained from the previous drills presented in this section.

Knife technique moves so utterly fast that the fighters are forced to become more cognizant of attack zones and positioning for counter attack. Knife play is far faster than any normal hand and foot exchange could ever be and it is therefore a useful tool for this purpose.

Over the years we have used a great many types of knife sparring to keep the activity as real as possible. If not kept real, the exercise loses its merit because the fighters take it too casually and make too many tactical mistakes. This is obviously counter productive to the purpose.

Side Note: Just prior to the release of this work, I discovered a new training tool in the form of a battery powered, electric shock blade that is simply perfect for this type of training. The shock factor makes the exchange very real in that there is actually a consequence for a missed stroke that translates to a good sense of what is real in the interplay.

We do primarily two variations of this drill, with several possible permutations as follows:

Both Armed

As it sounds.. Both fighters are armed in this version and hence the emphasis is on constantly covering your opponent's blade by positioning and alert action while simultaneously looking for opportunities to advance and attack. We allow not only bladed action in such an exchange, but also permit hands and feet, disarming tactics, etc. to liven the exchange.

In a both armed interplay, the fighters should seek to move both hands simultaneously to both cover and attack. One hand should be controlling the opponent's knife hand while the knife wielding hand moves to position for attack.

A. *Against a direct stabbing action to the center, I step outside, check with my left hand and simultaneously cut with my knife hand.*

B. *Against a high inward slash attack, I angle inside and check with my left hand while simultaneously cutting with my knife.*

C. *Against a rising stab, I redirect his attack to the outside while stepping forward and immediately attacking his groin.*

D. *Against a backhand slash, I step to his oblique and check his attack with my left hand while simultaneously slicing his outer knee.*

The exchange should be fluid, with both hands moving in harmony to achieve the objective.

Fighters should also experiment with both single and double edged weapons as such a change in utility can alter the playing field significantly and thus encourage more varied expression. This will also encourage the fighters to think tactically in terms of the possibilities of a single vs. double edged weapon.

This short section is in no way intended to relay "all things about the knife and its usage" but following are a few pointers if you have never engaged with a blade prior:

Stabs vs. slashes: A direct stab from a knife is by far easier to angle away from than is a slash. Therefore, you will find more often a better opportunity to disarm on a stab. By the same token, the flip side of this coin is that slashing on the part of being the attacker is generally a better way to keep your knife.

Knife grip: Grip is an arbitrary decision. An extended grip will allow for the advantage of range but is not as strong. And in contrast, an inverted grip allows for strength, especially of downward arcing stabbing motions but will sacrifice a range equal to the length of the knife blade in question.

Stance Choices: A stance is much like a grip in terms of any respective stance offering pros and cons within exchange. A forward stance (either leg forward) will allow for quick inward and outward mobility and so may suit an aggressive fighter well. However, the exposed front leg becomes a rather inviting target to the opponent.

While in contrast a lateral stance makes for easier rotation and countering and may suit the counter based fighter well. But this stance will make quick forward movement for attack all but impossible.

It is advised that all variables be freely explored for viability.

Perceptual Training #6 - One Unarmed

This is the second primary avenue of training we utilize with a bladed weapon.

In the contest variant where one fighter is unarmed, the engagement emphasis will change by necessity.

Limited engagement should be emphasized on the part of the unarmed fighter. The perspective should be one of trying to stay away from the blade and punish the opponent when it is feasible. Positioning will be of paramount importance.

6a. *Brandon attempts a backhand slash to my throat. I step in and check his elbow with my left and seize his wrist with my right.*

"Disarming should be attempted when presented but not emphasized in this type of engagement."

If there is an opportunity to disarm after some sort of punishment has been inflicted on the opponent it may be then attempted. Or, in the case of a kismet kind of opportunity that presents itself during the exchange, then yes, go ahead and try.

But a disarm should not be the emphasis of the exchange by any means. This is a rather foolish perspective and, once you begin doing this drill regularly, you will soon find out that this is true.

6b. *Moving closer, I fold his elbow into my chest for leverage and use my right hand to begin to bend his arm inward.*

"Disarms should be either accidental or incidental but not the sole focus."

The above point cannot be emphasized enough, but new fighters need to be reminded of this fact often. If you become overly focused on removal of the weapon prior to having compromised the opponent in some way, it is highly likely that the knife will be your undoing.

Remember, with a blade, it only takes one mistake. And the stroke that finishes you doesn't even need to be necessarily forceful, depending on the site.

6c. *I then use the leverage from my chest and both arms to force his own knife back into him.*

R.S.P.C.T. Tier 4 - Conceptual Training

Conceptual Training can be called the real heart of RSPCT in that this tier focuses on development of not only skills related to fighting prowess but emphasizes education on fighting *tactics*.

Anyone can learn to punch another in the face. But it is an awareness and knowledge of tactical overlay that separates the mediocre from the truly adept in the fighting arena.

This tier is broken into three broad areas of training; Bridging, Defending the Bridge and Breaching the Gate.

Each of these areas is quite extensive and require much education and training. And over the following few pages I will attempt to give the reader at least a general idea of that to which I am speaking.

But it must be understood that each area could easily be an entire work in their own right and I am not attempting to put everything I know about these subjects on paper here. I am merely endeavoring to give context for greater understanding.

It is important to explore each area thoroughly by using the aforementioned interchange of the "working phase" and the "live phase" until thoroughly understood.

First, let us define what a bridge is and, perhaps even more importantly, is not;

In the context of martial arts, a bridge is the span of distance connecting the two combatants. It is not physical in the conventional sense necessarily as fighting often happens on open ground. But it is never-the-less very real. One could make a military analogy to "terrain" certainly and this can at times be true, if the engagement happens in a location such as a public parking lot, a restaurant or an office. In other words, a place where there is indeed "terrain."

But for most intents and purposes, the bridge will simply consist of open space between two adversarial parties and this is what I am addressing here. The simple act of getting from where you are currently standing to where your adversary is standing.

So with that said... on with the bridging perspective.

Bridging: The bridging phase of any combative encounter is the most dangerous and should be approached with trepidation against a seasoned adversary.

Sure, it can be said that rushing forward with fierce aggression may catch any one opponent off guard, thereby winning surprise as your ally. But this tactic generally will not work against anyone except the most green of fighters.

Hsu Hong Chi was fond of saying your guard is like a house that you both built and now live within. Since you did indeed build it and have spent considerable time living within this same structure, you know where all the doors and windows are located. And therefore, you know how to stop drafts from getting inside. Obviously, in the "house" metaphor, your doors and windows are the perceived holes in your defenses and the drafts getting inside are references to your opponent's attack strategies.

A good fighter has spent considerable time honing his/her guard position and will have many "go to" moves in their arsenal to defend any obvious attack zone. Therefore, attacking what would be the obvious holes is generally a futile gesture.

There is an old Kungfu saying; *"He who moves first, makes the first mistake."*

If you approach the study of combat seriously with other like minded individuals, it soon becomes apparent that crossing the bridge first is perilous and must be done with a plan. Simply "throwing hands" and *hoping* something will land is a fool's errand at best. And at worst, it will get you seriously hurt in the face of a skilled opponent.

Defending the bridge: It should also be clear that since crossing the bridge is so perilous, then defending that crossing is equally perilous in the face of a well skilled and executed attack plan.

Make a mistake here and the aggressor will have achieved the upper hand. You will now be purely defensive. Which means that in short order you will succumb to the pressure of a skilled adversary. For the longer you stay purely defensive, the higher the probability of failure.

To again use my teacher's house analogy; your doors and windows will be thrown wide open allowing the drafts to pour inside, your foundation will be wrecked and your house will no longer be intact. This is now a condition where you have to play catch up to the aggressor and this is always a losing proposition. Momentum of attack is now on the opponent's side and this can be a very difficult thing to curb.

Breaching the gate: Once crossing the bridge has been successfully achieved, a good fighter will want to stay proximal to the opponent for as long as possible. This ensures the potential to maximize the encounter in favor of the attacker, keeping the opponent on the defensive for as long as can be profitable. Hopefully, until conclusion of the encounter. For to disengage before conclusion will mean that the bridging process will, by necessity, have to start all over again. And this time, the opponent has learned something about your tactics and abilities. They will be better prepared each time this occurs.

It is therefore of extreme importance that multiple tactics and strategies be developed over time so that the fighter has contingencies available and thus becomes less predictable. The study of tactics must take precedence in training once basic skills have been ingrained if the fighter hopes to achieve a level that is truly superlative.

Conceptual Training - Bridging through Combination

Combination attacks need to follow some fairly simple rules but beyond that, the only real limitation on such attacks are the fighter's own physical prowess, knowledge base and skill.

The general rules of combination bridging are only two; the rule of opposites and the rule of broken rhythm.

The rule of opposites is succinctly stated below in the following manner:

1) High/Low/High or Low/High/Low
2) Right/Left/Right or Left/Right/Left
3) Inside/Outside/Inside or Outside/Inside/Outside
4) Hand/Foot/Hand or Foot/Hand/Foot

2a. *A simple example of opposites combined with broken rhythm begins with a low line round kick to Alex's lower thigh.*

1a. *A simple example of opposites beginning with a set up utilizing a skipping low line left side kick to Alex's knee.*

2b. *Then moves to a high right palm strike toward his left ear to draw the guard upward and outward to engage.*

1b. *Followed by a right spinning back thrust kick to the mid-line as he attempts to move forward after the initial bridging tactic.*

2c. *Following up by wrapping the hand to control his parry and following with a left uppercut to the exposed zone.*

Broken rhythm, on the other hand, would be a cadence change. But such a change may be one of speed, tempo or utility. For example:

1) Two short lefts followed by a right.
2) Two quick hand strikes followed by a slower, long turning back kick.
3) Two rights on a returning circular or figure eight pathway (i.e. backfist into palm).
4) Two low line kicks from the same leg.
5) Two quick blows followed by a pause (to invite the opponent's counter). Which is then followed by implemented slipping to set up a counter movement; etc.

All the above examples will create a change in cadence which alters perception on the part of the opponent. And this is the goal.

3a. *A quick lead is thrown inside the guard to Alex's right cheek in order to draw a natural deflection across center.*

3b. *A rapid secondary follow up is thrown to Alex's now exposed left side head to which he responds by ducking downward.*

3c. *Feeling that he now has advantage, Alex rises up to my outside and attacks with a hook punch to my exposed head. I slip downward.*

3d. *And then roll to the outside as his hook punch momentum carries him past my centerline.*

3e. *I then hammer him with a straight overhand right, controlling his left arm as I move toward him.*

216

Opposites can be employed quite effectively by themselves in a combination attack as can a broken rhythm. But utilizing opposites *with* broken rhythm is a very easy way indeed to create perceptual problems in the opponent giving rise to opportunity.

There is nothing wrong with sticking to basics as a novice fighter until better skills are developed. Simple low/high/low and high/low/high tactics are easy to learn and adapt. But once basics have been understood, it is time to create sequences that are more deceptive in application.

4a. *I again attack with a quick left lead to Alex's high centerline. He checks off with his lead guard hand.*

A good combination attack will exploit several zones utilizing a blend of opposites and broken rhythm. A combination that exploits a low/high/low simultaneously with a right/left/right has a better chance of succeeding than a combination which utilizes only one of these parameters.

4b. *Alex then pushes down on my attacking hand, opening a space for his return right. I begin to slip away, drawing him further inward.*

4c. *I then complete my weave moving to his oblique right in the process setting up my counter movement.*

4d. *I now deliver a strong left to his head while shifting my body mass into him.*

4e. *Followed with a shift back the other way for a strong right finish.*

Likewise, a combination that employs three paradigms of opposites such as high/low/high in conjunction with both right/left/right *plus* inside/outside/inside has a much higher probability of success than the one that conjoins two paradigms.

You can see where this is leading by now but it still needs to be said... the goal of combination training is to learn to enjoin as many paradigms as possible into one sequence.

If you can create combinations that are an amalgam of multiple opposites *in addition* to infusing broken rhythm *and* adaptable footwork, angle of insertion *and* level changes then you have something very difficult to interpret indeed.

Any combination idea should be immediately tested with a less than cooperative opponent to determine viability before devoting time to hone the idea. Preferably, this stage is performed under the watchful eye of a coach to ensure that the correct determination is achieved.

Once a combination passes initial scrutiny, it should be gradually honed and tested over time, with as many uncooperative opponents as is feasible to make it your own.

And then, when the kinks have been worked out, that same combination should be tested against a very resistant opponent who is attempting at every opportunity to run their own combination ideas on YOU.

You will never truly know what is effective if you do not test it against those who are diligently trying to stop you from employing same.

When working combinations, the fighter should be cognizant of the following:

1) Simple works. Complex is never a good idea. With that said, "complex" is a relative term which will change many times over as the fighter evolves. What is complex today may become child's play tomorrow.
2) Remember, there is no "hoping" things will land. You work for the shot. You cultivate proper distance, timing and precise execution. You do not just "throw hands."
3) Learn the effective distance of your respective and various tools. The most common error made by new fighters is that of trying to attack from too far outside. You must learn to "stalk" your opponent and move on *your* timing, not his/hers.
4) Never.. EVER.. Look at a target zone before attacking. Learnt to "see" without ever looking directly AT anything.

A necessary attribute for a fighter is well trained peripheral and diffused, visual awareness.

Conceptual Training - Bridging through Progression

A progressive attack seeks to engage the opponent directly and provoke a specific response through engagement. This response will then allow the progressive attack to continue moving forward into the opponent's space.

Progressive attacks utilize more sophisticated structures than do combination attacks. Trapping and seizing skills are a staple of progressive bridging and so the fighter will have need to more fully develop his/her sense of touch to make progressive attack strategies work effectively.

Bridging through progression requires a more refined skill base to execute successfully. The fighter must have a good working knowledge of tactical positioning and angles of insertion. Good footwork is essential. And a real understanding of normal human response under threat. As subtle psychology is also part of any progressive attack strategy.

In a progressive attack, the fighter will engage the opponent actively; such as to punch forward under the guard, thereby drawing a defensive downdraft of the opponent's guard, and thus creating opportunity to trap that limb and progress forward.

This approach is illustrated in example "1a and b" below.

1a. *I deliver a quick lead right under Alex's guard. He takes the bait by dropping his lead guard to cover.*

1b. *His response allows me to now trap and progress my right hand forward in a secondary attack to his head.*

There are, of course, numerous permutations on the above theme. The fighter can employ a high line entry and then trap to expose the low line. You can move from right to left, or from left to right, utilizing the initial entry and response to proceed.

Or, the initial entry can be done on an oblique angle of insertion after first stepping toward the outside of the guard. You would first drive the initial blow in under the guard as entry is achieved on a tangent angle from outside and then, upon the opponent's engagement of that limb, float the attack in one continuous circle to another attack zone immediately above the point of engagement e.g. the head.

This second example is illustrated in sequence "2a and b" immediately below.

2a. *From an outside set up, I quickly step across center and dive my right fist under his guard. This draws a cover response from Alex.*

2b. *My right hand never stops moving. It floats off his downward pressure and progresses over the top into a palm strike to the head.*

3a. *I quickly seize Alex's lead guard hand and shoot a drilling fist toward his face, forcing him to engage his secondary.*

Progressive equates to aggressive.

Stride forward and seize the opponent's lead and when he/she moves to resist, use a direct grab control on the first limb forcing a panic response from the opposite limb. Then convert to control of the second limb and continue to move forward obliquely to the flank creating good opportunity and getting away from his opposite limb.

This strategy is illustrated in example "3a, b and c" on this page.

3b. *I will now seize his secondary and step obliquely, simultaneously delivering a palm strike to his back brain.*

3c. *I then release my grab on Alex's right arm and smash my right palm into his face, taking advantage of his forward momentum.*

Progressive bridging attacks can be extremely effective if the base skill and knowledge is already in the fighter. But the fighter must have not only this. He/she must possess bravery to make this method work.

Progressive bridging will require a comfortable confidence in getting inside and staying close to the opponent. And this means you are also at risk while operating this strategy.

Conceptual Training - Bridging through Cutback

A "cutback" is a term we use in my school to describe an interplay of angular stepping to achieve a positional advantage. A cutback can be performed to either the inside (by first setting up from outside) or also to the outside (by first setting up to the inside). It is also possible to conjoin the two to achieve an entry, a primary strike and a follow up strike in one sequence.

A cutback must, by utility, cause the opponent to shift upon the initial footwork phase. And then a swift movement must be made as the opponent shifts to create a less measured response, setting up the actual attack.

1a. *I make my first move by crossing from the outside to the inside and threatening Alex's face which forces him to check off the attack.*

1b. *I now quickly step to his flank and attack his exposed ribs, forcing a panic response of his left arm to cover.*

1c. *I then move forward again angling inside and crossing into his centerline while delivering a right palm strike to his head.*

An easy way to accomplish this is just to start purposefully angling to the opponent's flank until they begin to feel pressured by your position and the threat of the angle. Once they feel the need to adjust their centerline, and they will, you can make your initial cutback.

This first cutback movement must be believable to make the sequence work. You have to sell it! And the best way to do this is to make it real.

Remember, we don't feint. We attack. And we never attack in an empty way. An empty attack can be ignored and this achieves nothing.

A real attack cannot possibly be interpreted as empty. And if the opponent does not respond the way you would have liked.. Oh well, you strike with the first and go from there.

For a cutback to work as intended, distance is critical. And the most common mistake most fighters make with this method is moving from too far out in terms of range.

You must be close enough that you can reach the opponent on the second step. This is the only way to ensure a response that you can exploit.

Any attack through cutback must by necessity be delivered on a narrow angular vector off the opponent's centerline. I recommend a 30 degree angle for such utility.

If a wider angle is employed you will more than likely find the opponent stepping into you in mid stride and this is not desirable.

Oftentimes, a good cutback attack done at the proper angle and distance will have an added advantage of causing the opponent's vision to be partially occluded by his own defenses.

The example of "2 a, b and c" at the right of this page shows just such a tactic. The angle I choose for delivery in "2b" partially occludes Alex's vision to his lower line which then allows my round kick to his inner thigh to slip in unseen. Or at least, seen too late.

Study the "cutback" well. It can be a very effective strategy.

2a. *I again cut from the outside to cross the centerline drawing Alex's guard hand across and exposing an angle of attack on his flank.*

2b. *I quickly step to his flank and threaten his face. Alex wisely moves his lead hand back to check off this second attack.*

2c. *I take advantage of his obscured line of sight and slide a round kick up underneath to his inner thigh.*

Conceptual Training - Bridging through Invitation

In the Art of War, Sun Tzu talks about presenting a false front to the enemy in order to lure him/her into your terrain to gain advantage.

The I Ching trigrams that depict both broken and solid lines have also been likened to battle strategy. In this case it would be one broken line in front of two solid lines, equaling apparent weakness hiding true strength.

Suffice it to say that this notion has been around in one form or another for militaristic purposes for a very long time indeed.

Bridging through invitation is a tactic of presenting what appears to be a "too good to pass up" opening to the opponent and when he/she takes the bait,

1a. *In the midst of combat, I suddenly part my arms and expose my centerline inviting Alex to take advantage of my mistake.*

1b. *As Alex launches forward into a strong centerline crushing fist, I perform a rear cross step and parry his limb in the process.*

1c. *The movement continues with my left foot now swiftly stepping forward to complete my flanking position.*

1d. *Now the momentum of the two steps and torque of my waist is transferred into a palm strike to Alex's bladder.*

1e. *I then trap his limb and simultaneously deliver a crossing elbow to his exposed back brain to complete the sequence.*

223

moving adroitly to an advantageous position to seal the outcome in your favor. Such a tactic requires both perfect timing and position in relation to the opponent to be successful. To work, this gambit must appear weak but not so obviously weak to be transparent. Being successful with "bridging by invitation" requires a good *performance* on the part of the fighter executing this strategy.

In a military engagement, this tactic can be employed at the outset when the enemy is first approaching your current position. But this is not appropriate in singular engagements.

For singular combat, this is a tactic that is best employed in the heat of the moment when tensions are already running high. You want to ramp up the opponent's mind and perceptions so that they are in a truly combative mode, thinking to destroy.

You do not want their minds in a place where they are still calm, measured and calculating. Therefore, this type of tactic is *not* generally something to be done when the fight is just beginning. (Unless of course the opponent is deemed less than worthy, in which case it may still be employed even at the outset).

2a. *I seize Alex's lead guard and step into him, striking toward his head with my right fist, forcing a quick parry.*

2b. *In rapid succession, I disengage from his lead hand and deliver a left fist to the same target zone. Alex rotates and recovers his center.*

2c. *I then quickly drop my hands inviting his counter. Since he has recovered his center, he feels in control and takes the shot.*

2d. *I fade and counter with a low side kick to Alex's his knee. My range completely negates his attack in the process.*

224

When adrenaline is running high, reason is less on the forefront in most fighter's minds and they are running more or less on base instincts. So when you present your head to them by dropping your guard or you exposes your centerline to them by separating your guard, they will likely take the invitation as it is presented. It is simply too difficult to resist.

Oftentimes, a quick and punishing flurry followed by a presented opening can work well in this manner. The pressure put on the opponent, ramping up their defenses and their minds followed by what seems to be a mistake, an obvious opening, fuels their desire to respond.

Such as the example on the previous page where a quick one, two followed by a strategic fade and deliberate dropping of the guard is employed to draw the opponent into a high line attack.

Once the bait is taken, a stop kick is employed to interrupt both the momentum and mind of the opponent which will then lead to easy follow up techniques.

Another variation of this method is to repetitively attack the same zone with the same technique with the guard held intact, letting the opponent read the sequence and pick up on the physical cues. Then deliberately enter with a dropped guard, inviting the response gleaned on the part of the opponent and capitalizing.

For example: Jab, cross, front kick twice. Each time, keep your guard up when delivering and recovering from your kick. The opponent will be reading your cadence and looking for a return path after the kick which will not be there because of your high and maintained guard. Then, on the third sequence, deliberately step back and drop your guard after the front kick. When the opponent tries to go for what is perceived as a mistake and a resultant open high line, quickly step obliquely, redirect his limb and punish from the side.

Such tactics must be contrived and polished sequences that have been refined many times over in combat to be reliable. But once this is the case, they can be a very effective tool.

Remember, you are capitalizing on human psychology. You need to understand how a fighter's mind is processing data mid-fight to utilizes such tactics effectively. Experimentation ahead of the fact is an absolute must. Do not expect to be successful the first time you try such a tactic. You must be willing to "invest in loss" to learn such methods.

Conceptual Training - Bridging through Provocation

<u>Provoke;</u>   1. To incite to anger or resentment.   2. To stir or incite to action; arouse. 3. To bring on by inciting: *provoke a fight.*

Bridging through provocation is one of my personal favorite strategies. To utilize this method, great speed and a healthy degree of confidence in one's abilities are necessary components. My late teacher, Hsu Hong Chi used to refer to this method as "touch, go, kiss" at times and it was also one of his favorite tactics.

Provocation can take many forms in terms of actual usage and expression, but the central idea and theme remains the same. The fighter will passively (meaning without true commitment) engage the opponent, provoking a response. This response is then capitalized on in a continued sequence of attack.

Hsing I's Tsuan (drilling) fist is a good example of provocation. The first hand is passively lain onto the lead of the opponent's guard. And then, when the opponent attempts to stabilize the guard, the lead is jerked downward with sudden force exposing the jaw to the uppercut.

Or in the alternative if, after you pressure his lead guard hand, the opponent chooses to punch with the other hand instead... that hand is then subsequently wrapped and pulled downward in the same manner, also exposing the jaw to the secondary uppercut movement. Either way, if done correctly, you win.

When I was competing in Taiwan in the 70's, I fought a lot of Muay Thai based fighters. And they do love that round kick of theirs. They love it so much. And they have so much faith in it that if you give them the opportunity, they just

1a. *To provoke Alex, I quickly move in and pressure his lead guard hand with my own. He naturally presses back in response.*

1b. *Upon feeling the return pressure I seek in his response, I dive my same right hand quickly down to his ribs. He instinctively follows.*

1c. *I then come quickly over the top with my left palm to his head in one fluid sequence of attack. This is a simple provocation.*

can't seem to help themselves. And they have to take it as they see it presented to them. They simply can't seem to override that instinct very easily.

So when facing one of their ilk I used to stride forward, guard held high and probing theirs, deliberately exposing my ribs to that round kick attack of theirs. Once taken I would quickly turn and underhook their leg, pinning it to my body, drop and elbow on their knee, back hand their face and then reap their support leg. Oftentimes, they did not get back up. And if they did, psychologically the fight was already mine.

The provocation tactic illustrated on the previous page is one of a designed capitalization on the sensory. Passively touching the opponent's guard with moderate pressure and then suddenly diving underneath will provoke an instinctive, mechanical response of lowering that hand to follow. It is psychologically impossible to not do so given the sensory input. This then opens the high line of attack which is subsequently capitalized on with a swift secondary stroke of the opposite hand. Done correctly, the sequence is seamless and therefore effective.

Provocation is a way to preserve your guard while encroaching on the opponent's space. You do not come out of "your house" but instead force him/her to leave theirs to engage. This gives a useful advantage if understood completely.

There are many ways to construct a provocation based strategy. And they all have the same governing principle. You use one limb to encroach upon the opponent's space, what we call the "sphere of influence." At the same time, you are both preserving your defenses/guard *and* you are offering up what appears to be a good avenue of attack to the opponent.

One of my favorite quotes from old writings, a statement attributed to one of our Hsing I lineage ancestors, Li T'sun I, is; "When Li was challenged, he put forth his hand, strode forward easily and achieved his objective."

Sounds pretty much the same, does it not? Touch, go, kiss?

Conceptual Training - Reading the Stance

Reading the opponent's stance to determine possible exploitation should become a primary component of further training.

Our general guideline states; "Attack a low stance, sweep a high stance" which is sound advice. But there are many other points of consideration that must be learned as well.

1a. *Alex presents a deep stance, toe inward. Strong and able to move under me for throw. But not especially mobile against low line attack.*

1b. *In this case a good option would be a cross kick to the knee. It will fold his stance and keep him from moving under me.*

The following is by no means meant to be a complete list, but presented are a few points of consideration in relation to general stance and/or footwork. All of these and more should be studied and committed to the fighter's memory. Such tendencies and transitions must be observed on the fly and in context. And then exploited with appropriate counter strategies.

1) An "on the balls of the feet" stance (boxing, kickboxing, muay thai) is highly mobile but weak against sweep or throw.
2) The shuffling/bouncing footwork of the same boxing, kickboxing crowd can be timed on any forward step presenting a vulnerable knee.
3) A feet flat, low center of gravity stance (wrestling) is strong and resistant to takedown. But it is less mobile and can be exploited by attack to the very low line.
4) A forward weighted stance (many karate styles) places the opponent's hands closer, but leaves the lead knee vulnerable to counter attack by low side, front, round or cross kicks.
5) A side horse (ridiculous for actual fighting) leaves the opponent's lead knee vulnerable as in #4 and, in addition, makes it easy to get to the rear flank.
6) A rear weighted stance (Hsing I) is protected against sweep or easy attack to the low line of the lead leg. And it is aptly suited for quick forward mobility. There is no "but" here. Be careful when you face this stance.
7) A toe-out step across the centerline of the opponent in transition is almost always an early indicator of a round kick in the offing.
8) A toe-in step in transition almost always indicates a spinning back hand or a spinning back thrust kick in the offing.

228

9) A toe-in, weight forward stance will allow a swift passing of the guard to flank with the right technical sequencing. See illustration "2a, b and c."

2a. *Alex presents a high stance, front toe turned inward, rear heel raised. Quick for moving forward into my position.*

A good fighter must learn to recognize that all true attacks come from the feet and that both foot placement and stance orientation matter a great deal in terms of possible available avenues of exploitation. This should be studied at great length in live environments under the watchful eyes of a coach.

2b. *I quickly threaten the high line to force him to engage his lead hand for defense, keeping his mind off of moving forward.*

2c. *I then quickly step obliquely pressuring his defending limb to gain advantage. This stance is not suitable for a quick turn to his outside.*

To not study stance and the resulting possible avenues of expression is to miss vital, valuable and essential information in the face of an encounter.

This is especially true in the street, where it is likely that you will be dealing with more than one adversary at any given time. Being able to determine potential orientation can make the difference between success and failure.

Time factors are limited and quick exploitation becomes of paramount importance. Therefore, the ability to size up weakness or available avenues of attack and then implement the most appropriate tactical strategies in exploitation becomes critical to survival.

Conceptual Training - Defending the Bridge through Stop Hitting

Once, while being interviewed by Inside Kung Fu magazine about my teams and their fighting prowess in the 90's, the editor at that time asked me to clarify a statement I had made about bridging in general. The statement had to do with allowing the enemy to bridge if he/she wanted to do so and not attempting to stop that from happening. He thought I had misspoke but I then assured him that I had not made any error. I went on to say that if the enemy wished to do that job for us, we would happily allow that to happen.

This is for the reasons I have already mentioned earlier. It is the most difficult and peril ridden phase of the encounter. And if we can stay "in our house" while the opponent comes out of theirs... Well, that is just fine with us. We will attack once engagement is met.

1a. *As Alex lunges left to my face, I stop his momentum by shearing off with my right hand while striking his shoulder well with my left.*

1b. *I then capitalize on the stop by following up with a strong right palm to his head from my prior position.*

The immediate goal in defending any bridge is to *not defend*. Instead, a fighter should seek to convert the tide of the engagement to one of attack as soon as possible.

The attacker always has the advantage in terms of speed as he/she has only two necessary mental processes for any one attack. One, to see the opening. And two, to move toward that same opening. The defender must see the attack, interpret the trajectory and then respond. Three mental processes to two. The defender will always be a split second behind.

Therefore, defending for the sake of defending is futile and will cause a loss in the engagement sooner or later. The goal should be to both interrupt the mind and momentum of the opponent, converting same to your favor as soon as possible.

A good stop accomplishes both these tasks. A well placed stop should arrest the forward progress of either the limb in question or the body outright. And the resultant pain will then interrupt the opponent's mind thereby allowing you a few tenths of a second for the purpose of exploiting the stop and following up. Both a limb and body example of stop are presented in illustration on this and the subsequent pages. The stop is the precursor. Follow up is a necessity.

There is an old saying in internal martial arts; "He who moves first, makes the first mistake." My teacher used to talk about this a lot.

He would say that everyone always told him how they would really love to see two master level practitioners fight. He would laugh and say; "No. This-ah boring." Then he would compare such an encounter to baseball, saying if you had ever seen professional baseball being played vs. seeing little league baseball being played. "Little league more fun." he would say, "They make a lot of mistake. So more fun watch."

2a. *As Alex lunges right, I intercept and seize his right hand and stop his momentum by chambering and delivering a front kick to his ribs.*

2b. *As Alex attempts a follow up left strike, I trap with my lead and enter to his flank, delivering a left palm strike to his face.*

2c. *I then follow up with a crossing right elbow to his expose back brain, completing the stop sequence.*

"Major league less fun." he would go on, "Throw, hit, catch, out. Throw, hit, catch, out. This-uh boring. Same, same have two master stay fight. Lot of look each other. Not much moving. Then finally, one move and the other kill he. Finish. Boring."

This is the essence of the stop hit. Wait, watch, move to intercept and turn the tables on the opponent. Let them "make the first mistake" and then capitalize by swiftly moving on the opening they create by making their attack.

Offense, or in this case, counter-offense truly is the best defense. Seek to move forward easily. Move back only as a strategic ploy in order to then move forward. Flow into the gap created by the opponent's attack and exploit to your advantage.

Conceptual Training - Defending the Bridge through Triangle Stepping

Triangle stepping is a specific patterned footwork taught within our internal martial arts system.

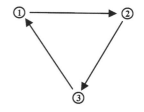

If done properly, it can be a useful ploy in countering the opponent's attempts to encroach upon your space.

This tactic is simple in principle, but it does require precision and a very established sense of timing in actual practical usage.

To apply this pattern in a combative exchange, the fighter will first deliberately step obliquely (1), flanking the opponent as the lead technique is thrown.

Once there, the fighter will wait briefly, strategically drawing the secondary attack. Then, as the opponent's secondary materializes, the fighter will again step obliquely across the grain (2) flanking the opponent once again.

1a. *As Brandon attacks right, I have stepped to his oblique while checking his attacking limb, waiting for the secondary.*

1b. *As Brandon realigns his center to deliver a left follow up to my new position, I quickly step to his opposite flank, checking and waiting.*

1c. *I then fade back a step and drop my hands, inviting him to pursue my position, leading his mind.*

1d. *As he takes the bait with a high right hand, I perform my foot change and enter to his right flank, checking and striking as I do.*

This second positional flanking will now be quickly followed with a fade back to the original starting point (3) to draw the opponent's tertiary (to maximize potential, it can be useful to drop one's guard at this juncture so that the obvious high line zone is taken).

Once the opponent pursues with a tertiary attack, the fighter will make a "half foot change" to gain sudden momentum back to the first position (1). This time, however, a counter-attack sequence will be initiated upon entry.

The basic concept is illustrated on the prior page. As is true with all useful things, this tactic will require practice to implement successfully.

To utilize triangle stepping in a effective and efficient (kinetically speaking) manner, the fighter needs to be cognizant of a few key points;

1) The fighter needs to keep good balance at all times within the footwork pattern.
2) The fighter needs to keep an attitude (balance point) that is slightly forward, even when moving to the rear from position 2 to 3. A forward attitude will allow for a quick return.
3) If your attitude (balance point) begins to move toward the rear, the resultant change will be too slow and cumbersome to be of any real use.

A good way to practice this footwork in terms of understanding the proper attitude (balance point) is to practice performing the foot change by itself first without the angular stepping and do not actually put the second foot down right away. If your attitude is proper, you should have a feeling that you will fall flat on your face if you do not quickly position the new foot forward. If you can stand on the one foot without this sensation, your attitude is too far to the rear.

You can then augment the kinetic potential further in the foot change itself by standing in a front stance, with your hands against a heavy bag. Change feet and immediately push the bag forward when the changing foot hits the floor. Kinetic potential should be transferred almost instantaneously from the changing foot through your hands, moving the bag strongly. This should happen just slightly before your new forward foot touches down. (Note that this is an exercise only. In true usage, you want the new forward foot to hit the ground just as you strike).

Once you have mastered the basic mechanics of the foot change and proper attitude, take the full pattern out for a test drive or two before trying it in combative circumstances. If you do your homework, it will swiftly become a viable tool within your strategic arsenal.

Conceptual Training - Defending the Bridge through "Dog Chase"

"Dog Chase" is one of the central concepts within our internal martial arts. And one that I have experienced in my lifetime thousands of times. Of course, my teacher instructed me on this notion and taught me to apply it in a combative context. And that is certainly *one* avenue of experience for yours truly.

But I have also raised and kept German Shepard dogs for most of my life and, as a result, I have had countless hours of direct experience and loads of fun with my dogs through the years with regard to this concept.

As discussed earlier, if you have ever played with a large dog, you have experienced the concept of "dog chase." A big dog will bring a toy to you and dare you to take it from him. When you do, he will move just out of your reach. And then, as you withdraw your hand from the attempt, he will follow your hand right back in again.

1a. *As Brandon lunges right to my face, I step my rear foot back a bit and shift my weight away from the attack, loading my thrust potential.*

1b. *As he withdraws his limb, I follow in on the heels of his withdrawal controlling the limb and delivering a high crossing elbow.*

As mentioned above and previously, Dog Chase is a central core method for us and, as such, is incorporated into several of the tier one reflexive drills of RSPCT. So we begin training the concept very early on in the fighter's developmental phase.

To exercise this strategy the fighter must develop an excellent sense of proper distance and must become adept at staying proximal to the opponent at all times. This means the fighter must be comfortable being close to his/her opponent's attacks.

Once developed, the strategy can be effective against a variety of different leads. Short, long, angular or circular... all can be dealt with by employing this skill once it has become fully developed in the fighter.

This technique is especially useful against a quick opponent that attempts to get in and out of your influence fast. The Dog Chase method, once polished, can allow you to catch such an opponent on their withdrawal and turn the tables.

Conceptual Training - Defending the Bridge through Grounding

Wrestling/grappling has been a part of the martial tradition for thousands of years. We have always had to deal with attempted takedowns in any true fighting context and we have always trained for such contingencies.

But in the recent climate of mixed martial arts, wrestling/grappling has experienced a sort of resurgence in popularity. And, as a result, far more opponents in the modern climate are prone to attempting such takedowns as a first gambit strategy than ever before. This has become such a popular go to strategy that the phrase "ground and pound" is now a staple of the mixed martial arts vernacular. Since so many opponents are predisposed in their attempt to take you down within the initial context of engagement, it is essential to develop solid grounding skills to be able to mitigate such tactics.

2a. *As Alex attempts a shoot, I brace to receive inserting my right hand inside and under his left while placing my left hand on his head.*

2b. *I then allow his momentum to carry past me and overturn his body by lifting his left shoulder and pressing down on his head.*

To "ground" an incoming opponent's attempt at a takedown, you must understand the nature of force vectors and physics. You cannot stop such momentum from happening, but you can learn to direct momentum in a productive manner.

The fighter must learn to quickly drop his/her mass, thus lowering their center of gravity to receive the incoming force. And then quickly and skillfully redirect the opponent's momentum in a narrow line to the side and behind.

Simply put, the opponent's momentum is directed down and through you in an effort to bowl you over to the rear. You cannot *stop* this. The forces involved are too great and if you try to stop such force, you will most certainly fail.

So the fighter will allow the established momentum to take its natural course with only slight modification. This is the most efficient course of action and can be done with very little strength in the effort. Done correctly, the fighter will be in superior position for strike or whatever other tactic they may prefer in the circumstance at hand.

Conceptual Training - Defending the Bridge through Sticking

Sticking is a concept that is not unique to the internal martial arts by any means. But it is one

1a. *Alex attacks with a high right hand to my face. I ward off the blow by a narrow turn of my core and engage my lead guard hand.*

1b. *Alex then uses an inverted fist to my ribs. I hinge my elbow and stick to the second movement following it downward from outside.*

1c. *Alex progresses his attack by circling his right fist upward. I once again stick by following the trajectory, this time on the inside.*

1d. *I now attack with a backhand strike to the face while controlling Alex's right hand. He is forced to engage his secondary to defend.*

1e. *I move to indirect trap from underneath, suppressing Alex's left forearm across his centerline in the process.*

1f. *I now have both his hands to his right side and with his left side undefended, I enter with a knife hand strike to his neck.*

that we spend a great deal of time honing for available use. Other arts use sticking as well. Judo, Aikido and yes, wrestling based arts also use sticking in their own contexts.

Human beings have a remarkable sense of touch. Most current estimates place approximately 2500 nerve receptors per square centimeter in a human fingertip. And because we are "tool users," a great deal of our brains are tied directly to our hands.

It only makes good sense to put that relationship to use in a positive context for martial arts. And internal martial arts has incorporated this basic fact into our training for hundreds of years.

For internal martial artists, sticking qualities are developed through endless hours of push hands training. For the sense of touch, once properly trained, cannot easily be fooled. Whereas a fighter who is reliant on visual acuity can be feinted easily out of position, a fighter who has been trained well in sticking skills is not so easily tricked.

Sticking can allow a well trained proponent to literally "smother" an opponent's movements as they are happening. Virtually at the very moment the opponent has an idea, it can be read through the touch we have on their bodies. Their body core will give away their intention as it is evolving and we can learn to read that intention through contact with our hands and limbs.

To try to engage someone who possesses truly high caliber sticking skills can feel at times as if you are trying to step, strike and kick your way through molasses.

To demonstrate such skills, my teacher used to place his hand lightly on one of ours, close his eyes and then dare us to try and pull our hand away by any means we could. We would try and try, even try stepping quickly away while pulling our hand from his. But none of us could ever succeed. His hand would stay on ours no matter what we did to pull it away. I can now do this same demonstration as any of my own students can attest.

Sticking can be useful against many types of attack but it is an essential skill to have against a fighter that understand multiple attacks with the same hand via circular return pathway. If you do not possess such skill, you will be hard pressed to defend against such an adversary.

Remember, sticking skills are based upon developing sensory touch. You cannot "muscle" your way through such a tactic. You must remain light, sensitive and alert to changing pressures that emanate from the opponent's limbs and body core.

My teacher used to remark when talking about such his own sticking skills (which were in a word, exemplary); "I never lead. I only reflect or follow."

In trying to develop sticking skills to a zenith of ability, those are words to live by indeed.

Conceptual Training - Breaching the Gate through the Nine Gates Theory

This concept it talked about earlier in this work as it is part of the "24 stems." The nine gates are offensive targeting zones designed to either cross, separate or coalesce the opponent's guard to one side. The locations are delineated in that chapter.

Again, the perspective is that by initiating one's attack sequences to the corners, one can expect to expose the center zones of the body to secondary and tertiary attacks.

As can be seen on this page, attacking a central zone leaves too many possible defensive actions to be able to plot a reasonable follow up sequence. The opponent's response becomes wholly unpredictable which then places the context into the realm of "I hope this lands" and this is unacceptable.

A. Against a left lead, Alex can choose to parry with his left hand.

B. Against a left lead, Alex can choose to parry with his right hand.

C. Against the same left lead, he can choose to simply evade to his left.

D. Or he can choose to evade to his right against this attack.

E. He can even choose to simply move away. All valid choices against this left lead to the high line. And there are others as well.

238

Attacking the corner zones will necessitate one of two options on the part of the opponent. Either a direct engagement or an evasive maneuver which will be limited in scope. If zone three is attacked such as in the examples below, the opponent is now limited to a direct engagement with either hand (such as illustrated below). Or, the opponent is limited to evasive movement either to the rear or toward his right side. In other words, he is limited to four predictable responses all of which will yield a zone two, five or eight opening immediately thereafter.

In the event that the attack is sloppy, and the opponent is able to slip underneath, you will still likely have a centerline zone available on secondary. Of course, timing the attack well, utilizing proper distance and angle of insertion so that the opponent is more pressured to directly engage your primary attack is more likely to succeed in a secondary opening.

Sometimes, a skilled opponent must be attacked at two divergent corner zones with the primary and secondary attacks to expose a central zone for the tertiary attack. For example; a right round kick into zone nine followed by a high line right to zone three will yield a centerline target for the tertiary attack regardless of which hand or cover strategy the opponent employs.

The best way for the fighter to develop true understanding of the nine gates theory is to explore potential options in live scenarios to find out what works and what doesn't work. The practice should be gradually ramped up and protective gear worn so that true response is logged and understood.

It is also helpful to have the watchful eye of a coach supervising for the most objective feedback possible.

1c. *Either of these responses will now leave zone five open for my secondary attack. This is the basic idea of the nine gates strategy.*

1a. *In this example, I specifically attack Alex's number threes zone with a knife hand. He can still parry left but cannot evade left.*

1b. *It is less likely that he will parry right given this same attack, but if he does, the same zone number five will still be open.*

Over time, the fighter will begin to understand how certain movement will trigger predictable, patterned responses and this knowledge can then be used to regularly and efficiently exploit such habits in the opponent. Repetition is key.

Conceptual Training - Breaching the Gate through Folding

Folding is the concept of learning to blend different ranged weapons seamlessly as you engage and close on the opponent. Or, in the alternative, as you and your opponent disengage and move away from one another (we call the latter "unfolding").

1a. *As Brandon and I close into clinch range, I redirect his overhand right and immediately strike his low line.*

When learned and implemented correctly, folding is one of the skills that make for old sayings about Hsing I practitioners. Sayings like; "feels like walking into a saw blade," or, "It feels like he has more than just two arms and two legs. I felt like I was in the grips of an octopus."

Folding in combative expression is accomplished by utilizing whatever defensive action may be offered up by the opponent as impetus to change to the next weapon in the chain. Hand folds to

1b. *Continuing the flow of the counter sequence I fold my elbow into his high line, still controlling his right limb.*

1c. *The elbow stroke is turned into a neck hook and his body is cranked downward using both my hands for positioning.*

1d. *A right knee strike is now delivered to his head, continuing the folding process of the counter sequence.*

1e. *And now a final elbow is delivered to the back brain completing the flow of this sequence.*

elbow when the hand has either been parried, or the hand strike has been successful, creating the next logical weapon/target relationship. Elbow folds to knee and knee back to elbow as you continue to encroach forward on the opponent. Knee folds to elbow, elbow to fist and fist to foot as the opponent attempts to cover up and disengage, etc.

The fighter should seek to use natural combinations that link together via mechanical attribute. The idea is to create a seamless kinetic flow. The movements, and weapons chosen within the sequence, must "fit" or the sequence will be cumbersome in usage.

Stepping and footwork must match the distance and utility of each weapon in the sequence or you risk becoming quickly off balance.

Following is a short list of good places to begin exploration of the idea of folding/unfolding. Obviously, what is good on the right also works on the left, etc. Throws and locks are not included in this list because the permutations are quite literally endless, but they are natural adjunctions once the concept is understood.

Folding:
1) Right hand to right elbow (right foot forward).
2) Right elbow to right shoulder. *Shoulder range is always equivocal to head butt range, so both weapons become viable in such a circumstance* (right foot forward).
3) Right elbow to right knee (left foot forward).
4) Right elbow to left knee (right foot forward).
5) Right knee to left elbow (right foot steps forward).
6) Right kick to left hand (right foot steps forward).

Unfolding:
1) Right shoulder *head butt viable* to left elbow (if right foot is forward).
2) Left elbow to left knee (right foot is forward).
3) Left knee to right hand (left foot steps forward).
4) Right hand to right kick (left foot is forward).

The fighter should run these combinations in a free form environment, first using several more cooperative opponents and then against uncooperative opponents with safety gear.

You must be willing to *invest in loss* to gain such skills as they do not come easily. You can expect to fail to properly implement folding for quite some time until you become intimately familiar with all of your tools and their effective distances.

Conceptual Training - Breaching the Gate through Double Attacks

We've all heard the expression "two heads are better than one." Well, in the martial arts, two attacks simultaneously *can* be better than one in the right circumstances.

Double attacks, when used creatively and sporadically, can be an excellent way to breach the opponent's defenses. Like any good technique, if you make the mistake of overuse it may cease to work for you entirely against any one opponent.

There are four classic types of double attacks:

1) Two hands simultaneously.
2) A hand and a foot simultaneously.
3) One hand used twice via circular return.
4) One leg used twice via circular return.

The pro of a double attack is that it bifurcates both the opponent's defenses and his/her mind. This can cause a few moments hesitation on the part of the adversary in relation to processing the incoming data of the fight. This hesitation, in turn, can then lead to a momentary window of opportunity for you to move into a better position and finish.

1a. *I close with Brandon by stepping in and provoking him, pressuring his guard.*

1b. *When he resists my pressure, I seize his limb and simultaneously deliver a left fist to his head and a right cross kick to his knee.*

One strategy is to employ such techniques after a series of one/two combinations have been thrown. With a sudden change of tempo, slip one of the doubles into the middle of the mix. This strategy can work well against a more seasoned opponent as it creates a natural break in the rhythm of combat that can be hard to read.

If you utilize the above strategy by employing either two hands simultaneously, or a hand and a foot simultaneously, it can have the effect of a sudden "shotgun" blast on the opponent's mind. They generally see and respond to one of the attacks while the other slips through unchecked.

Another strategy is to utilize a double attack as a lead technique if you have observed certain tendencies in the opponent that might give rise to such an opportunity.

For example, if you notice that the opponent always drops his lead hand to block a front kick (very bad idea) you can quickly pop the same leg upward into a head high round kick. You do have to practice the core mechanics to make this viable or the second kick will be too weak to be of any real value.

2a. *Observing a tendency in Brandon to drop his hands, I provoke him into his response pattern with a front kick to the midline.*

2b. *As soon as he makes contact by lowering his hands to stop the front kick, I turn and arc a round kick up to his neck with the same leg.*

A skillful technician knows how and when to employ his/her tools and those tools that are specialized require even more careful planning than other more mundane tools may require.

In other words, you can probe with your jab all day long with precious little consequence other than you hit or you miss. A jab is, in most fighters, an uncommitted blow that can be retracted swiftly if the enemy attempts to move on you.

A double attack, however, must be fully committed to be effective. It must be powerful to work as intended. And with such commitment of power and body authority behind the technique, you will be hard pressed to swiftly withdraw or change to defensive attribute. So this method should be studied well and implemented carefully and with thorough planning.

Explore the options in training by trying to locate seamless leads for circumstances of tempo change and insertion of the double hand method or the hand with foot method. In example: From right guard, lead right lunge, followed by trap left and simultaneously strike right high while cross kicking low from the rear left foot.

To utilize the same hand or foot twice via circular return method, you need simply look for repetitive defensive patterns in the opponent that may be exploited in this way. A patterned response is ripe for such a tactic.

Conceptual Training - Breaching the Gate through Flanking

Many times over the years I have had pupils who come from other backgrounds and styles express amazement at the sheer volume of information and technique that we possess on skills relating to achieving flank position on the opponent.

I have always found this amazement in them somewhat amusing for two simple reasons. One, the notion of "outflanking" your enemy is a standard tactic within military circles. And two, for our discipline, we consider this ideology fundamental and are exposed to the idea in numerous forms from a very early point in our training.

On sheer mathematical probability there is, generally speaking, no better position than on the opponent's flank (of course, barring being directly behind which is difficult to achieve in a one on one scenario). Once on the flank, you have a sheer numbers advantage in terms of weaponry. At close quarters you have both hands, both elbows and both knees available for easy use while the opponent is limited to only one side of the body for defense and counter-offense until he/she is able to rotate their centerline again to your position.

1a. *I step in and push on Alex's lead hand, getting him to firm up his position against my advance.*

1b. *As soon as he does so, I cut quickly inside across the centerline and threaten his high line to engage that same guard hand.*

1c. *Alex's response leaves him vulnerable to a flanking step and an attack to his lower right rib cage, of which I quickly take advantage.*

1d. *I continue the sequence by trapping his right hand downward and circling my right over for a palm smash to his chin.*

There are numerous ways to employ the concept of flanking in any singular or multiple scenario and there are far too many permutations to detail in this short section. But in general terms, they all follow certain rules of engagement as follows:

1) Attacking on the flank requires precise stepping and a near perfect understanding of the distance relationship that exists between you and your opponent.
2) The angle employed should be a narrow one, near 30 degrees in step to avoid the opponent being able to simply close the gap up the centerline while you are mid-stride.
3) Each stride should feed additional momentum to the successive stride, so that by the time you reach your opponent you have a great deal of kinetic potential at your disposal.
4) You should be able to reach your opponent within one and a half strides if the attack comes from a static guard. Or within two strides if implemented from a moving guard.

Although we do employ wider angles in counter-offensive flanking techniques, specifically a 45 degree angle for hand technique and a 60 degree angle for leg technique, we advocate an angle of 30 degrees for offensive attacks of the hands.

A 30 degree angle makes for swift side to side movement on entry. It is enough to confuse the opponent's mind as to your trajectory but not yet wide enough for the opponent to easily step inside your change.

Also, this narrow angle of entry will smother the opponent's leg technique and force them to seek to disengage a bit in order to find a good angle of counter attack.

This works to your advantage in that you already have superior position. When the opponent attempts to disengage to counter, you will be able to "stick like glue" and continue to rain your offensive movements in on them.

Done correctly, the opponent will be playing "catch up," jockeying for a recovery position throughout the entire engagement.

Flanking can be the tactic of choice at all times once it is sufficiently understood and polished. This method can get you inside and then keep you there long enough to finish the engagement.

You may also seek to combine flanking skills with any of the other concepts for a double or even triple threat on entry. A multi-tiered strategy is a very hard thing to defend indeed.

Conceptual Training - Ground Fighting Perspectives

Our ground fighting perspectives can be summed up fairly easily in three sentences...

1) Don't go there unless taken there.
2) Two; If an attempt is made to be taken to the ground, you must be willing to go.
3) Three; when taken to the ground, strike first and foremost, then get up.

There is a great deal of discourse nowadays on ground fighting. And it should by now be clearly understood that when talking about the ground in relation to fighting, a definite separation of a sport context and a reality context needs to be factored into the perspective. The two contexts are not identical by any means.

1a. *As Alex enters clinch range with me, I get the jump on him in position and step behind him for an outer reaping throw.*

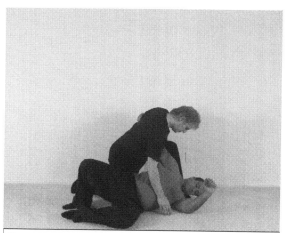

1b. *Realizing that he has been beaten, Alex wisely chooses to go to the ground in sacrifice positioning his right arm around my torso.*

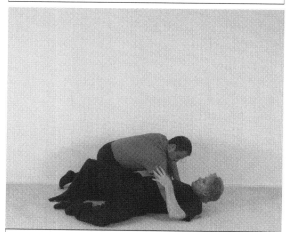

1c. *Alex now uses the momentum of my own throw against me by rolling tightly under me while pulling my torso over him.*

1d. *Alex continues the momentum of his sacrificing roll and, now in top position, delivers an elbow stroke to my jaw line.*

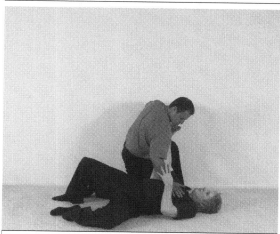

1e. *Alex then positions himself to get up by pushing on my chest and tabling one knee. He is ready in the case of other adversaries present.*

I often interact with those of the martial arts sporting world that seem to hold no distinction in their minds of this difference. Sport fighting is NOT street fighting and perspectives must, by necessity, shift when dealing with vastly different scenarios. To not acknowledge this is a mistake that could cost you dearly.

No matter what is said, the following undeniable facts remain... One, going to the ground for any length of time in a multiple encounter is folly. Two, if you stay on the ground for long in the context of a street encounter, you maximize your potential of loss exponentially in terms of the chance a friend of the foe will join in while you are tied up (friends don't jump into the ring in a sport context).

In any situation where you end up on the ground, the goal should always be to injure the opponent quickly and get up to handle additional threats.

The fastest way to do this is to either strike or break something and breaking something is easier said than done. It takes far more to break a joint or bone that is supported by muscle, tendon and adrenaline than many seem to think. So striking simply makes sense in terms of speed and efficiency.

If you instead take a perspective of trying to hold, pin or submit your adversary you can be making a critical mistake in any street confrontation.

No matter the position, it will always be possible to *slide* your hand to the eyes, throat or groin. None of these targets require much force to injure. Therefore the stroke does not need to come from any distance what-so-ever. It can simply be slid into place. Accuracy is then a given in such situations. And if you put your finger into their eyes, throat or groin, they WILL let go.

Now, as for training on the ground, we train a variety of skill sets and nothing is left undone. It is important to train fully for the ground phase of combat. It may or may not happen, but you must be ready.

A good fighter should cover the following areas in training:

1) Takedown and positional advantage (follow your opponent to the ground and seek control).
2) Conversion of force momentum (seek to yield willingly while being taken down, sacrifice and convert the existing momentum to a position of advantage for you).
3) Seamless striking techniques from take down or reception of take down (in order to disengage and get up swiftly).
4) Passive controls and conservation of energy techniques.
5) Submissions and counter submissions.

Once a fighter has absorbed key information from all five areas, he/she will be more capable of dealing with the ground adroitly.

R.S.P.C.T. Tier 5 - Tempering Training

There is a very old saying in the martial arts world; "Accentuate your strengths and cover your weaknesses." The Tempering tier is exactly what it sounds like... Identify any weaknesses in the fighter and prescribe specific combat exercises to strengthen the deficient areas.

We go through two stages in this tier. The first is to focus the fighter's time in training on all deficient areas in terms of regular drills already learned. A deficiency can be the result of an actual physical deficiency certainly. For example; a lack of either upper or lower body strength can contribute to a deficiency in certain throwing modalities. But oftentimes, a deficiency will be simply the fighter's lack of complete comprehension of a specific concept that was to be gleaned within regular training. So it is always best to start there and make sure that he/she does completely understand what was/is to be learned.

Once we exhaust those possibilities through regular drilling, then we designate the restrictive combat exercises found in this section to temper those deficient skills further. These exercises are restrictive by design to force the fighter out of his/her comfort zone in the process.

By forcing the fighter to think outside his/her respective box, a more well-rounded fighter will emerge at the end of the tempering process.

Below is a flow chart we use for determining how time is best spent in further development:

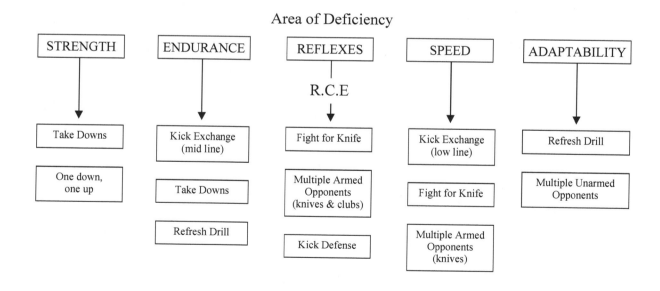

Area of Deficiency

Again, note that R.C.E.'s (restrictive combat exercises) are always done under the watchful eye of a coach so that the fighter may receive constructive feedback on their performance. We often film the sessions and then watch the films with the fighters to make this the most productive use of time possible.

Tempering Training Drill #1 - Kick Exchange

Certain fighters have trouble developing their leg techniques. Perhaps they have become too reliant on their hands and throwing skills. Perhaps it has been determined that they simply have too few leg techniques in their arsenal.

By taking hand technique out of the equation for the most part and placing the emphasis on leg technique repetitively and exclusively, the fighter will begin to develop a more well rounded approach to kicking, sweeping, reaping, checking, etc.

Under the watchful eye of a coach, new perspectives will open up and new combinations will be born. The coach will guide in terms of missed opportunity and perspective.

1a. *As Brandon opens with a right mid-line round kick under my guard, I step in and circle my lead hand down, underhooking his leg.*

1b. *As I fire back a right leg round kick to Brandon's mid-line, he angles forward and in while deflecting the kick force past him.*

1c. *As Brandon returns a low line round kick to my right support leg, I step back and check with a left inner iron wall.*

1d. *I then quickly attack Brandon's support leg with an left low side kick to his knee. Brandon quickly withdraws and changes feet.*

1e. *As Brandon delivers a right round kick off his foot change, I step inside the range of the kick and strike his chest.*

The fighters should initially limit themselves to minor leg combinations. First, exchange just one strong, focused kick back and forth. This can be, at first, even relegated to the same kick in exchange over and over again to learn proper distance and angle of that particular technique.

Once the fighters become more adept with a one kick exchange, then combinations of two kick exchanges can be implemented. And again, the combination can be fixed just to enforce a strong understanding of a particular technique.

We often use this restrictive combat exercise to incorporate new ideas, techniques or specific combinations into our fighter's arsenals.

For example; Double kicks, learned earlier, can become a focal point if it is determined that they are not yet combat viable. Often, by limiting the exchange, little used tools become very sharp implements.

No matter what limits are imposed, the emphasis should be placed upon precision in exchange, working for and capitalizing on specific openings in both offense and counter offense.

As skill grows, hand technique can be re-integrated gradually, broadening the exchange, but still emphasizing leg technique development.

Tempering Training Drill #2 - Kick Defense

There exist fighters out there that have honed their leg techniques to a level that can both punish you *and* keep you from closing with them if you are unfamiliar with such tactics and you have not adequately developed your counter tactics.

I know people who have low line kicking down to such a science that they will punish your legs to the point of complete uselessness. I am such a practitioner, as are many of my pupils. You cannot close with an opponent if your legs ache and they are unable to support your weight.

2a. *As Alex attacks with a straight front thrust kick, I cross step to the side and hang his leg while beginning to pressure his upper thigh.*

2b. *I step through and continue lifting his leg while exerting greater pressure on his thigh. He will fall backwards (not shown).*

Therefore it is wholly necessary to work against such tactics and technical savvy on a regular basis to be able to weather the effect when used against you.

This limited combat exchange should designate one fighter as "the kicker" and the other as the counter offender. All methods acquired earlier should now be honed to more workable tools or developed further.

1a. *As Brandon delivers a right skipping side kick to my mid-line, I step to his flank, underhooking his leg and direcing the kick past me.*

1b. *While momentarily hanging Brandon's leg, I deliver a low side counter kick to his exposed knee.*

During the course of the exchange, the counter offender should work on:

1) Foot changes to deal with multiple low line kicking attacks.
2) Angled stepping to facilitate counter kicking techniques from better position.
3) Kick shearing techniques.
4) Leg trapping and throwing methods.

All should be repetitively worked until polished and useable under live circumstances.

The practice should be gradually ramped up in pace and intensity under the watchful eye of a good coach. Safety gear (not shown) should be implemented to keep the contests as real as possible but to avoid unnecessary injury while training.

Even though all of these tempering drills are limited combat exercises, the intensity needs to be ramped up gradually and consistently until eventually the same level as any unlimited encounter or exchange to reap the most positive benefit.

Fighters do not profit without realism in practice.

Tempering Training Drill #3 - Take Downs

I am a firm believer in practicing all facets of combat. Long before MMA became popular, our internal martial arts school of thought was working takedowns, counters and submission in addition to all manners of striking, kicking, Chin Na (seizing/locking) and shuai (throwing).

This perspective was espoused in Hsu Hong Chi's school in Taiwan and was drilled into me from a very young age. All ranges of combat were considered a natural and normal part of the fighting construct and all were studied and practiced until skills were honed in all areas.

Our primary perspective has been mentioned before elsewhere in this work so I will not repeat that here. In this instance, for the purpose of this R.C.E. (restricted combat exercise), we focus on all aspects revolving around the takedown, conversion of the takedown and final submission to conclusion. But the focus in training is limited to *only* those three facets; the takedown itself, the conversion of the takedown attempt, and then the submission by one of the fighters once the contest actually goes to the ground.

To get the most out of this R.C.E., the fighters should work independently in live time. They

1a. *The drill begins each time from clinch range as one fighter looks for an opportunity to take the other down.*

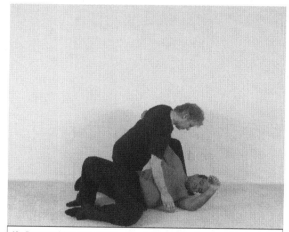

1b. I get position and execute an outer reap take down on Alex's right side. As he goes down he is to be looking for a chance to convert.

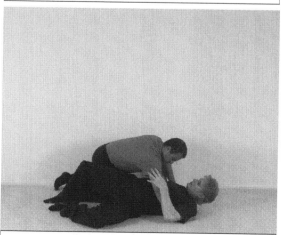

1c. *Alex uses the momentum of my throw pulling my torso over him to gain the top position in this exchange.*

1d. *Alex now delivers an elbow stroke to my jaw line. I would be looking for submission at this time having no chance to convert.*

252

should NOT take turns (although this can be done for a limited time in the beginning if one is less familiar and this can be productive).

The engagement begins each time from a clinch position. As one fighter gets an opportunity, an attempt at a takedown ensues. The opposing fighter should attempt to convert the energy of the takedown if possible in what is commonly called a "sacrifice" (one example shown on the previous page against a common front cut/outer reap). When and if the conversion is made successfully, the converting fighter should attempt to punish and get up. If this cannot be done, the contest should go to finishing mode through submission.

Remember the key points of this R.C.E.;

1) Upon takedown attempt, look for conversion through sacrifice first and foremost.
2) Once a conversion is successful, look to punish and *get up*.
3) If, and only if, momentum can no longer be converted and has run into the ground, should a fighter look for submission.

It is often possible to convert as many as three times before momentum runs into the ground completely and a submission is the only choice left. This notion should be explored fully. The fighters should NOT develop tunnel vision and immediately look for the submission.

Tempering Training Drill #4 - One Down, One Up

One up one down is fairly self explanatory except for certain obvious focal points. In this restricted combat exercise, each engagement starts with one fighter in a downed position while the other fighter is upright.

These different starting positions should be randomized once both fighters become more acquainted with the protocol of the exercise. Patterning must be prevented.

The contest ends and is restarted under any of three conditions:

1) The downed fighter gets up.
2) The upright fighter enters and compromises the other by control and strike.
3) Either fighter is submitted while on the ground.

Each fighter has very different roles and goals in this contest and must behave accordingly to each intention.

1a. *Brandon attacks from "up" position. I seize his hand, positioning my right leg behind his knee and my left in front of his ankle.*

1b. *I pull Brandon's hand down and across his front, turning him away from me while I begin to scissor his lead leg.*

1c. *I continue scissoring his leg and simultaneously pressure his right hip with my lead hand to take him down.*

1d. *The dual pressure on his frontal frame result in a take down against his position. I would now move in to follow up.*

The *upright fighter* attempts to find an opening for entry with any type of striking technique in an effort to compromise and incapacitate the downed fighter while simultaneously avoiding becoming embroiled in a ground battle. But, if such a ground tussle does indeed occur as a result of the down fighter's prowess, the upright fighter must willingly go to the ground until submission conclusion.

Meanwhile, the *downed fighter* must exercise the lower basin theory completely, using "feet as hands and hands as feet" and all parts of his/her body as points of leverage for both bringing the upright fighter to the ground level and then applying a submission for conclusion.

Done properly, this contest will strengthen aspects of both the upright and downed fighters' repertoires. This restricted combat exercise serves no purpose if both fighters do not stick to their respective roles so this must be enforced by the coach/referee's watchful eye.

Tempering Training Drill #5 - Fight for the Knife

Adaptation and the ability to think outside the box is a trait highly prized by many elite branches of the military. To be able to adapt and overcome adverse and unusual circumstances is a skill set that goes beyond daily utility.

This R.C.E. is a training exercise that is about perception, tunnel vision and tool usage. And by tool, I do not simply mean the weapon that is involved in the drill. *That* would, or could, be the "tunnel vision" aspect of the exercise.

Most fighters will focus on trying to *possess* the knife in order to *wield* the knife initially. Because of the perception that this represents an extreme advantage to win the encounter.

1a. *As the contest begins, the knife has just been thrown in from the side between our positions.*

1b. *Brandon makes an overly zealous move for possession of the knife thinking to attain rapid advantage in the contest.*

1c. *I immediately close on his position and attack his exposed head with a right downward palm strike.*

1d. *I follow rapidly with a knee to his face while he is still reeling from the palm strike of the prior attack.*

1e. *I then conclude with a downward elbow stroke to his exposed rear neck to conclude the contest round.*

Now I'm not going to deny that this can be true if done properly. But the exercise itself is about understanding that to be overly focused on a weapon as an "advantage" can be folly in and of itself. And that like any strategy or advantage, if not executed properly there may indeed be a negative surprise.

The contest starts by having a third party toss the knife in from the side both arbitrarily and randomly. This person usually also acts as referee and his/her job is not to make the contest "fair" but to make the contest "diverse."

Therefore, sometimes the knife should be deliberately thrown nearer one fighter than the other. Sometimes distal to both. Sometimes in the center. Or sometimes in the air as "begin" is being shouted to start the contest. Diversity and conflict, that is what we are after here.

The contest ends when any of the following conditions are met:

1) One fighter is finished by the knife via vital stab or slash.
2) One fighter is incapacitated by a sequence of hands and/or feet.
3) One fighter is compromised or incapacitated by numerous knife wounds.

Both fighters should attempt to get the knife, yes. But they should also utilize all other weapons in their arsenal to both stop the other from possessing the knife and to try to possess the knife for themselves.

We have our own scoring/rules system for this R.C.E. but you can feel free to modify as suits your purpose. Our normal method is as follows:

1) A point is won by *any* strong/damaging blow by a hand or foot technique (the impact should be tangible to both eye and ear to count).
2) A point is won by *any* penetrating cut by the knife (shallow scratches are not counted).
3) A penetrating knife wound to an interior major vein/artery structure on any limb causes both loss of point *and* loss of function of that limb (damaged arm is put behind the back and a damaged leg causes either hopping on one or going to one knee).
4) A pierce or slash of the knife to a vital spot/organ is automatic loss/victory.

We generally play to five points but sometimes extend for endurance training. Our rule set is designed to force both fighters to adapt to an ever changing balance of power and adjust their strategies on the fly accordingly. It has always worked well for us.

Gearing up fully is highly recommended as this contest can get rather intense.

Tempering Training Drill #6 - Multiple Opponents Unarmed

Multiple opponent scenarios are an unfortunate part of engagements that happen in the street, public places like bars or, if you're in private security, in the course of your job.

Such scenarios can be intimidating and risky. In a multiple opponent scenario, you have four main objectives.

1) Get to the periphery of the circle so that you can either stack (the act of lining them up so that both their line of sight, and direct line of approach, to you is now impeded by one of their comrades) or herd (the act of moving yourself bodily to a position or positions that forces the opponents to "coalesce" while chasing

1a. *Faced with two unarmed opponents with myself positioned between both adversaries and my back against a wall, the contest commences.*

1b. *Alex, being slightly closer to me, attacks first with a right punch to my head. I redirect and shift my weight, keeping my eye on Brandon.*

1c. *Brandon immediately attacks with a left to my face. I step my left foot toward Brandon's flank while parrying his attack past me at a narrow angle.*

1d. *I continue moving away from Alex, stepping through with my right while seizing Brandon's left arm and wrapping his neck with my right arm.*

1e. *Still in motion, I swing my right foot back behind Brandon, securing my hold on him and placing him squarely between myself and Alex.*

257

1f. *As a determined attacker, Alex begins to encroach on my position to aid his fellow attacker.*

1g. *In response to Alex's continued pursuit, I leverage Brandon's body and head back, using him as a shield on my position.*

1h. *As Alex continues forward to strike at me again, I expend my temporary shield, shoving Brandon forward into Alex's strike.*

1i. *I now disengage from Brandon, having accomplished my goal of getting to the perimeter to escape. A new scenario will now begin.*

you, thus crowding one another) thereby allowing you to take advantage in that they can neither surround or work as a team against you immediately. And allowing you to now work the periphery of the group.

2) When possible, use one of them as a shield against the others' encroachment on your immediate position.

3) If terrain can be utilized for the same purpose of shielding, stacking or herding, this should also be done.

4) Escape at the earliest opportunity.

Objective #4 cannot be emphasized strongly enough. I personally have had the misfortune of being in several multiple opponent encounters on the streets of Taipei, Taiwan and a few more here in the states. In such an engagement, even with a great deal of skill, you will take more and more damage the longer you stay engaged. Therefore, it is wise to understand certain strategies to maximize your chances of reducing the odds against you quickly. But moreover, it is wiser to understand that "he who fights and runs away, lives to fight another day." You really need to recognize when the odds are too great and seek a timely exit. The mindset of "staying in it to win it" is a false one in such circumstances. Survival is the win here.

Tempering Training Drill #6 - Multiple Opponents Armed

Dealing with armed assailants in multiples is a very scary business indeed and if you do not have *exceptionally* GREAT standup skills, you are not going to survive.

This is a situation where moving with extreme urgency is the venue of the day if you are to survive the encounter.

Working the peripheral now becomes a matter of necessity. For if you stay in the center, between two or more opponents when a weapon is involved, you have zero chance of survival.

In this type of encounter, stacking can still be a viable strategy. You would employy

1a. *Faced with a dire situation of two knife wielding assailants, one at my front and one at my back, the timing and movement must be specific and quick.*

stacking as a temporary outlook used only to get you to a better position in order to secure your escape.

Shielding can also still be viable but it is far more risky as you must be sure that you can control the opponent's weapon while you simultaneously control him/her.

Herding also, if again done on the way to escape, can still be useful. But you are no longer looking to engage in any of these manners. You are looking to exit.

1b. *As Alex attacks, I deflect his knife hand while simultaneously rotating and pushing Brandon's knife hand across his centerline removing any easy vital stroke for now.*

1c. *I continue stepping around to Brandon's back, pressing his knife hand into his body and clamping his head with my left arm at the same time to accomplish my escape.*

Corner strategies no longer apply. Nor do any number of terrain based strategies unless such terrain literally puts a barrier between you and your assailants.

In such scenarios; speed, precision and limited engagement are of essence.

Striking to disable is the only real option. Becoming tied up for any length of time will spell certain doom.

Elsewhere in this work, I have talked about disarming a weapon being of either an "accidental" or "incidental" nature and this is still the credo of the day here.

If there appears an opportunity to disarm in a rather matter of fact and incidental way, then yes, this can work. The reality is that this will seldom be the case. If it is an equalizer you seek, you are better off removing your belt if wearing one. Or a hard soled shoe. Or picking up something else that is in the vicinity.

This is a more effective disarm strategy in such instances as it requires far less time in any one engagement. Such implements are far easier to procure. And they can then be employed to strike the surface radial or ulnar nerves of the assailant's knife wielding limb, possibly resulting in a drop of the assailant's weapon. Also, because of the faster deployment of such implements, it is less likely that another assailant will get to you while you are tied up trying to disarm.

If time permits, pulling off your shirt or jacket and wrapping it around one arm to create a temporary shielded buffer while you quickly exit can be a useful strategy. But there is not always time to implement such and things transpire very quickly when blades are involved.

Realistically to survive, you must expect to get cut. It will be a sheer miracle if you do not. And so a working knowledge of your own anatomy is of great value. Protect your vitals at all costs and get away at the earliest opportunity.

A few final comments on multiple engagements come courtesy of my teacher:

Hsu Hong Chi used to tell us that several on one is a bad situation and several on one with weapons will be potentially lethal so it is best to avoid such events completely if at all possible. This, of course, makes very good sense.

But he also used to say that if you can capture the psyche of the group, you have a better chance of surviving and one of his favorite strategies revolved around making the first adversary look so utterly bad (and he meant ugly bad) that the others feel fear for what may befall them and that this fear in them can buy you just the amount of time you need to plot and execute your escape parameter. He is right. I have seen, first hand, the truth of this perspective.

He also used to say that to grapple in such circumstances was sheer folly and would likely get you severely damaged if not worse. He was right about that as well. I have also seen, first hand, the truth of this perspective.

To be able to survive such encounters requires both knowledge and great skill. What it does NOT require, is false bravado.

Tempering Training Drill #7 - Refresh Drills

Refresh drills are where we put it all together. Everything thought to be learned and understood in all prior fighter training is now put into the metaphorical crucible for testing and refinement.

Refresh drills are kind of like playing what we called "king of the mountain" when I was a child. One boy stood on the top of a small hillock or mound of dirt and the other boys tried to clamber up the hillock and throw him off while he attempted to cast them down before they could achieve that aim.

In our martial arts version, the difference is that each adversary that scales your mountain and assails your position is a specialist in a specific method of attack. And for the most part, he is to stay in character for that specialty and force you to adapt quickly to whatever that may be.

Refresh drills are a restricted combat exercise where not only specific skill sets and technical attributes are tested and scrutinized. But also, each fighter's conditioning levels and mental adaptability are put under the gun.

1a. *Brandon jabs left and I redirect and adhere to his jab, maintaining my frame and staying proximal for the next attack.*

1b. *As Brandon throws his secondary right cross, I turn my body and redirect his limb and simultaneously check his elbow.*

1c. *I now press Brandon's arm downward, opening the space for a neck hook and shoulder bar combination...*

1d. *... which does not materialize because Brandon immediately tries to uppercut my jaw. I respond by turning and catching his elbow.*

When we do refresh drills, there is one fighter. He/she stays on the mat until told otherwise. The length of time can vary depending on where that respective fighter is in terms of their individual conditioning. We wish to push the limit each time in each respective fighter.

There will be a pool of opponents, usually at least six in number:

1) One hand specialist (this can be from any persuasion but we generally draw this category from our own systems).
2) One a kicking specialist (TKD, Savate, etc.).
3) One a grappler (wrestling, BJJ, Judo, etc.).
4) One is a western boxer.
5) One is a kick boxer.
6) One wields a weapon (knife or club).

The opponents are ushered in one after another in a seemingly (to the fighter) randomized way, although a good coach always has a plan and purpose behind the chosen order of appearance given individual fighter weaknesses and/or strengths.

1a. *Alex attacks my left knee with a cross kick to which I respond with a simple foot change to avoid and stay proximal for counter.*

1b. *Alex responds with a round kick to my inner left thigh. I shift my weight forward and rotate into the kick, jamming his knee.*

1c. *Alex attempts a mid-line round kick against my position. I circle my right arm underneath and hang his leg for throw.*

1d. *Alex delivers a front thrust kick to my centerline. I angle away from the attack and hang his leg with an underhook of my left wrist.*

In any given practice, the coach will motion in fresh opponents *from varied angles* to the fighter on the mat, attempting at every turn to challenge both awareness and adaptability. Frequently, the opponents will be waived in on the fighter's blind side forcing the fighter to receive fresh opponents at angles other than directly ahead. This forces the fighter to be alert and adapt to an ever changing set of variables, sharpening overall awareness in the process of honing key skills.

And because of the "freshness" of the opponents being waived in one after another, the fighter's stamina will of course be tested in the process. But more importantly, as fatigue settles in, the fighter's deepest and most ingrained *mental* conditioning will be revealed to the coach's trained eye. This information will be invaluable in determining what tools need the most sharpening and what tools are not even present. For as the fighter fatigues, their most ingrained training will take over.

Again, as I have stated before, what I call the "flail factor" surface in the fighter when pressure is at its greatest. And "rather than rise to your level of expectation, you will instead sink to your level of truly ingrained training." The combination of fatigue and continued pressure from fresh, relentless opponents will reveal quickly what is truly ingrained and what is not ingrained in each respective fighter.

Properly structured refresh drills will bring the fighter's mental state to a point that is as close to possible of an actual, no holds barred encounter as can be approximated in any training only environment. The fight or flight adrenal responses will be triggered and manifest the fighter's most base and ingrained skill sets, revealing any weaknesses readily.

And just when the fighter thinks they are getting a handle on things, we change the drill up with multiple opponents. Multiples are mixed and matched... weapons and unarmed, different skill sets for each, etc., raising the stakes ever higher in the name of triggering such responses in the fighter. For pressure testing is the only way to really clearly reveal such tendencies. And a good refresh drill is about the most severe pressure you can bring to bear on a fighter short of an actual street encounter.

For a refresh drill to approach this context, protective gear (not shown) must be worn on both the part of the fighter and the opponents and the contest ramped up to the highest level possible within safety tolerances.

Done properly, a well run refresh scenario is very rewarding in its capacity to show the fighter new perspectives, new insights, established strengths, developing weaknesses and levels of mental and physical conditioning that are crucial to furthering their respective skill sets.

Not to mention, they can be a helluva lot of fun!

"One of these days the world is going to become so politically correct
that it risks offending itself out of existence."

Mike Patterson; 1996

How to close this work was something I thought about for a good long time. And because of a few events that had occurred just as I was winding up, I decided to go with my known strength.. A concise summary combined with a few insights I have gleaned over my long involvement with internal martial arts.

Some of these statements will by no means be popular, hence the opening quote which I coined back in the 90's when I first started speaking out about what I believed regarding the internal martial arts, both the facts and the myths.

One of the events that spurred this ending was that I have recently been besieged with frequent questions from both students and constituents regarding fighting and conditioning. The current consensus seems to be that you should "ramp up" about six weeks prior to a fight to avoid any "burnout." I chuckled. This is the mindset of someone who trains for sport only.

One fellow said that Lei Tai rounds had now been dropped to 1:30 with the final at 2:00 mins. I found myself thinking my how they have lowered the bar. And, no wonder we used to walk all over so many "so called" professional fighters on the platform when I was still coaching.

You know, you can be the faster fighter. You can be the stronger fighter. You can be the more powerful fighter or the better technician. You can have the best fight strategy, the best coach... But that ALL leaves you when your conditioning leaves you. When you're out of gas and the opponent isn't, you lose.

Conditioning should be a year round thing. You should never let it slack as it will leave you quickly. Training, no let me make that true training, is for life. You train ALL the time. That way, you are always ready. Whether that may be a fight for your life, or a fight for your health. And training should be about the whole. It's a package deal.

Training is for life. Many aspects of Internal Martial Arts have been recently shown to be of great benefit in potentially even slowing down the aging process. As this book goes to press, a recent University of California study showed that people who regularly meditated over a three month period had more active telomerase, an enzyme that helps preserve telomeres. Telomeres are special strands of DNA that cap off each of your chromosomes, protecting them from any mutation when your cells divide. And when your cells are no longer able to effectively divide, they begin to deteriorate. Internal martial arts is moving meditation in all aspects of practice. So, training is for life.

Modern sport combat is a dual edged sword. It does allow a venue to test your skills against a variety of different types of fighter, or at least that was the original intent, which was good. However, now that the structure has been in place for many years, you will see that most of the fighters tend to use the same techniques, the same holds, the same everything. The reason is simple. There are rules and they are fighting for money. Why should a professional fighter spend time developing a technique that is disallowed in the ring? He should not. So status quo tends to become the norm and this is exactly what is happening.

As a result, we are seeing a sort of devolution of the arts as a result of sport combat. A limited paradigm of perception dictated by both the rule set and the perception of what "works" in the ring. This is unfortunate, but wholly expected and natural.

This is not the original intention of training. And it is moving us further away from the truth or what training should be. But I digress. This book is about the combative aspects of Internal martial arts and specifically that of Hsing I so I will get off that soapbox here.. Well, mostly.

So as I said in the outset, RSPCT is a synthesis... a distillation... a fast track. Will it make you a better fighter? Yes. If you practice the drills presented here regularly and understand what the real "root" of internal arts mechanics are all about. So what are the "roots?"

1) These arts are circular, three dimensional movement structures. Every action has a forward or rearward weight shift and/or step, combined with a right or left rotation, combined with a rising or falling action (this last is done primarily in the thorax through use of the intercostals muscle structures, although level changes are also often incorporated into this as well).

2) Everything proceeds from, is moved through and delivered by.. the core of the body then timed with the step. This allows for maximum transfer of momentum to the limb.

3) The arms remain in "frame." This allows a simultaneous protection of the centerline to be married to a short, sharp delivery system.

4) The shoulders never leave their natural seat. Elbows must reside in a downward instead of outward position (this ensures maximum integrity of any one stroke). And the head is always erect, even when slipping, which maintains positive balance.

5) We do not "lean." Leaning takes away from the body's natural balance, forcing it to use its stabilizer groups to compensate and destroys structure in the process, yielding substantively less power in the process.

6) Relax. True cultivated relaxation reduces the antagonism in the muscle structures, increasing velocity. Relaxation also conserves energy. And relaxation makes for a more strongly grounded disposition while simultaneously allowing for a nimbleness in change.

If you practice the RSPCT structures regularly, you will begin to feel the natural kinetic flow of one action into the next as it was designed. Falling will naturally generate rising. A step and sink to the left while rotating leftward will naturally give potential to generate power while stepping and rotating right. An uppercut will expand the thorax which then naturally prepares the body to contract the abdominal wall in motivating a front kick. And then that contraction will immediately prepare the expansion of the forward action of the pelvic girdle for power, etc.

RSPCT drills were constructed utilizing the internal martial arts body mechanical principles of motion. For you see, when you have done this as long as I have, you do not know how to move any other way. So it is all there, in a simple and transparent methodology. A practitioner need only to do the practice and allow themselves to feel. Although I would be remiss if I did not mention that a good coach's watchful eye can ease the process of assimilation substantively and hasten the development of true skill.

Is the study of RSPCT a better way than the classical approach to internal martial arts training? No. It cannot be as it is a distillation only. There is no substitute for total training in the internal martial arts. The knowledge base is immense and the study of the complete style develops a technical and tactical mind that cannot possibly be approached by the study of RSPCT alone. Remember, yours truly was trained classically and it is only because of that lateral, big picture understanding that I was able to create RSPCT in the first place.

As for the martial aspects, I was trained the old way. The perspective of; "Can you use what you know for fighting" was primary. Style was secondary to efficiency of combat. That is not to say style is unimportant. Style is important. Don't let anyone ever tell you different. Style is an amalgam of principle, technique and tactic forged together into a seamless entity of motion. The amalgam is the means to understanding the how, why, when and where of combat. If you study the eclectic way, you will end up with some useable tools, yes. But you will then, by necessity, have to re-invent the wheel to make it seamless. And seamless movement is what must be the norm for truly effective combative skill.

What I am saying is that this is the "martial arts." The word "martial" comes first in that name. If the emphasis were to be any different, it would be called "art of the martial" and it is not.

The second event was that a student asked me the other day as we were finishing up an RSPCT workout; "Shrfu, why did you train so many people specifically for the ring back then?" Well, I NEVER trained people for the ring. I taught them how to use their training FOR the ring. There is a big difference.

Again, true kungfu is for life. The fighting aspect comes out of the overall discipline and if you want to become a better fighter, then you train your skills diligently for that purpose. Then, if you want to fight in the ring, you find out what the rules are and you make selective tactical and/or targeting decisions based on those rule sets. If the rule says don't kick the knee, well then, you don't kick the knee. But you throw the same kick that you always train to a target that is allowed. If the rules say don't elbow the back brain, you don't elbow the back brain. Instead you elbow the side face under the ear, the clavicle, etc. You DO NOT train anything away. You train as you always did.. For life.

Training is for life...

Printed in Great Britain
by Amazon.co.uk, Ltd.,
Marston Gate.